MW00397050

NO BULL

~~NOBLE~~ REVIEW

FRAME-WORK EDITION

U.S. HISTORY & GOV'T REGENTS

A no-nonsense approach for in-class review and exams

by Jeremy Klaff & Harry Klaff

About the Authors

Harry Klaff taught high school social studies in the New York City public schools system for 34 years. In 1993, he was the honored recipient of the John Bunzel Memorial Award as NYC's social studies teacher of the year. As a member of city-wide Justice Resource Center, he helped write numerous curricula in law-related education. For many years, he created the annual Model City Council project, in which students took over New York's City Hall for a day-long simulation exercise.

Jeremy Klaff has been teaching AP History classes for over a decade. His website, www. mrklaff.com has been utilized by teachers and students across the country for review materials as well as original social studies music. Jeremy has been a contributor to H2 network, and has published Document Based Questions for Binghamton University's Women's History website, womhist.binghamton.edu. He has conducted staff developments for "Entertainment in Education" at both the high school and college level.

© 2019 by No Bull Review™. Reproduction in whole or in part without written permission of the publisher is strictly prohibited.

This book might contain product names, trademarks, or registered trademarks. All trademarks in this book are property of their respective owners. If used, they are for non-biased use, and we do not encourage or discourage use of said product or service. Any term suspected of being a trademark will be properly capitalized.

The authors of this book make no warranties based on misinformation, or information excluded from these pages. The author shall not be liable for any positive or negative test scores achieved.

Cover Artwork by Stephanie Strack

Table of Contents

The No Bull Approach

No Bull Review…"because your review book, shouldn't need a review book!"

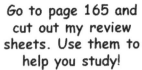

Go to page 165 and cut out my review sheets. Use them to help you study!

This book is a concise and to the point review for United States History. Our goal here is to give you a great review for both in class and standardized testing. The No Bull approach is to cut through the fat, and give you what you want.

We, as authors of No Bull Review, are teachers. For years, we have been speaking to students to find out what you want in a review book. The answer? No Bull. You want the facts, clear and to the point. And... you want review questions. Lots of them.

At the end of this book you will find an intense review. We advise you to know the terms and definitions on the *No Bull Review Sheet*.

The practice questions in this book are our own creation, and are based on the style of questions commonly used in the curriculum. They are questions that evaluate the most important themes of United States History.

We hope you enjoy the No Bull approach. Thank you, and best of luck.

– No Bull Review

Colonial America, Before 1763

Before conquest, American Indian cultures thrived in the New World. However, conquerors from places such as Spain, Netherlands, and England, had different economic, political, and social desires. Ultimately, it would be the British colonies which would dominate the East Coast. The new America displayed a Great Awakening of religious thought, some rebellion in Jamestown, and even a representative government in Virginia. Witch-hunts, self-rule, and a constitution in Connecticut foreshadowed the future founding of the United States. However, after the French and Indian War, the honeymoon of *salutary neglect* came to an end.

See map on pg. 184 for details of American Indian (Native American) cultures before conquest.

HERE IS WHAT YOU NEED TO KNOW:
Question: What should I know about early Spanish settlements?

Answer: Spanish conquistadors (conquerors) were the first to arrive in the New World. ***They brought over domesticated horses.*** They also brought over a lot of crops, animals, and diseases such as smallpox. This massive cultural interaction between two world hemispheres is called the ***Columbian Exchange***. To extract valuable resources (most notably gold), they set up a system of forced labor called ***encomienda***. African slavery would eventually replace *encomienda*. Spanish settlements were strong in:

1. Florida - St. Augustine was settled, and today is the oldest city in North America.
2. New Mexico - Santa Fe became a capital. ***Pueblo Indians revolted*** in 1680 against Spanish rule and the spread of Christianity. Many Spaniards resettled in Texas.
3. California - The Spanish continued to spread Christianity throughout the western portion of North America. The Franciscan Order later set up 21 outposts/religious centers known as ***missions*** between 1769-1833.

Question: What important interactions occurred between Europeans and Native Americans?

Answer: The Spanish and Portuguese generally looked at the natives as inferior. Spanish philosopher Juan Ginés de Sepúlveda defended colonization and the harsh treatment of natives as natural. Bartolomé de las Casas, on the other hand, believed colonization was immoral and brutally cruel to the natives. Nonetheless, Europeans continued a superior attitude towards Native Americans.

Aside from Spain, Portugal was also an early force in the New World and was powerful in South America in Brazil. The French and Dutch had strong trading ties with the Native Americans (specifically, the fur trade was vital to the French). Intermarriage was common between Europeans and Native Americans. This intermarriage created a new ***Mestizo*** culture. However, the English tended not to intermarry. Our story now shifts to the English.

Definition: Indentured Servant

These were "adventurers" who traveled to the New World and settled mainly in Maryland and Virginia to work ***tobacco*** fields in the English Colonies. They generally labored from 4 to 7 years in exchange for the voyage over. They were given freedom dues (tools, land, etc.) after their time was served.

Question: Near what waterway was much of Virginia's tobacco harvested?

Answer: Chesapeake Bay. Jamestown was founded by an English joint-stock company called *The Virginia Company of London* in

1607. They awarded *headrights*, or land grants, to spark immigration. If you see 1607 as a time frame on an essay, you are expected to write about Jamestown and the Chesapeake.

The bulk of tobacco farming took place near the Chesapeake Bay in the Maryland and Virginia area. Much of the work was done at first by indentured servants. Slaves would take over Southern fields soon after. It is important to know that indentured servants were farming tobacco *before* African slaves.

Note: Southern English colonies were settled for economic reasons. The Northern English ones were predominantly religious settlements. Many died in the early years of settlement, as famine, disease, and conflicts with Native Americans were all too common.

Definition: Bacon's Rebellion, 1676 (100 years before 1776)

Nathaniel Bacon led farmers in a rebellion against rich planters, the governor (William Berkeley), and American Indians in Jamestown. The rebellion led to the burning of Jamestown, but fizzled out when Bacon died. It is significant because it is a colonial indicator of class struggle and political discontent in the United States, 100 years before its founding.

Question: Puritans or Pilgrims...who were the Separatists?

Answer: The Puritans wanted to "purify" Catholic influences within the Protestant (Anglican) Church of England. Most Puritans were *Non-Separatists*. They did not separate from King James I, who was the head of the Church. They settled at Massachusetts Bay under *John Winthrop* to establish a religious community known as a *"city upon a hill."*

Pilgrims were *Separatists*. They settled in Plymouth, Massachusetts and preferred to *separate* from the Church of England rather than reform it from within.

Tip: On Thanksgiving, people like to *separate* their turkey from their stuffing as they talk about the story of the Pilgrims. Pilgrims also liked to separate.

Definition: House of Burgesses, 1619

England's Virginia Company allowed Virginians to elect representatives to a legislature. The House of Burgesses became the first representative government in the New World, and a model for the future Legislative Branch of the United States.

Definition: Mayflower Compact, 1620

The Pilgrims pledged justice, equality, majority rule, and direct democracy on the voyage over on the Mayflower. This is yet another example of self-government in the New World. In some places in New England, *town meetings* of local propertied men created laws.

Question: What colony had the first constitution?

Answer: Connecticut in 1639. The *Fundamental Orders of Connecticut* were written as the first constitution of its kind in the colonies.

Definition: Anne Hutchinson and antinomianism

Anne Hutchinson questioned the Puritan religious establishment of Massachusetts Bay. She believed that faith alone was critical for salvation. This is known as antinomianism. She was banished for challenging church authority in 1637.

Definition: Salem Witch Trials, 1692

In 1692, young Puritan girls were accused of witchcraft, which was illegal in Massachusetts Bay. After fingers pointed in every direction, twenty of the accused were executed. The significance of the trials is more important, as this was an early case of mass hysteria. In an essay about the Red Scare of 1919, or McCarthyism of the 1950s, a reference to witch-hunts in colonial times is a nice connection.

Definition: Metacom/King Philip's War

There was a war fought from 1675-1676 (same year as Bacon's Rebellion) between the colonists and Native American tribes of New England who were united by Metacom (King Philip). The colonists ultimately defeated Metacom, but the conflict destroyed many Puritan towns and the economies within. A different conflict you should know about is the *Pequot War*, where colonists teamed up with other Native Americans to defeat and deplete New England's Pequot Indian population.

Question: What colony was founded for religious freedom?

Answer: Rhode Island

Roger Williams supported separation of church and state, and founded Rhode Island as a religious retreat for persecuted people such as Jews and Quakers. Its early neighbors called the colony "Rogue" Island. The country's oldest Jewish synagogue still stands in Newport.

Question: For what religious sect did William Penn found Pennsylvania?

Answer: Quakers

Pennsylvania had no established church, which therefore made the colony more tolerant than places governed by the Puritans. Religious toleration was part of what Penn proclaimed to be a *Holy Experiment.* However, religious differences in the colony hurt its long-term success. Another colonial form of tolerance important to know is Maryland's *Act of Toleration*, which granted freedoms to Christian sects.

Definition: Great Awakening

Even after the Half-Way Covenant, religion was losing its influence in New England. The Great Awakening was a religious revival in the mid-1700s. Led by *George Whitefield* and *Jonathan Edwards*, the movement expressed theatrical emotion towards religion, and condemned sinners. New Lights, or those who favored the movement, looked to eliminate sin from the colonies through the lessons of the scriptures of both the Old and New Testament. Presbyterians and Baptists increased in number. Quakers were less affected.

Still, many colonists were *Deists* who believed that God created the world, and then allowed natural law to take over.

Definition: John Peter Zenger Trial, 1735

The court's decision from this trial affirmed freedom of the press in the New York colony. Journalist John Peter Zenger was put on trial for printing something negative about colonial governor William Cosby. Zenger's attorney, Andrew Hamilton (not Alexander) argued that if something printed was true, then it can't be libel (libel means *false* printed statements). The jury agreed. Zenger was not guilty.

Definition: Middle Passage

Because of an abundance of land, there was a high demand for labor. The same European superiority that existed regarding harsh treatment of American Indians was also applied to African slaves. The Middle Passage was the *Triangular Trade's* journey which brought slaves from Africa to the Caribbean. As for the Triangular Trade, molasses from the Caribbean was brought to New England, distilled into rum, and then traded to African kings for the slaves. The Transatlantic Slave Trade would not be phased out in the US until 1808. For more on slave life in the US, see pg. 44.

Definition: Stono Rebellion, 1739

In South Carolina, there were rumors of slaves escaping to Spanish-controlled Florida to receive freedom. A slave named Jemmy recruited others in South Carolina looking for "liberty." They gained ammunition from a local shop, and went on a killing spree. Whites in the area returned fire, and the rebellion ended. It led to slave codes, such as the Negro Act of 1740, which prevented slave assembly, education, and property ownership. Thus, strict racial divisions continued to evolve before the United States was founded.

Definition: Mercantilism

Mercantilism is an economic system where the European Mother Country (in this case, England), extracted the raw materials produced by its colonies and sold them finished goods. The sole purpose of the colonies was to make the Mother Country rich and self-sufficient.

Before the American Revolution, a series of *Navigation Acts* stated that the colonies had to exclusively trade certain items, such as sugar and tobacco, with Britain. All trade had to be done on British or colonial ships, and goods destined for other nations had to first go through British hands. The Navigation Acts weren't enforced extensively until 1764, and smuggling was common.

Definition: Salutary Neglect

Because the British were thriving from mercantilism, they were willing to look the other way when it came to certain trade laws, and the governing affairs of the colonies (the expression was "let sleeping dogs lie"). This process, known as salutary neglect, ended after the French and Indian War when the British needed more revenue.

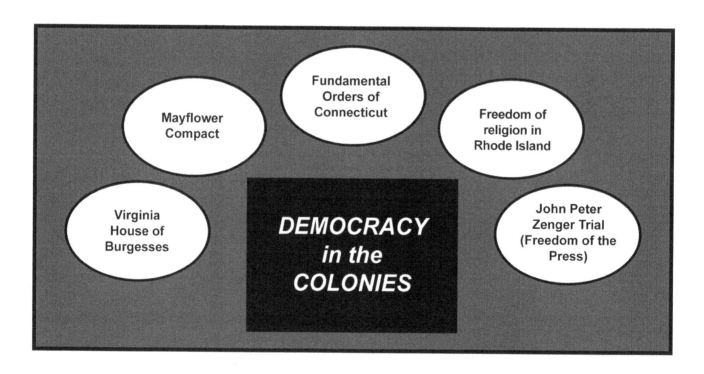

Question: What major events do I need to know about the French and Indian War, 1754-1763?

Answer: Remember, the colonists *are* British in this war! The British are the good guys! The British and colonists were fighting the French and Native Americans who had united to create a profitable fur trade. In Europe, the conflict was called the Seven Years' War. *Note:* Not all Native Americans supported the French, as the Iroquois Confederacy—made up of the Six Nations of the Mohawks, Oneidas, Onondagas, Cayugas, Senecas, and Tuscaroras—sided with the British. You should know:

1. *The Albany Plan of Union*, 1754 - Benjamin Franklin had a belief that the colonies had to unite to win the French and Indian War. He created the famous "Join or Die" cartoon in support of a united government. The plan failed in Albany, but the message stuck for centuries.

2. A young George Washington was engaged in conflict in western Pennsylvania at Fort Duquesne, near modern-day Pittsburgh. He surrendered at Fort Necessity.

3. Battle of Quebec - William Pitt of Britain changed the war effort to concentrate more on Canada. The French lost at Quebec. Many of them now speak English.

4. Outcome of the War - The British won and formally controlled the 13 colonies and areas to the west. But, how were the British going to pay for such an expensive war? The following decades of taxation would help lead to the Revolutionary War. Salutary neglect was over.

5. After the war, a group of Pennsylvania frontiersmen killed 20 innocent people of the Conestoga tribe. These *Paxton Boys* also resented the rising influence of eastern interests. A large group marched on Philadelphia in 1764 to demonstrate the grievances of those on the frontier. Benjamin Franklin and others met the mob, and promised to consider their concerns.

See pg. 181 for a quick guide to Colonial Geography, and pg. 184 for details of early American Indian (Native American) cultures

Review Questions

"Having undertaken, for the Glory of God, and advancements of the Christian faith and honor of our King and Country, a voyage to plant the first colony in the Northern parts of Virginia, do by these presents, solemnly and mutually, in the presence of God, and one another, covenant and combine ourselves together into a civil body politic; for our better ordering, and preservation and furtherance of the ends aforesaid; and by virtue hereof to enact, constitute, and frame, such just and equal laws, ordinances, acts, constitutions, and offices, from time to time, as shall be thought most meet and convenient for the general good of the colony; unto which we promise all due submission and obedience."

– Mayflower Compact, 1620

1. Which of the following would be a relevant continuation of the above statement?
    A) An elimination of class distinctions
    B) The equality of all people
    C) The creation of a centralized court system
    D) A democratic government in the US

2. Why was the above community set up in North America?
    A) To bring religious freedom for Separatists
    B) To establish a tobacco planting joint-stock company
    C) To spread Roman Catholicism through missions
    D) To secure raw materials and gold for the Mother Country

3. Which colonial entity would have a similar impact on the early United States?
    A) House of Burgesses
    B) Dominion of New England
    C) Navigation Acts
    D) Encomienda system

Answers and Explanations

1. **D**. The Mayflower Compact foreshadowed a democratic form of government in the United States.

2. **A**. Pilgrims were seeking religious freedom in the colonies. They separated from the Church of England and established a settlement in Plymouth.

3. **A**. The House of Burgesses was an early representative democracy in Virginia and therefore, another example of foreshadowing democracy in American History.

Short Essay Question Set

Document 1:

Source: Benjamin Franklin. "Join, or Die." Page 2. Woodcut from the *Pennsylvania Gazette*, Philadelphia, May 9, 1754. Serial & Government Publications Division, Library of Congress

Document 2:

The following is an excerpt from Edmund Burke's *Speech on Conciliation with America* given in the House of Commons in 1775. Here he reflects on British relationships with the colonies from c1607-c1763.

When I contemplate these things; when I know that the Colonies in general owe little or nothing to any care of ours, and that they are not squeezed into this happy form by the constraints of watchful and suspicious government, but that, through a wise and <u>salutary neglect</u>, a generous nature has been suffered to take her own way to perfection; when I reflect upon these effects, when I see how profitable they have been to us, I feel all the pride of power sink, and all presumption in the wisdom of human contrivances melt and die away within me. My rigour relents. I pardon something to the spirit of liberty.

- **Describe the historical context surrounding documents 1 and 2**
- **Analyze Document 1 and explain how *audience*, or *purpose*, or *bias*, or *point of view* affects this document's use as a reliable source of evidence**

Revolution and the Constitution, 1763-1791

To pay for the costly French and Indian War, the British had to tax their subjects in America. The Stamp Act, Sugar Act, Townshend Acts... surely the colonists would understand the need to pay for the British Army...right? Gradually, the colonies pulled away from Britain, used their *Common Sense*, and declared independence. After losing many of the early skirmishes of the Revolutionary War, the Battle of Saratoga proved to be the turning point the Americans needed. After France and other European nations aided the cause for independence, Britain surrendered, and the 13 colonies became 13 states. But how would they legislate? After a failed Articles of Confederation, a strong and everlasting Constitution was ratified in 1788.

HERE IS WHAT YOU NEED TO KNOW:
Definition: Proclamation of 1763

This British law stated that colonists could not settle west of the Appalachian Mountains. The Americans were furious, but the British were attempting to protect them from Native American raids led by chiefs such as *Pontiac*. For the colonists, this would be one of the many arguments they would have with King George III and Parliament.

Definition: Sugar Act (American Revenue Act), 1764

As mentioned in the Colonial Era, the *Navigation Acts* were rarely enforced until 1764. That year, in an effort to raise money, British taxes were placed on imports of sugar. The Sugar Act intensified the cries of "no taxation without representation" that would be heard before the Revolutionary War. This statement meant that the colonists had no way to control British policy because they lacked seats in Parliament. But even with a seat, they would have been outvoted. The British believed the colonies were indeed "virtually represented" as Parliament was passing laws in the interests of all British subjects...wherever they happened to be in the world.

Definition: Stamp Act, 1765

Prime Minister George Grenville said that a royal stamp had to be placed on the parchment of printed materials and official legal documents. Of course, that stamp was taxed. The Stamp Act was a *direct* and *internal* tax. The direct tax was added to the purchase price (which went directly to the government). An internal tax was on items within the colonies (external taxes came on imports). The Stamp Act was repealed after colonists protested and Benjamin Franklin lobbied Parliament. Although the act was repealed, Parliament passed the 1766 *Declaratory Act* that affirmed Parliament's *"full power and authority to make laws...to bind the colonies...in all cases whatsoever."*

Definition: Townshend Acts, 1767

After the Stamp Act was repealed, Parliament passed the Townshend Acts (named for British official Charles Townshend). They were external and indirect taxes (included in the price) placed on imports such as paper and tea. To avoid these duties, many colonists smuggled. To combat smuggling, English customs agents investigated homes with *writs of assistance*, or permits (which acted as search warrants) for search and seizure.

Definition: Boston Massacre, 1770

This massacre began as a protest against British rule and taxes. It escalated into a mob in the streets of Boston. Things got out of hand when people hurled snowballs and rocks at the

British troops. The soldiers fired guns, killing Bostonians such as Crispus Attucks (a free black). John Adams successfully defended the British troops in court. The event displayed the escalating tension in the area.

Two years later in 1772, another massacre occurred, this time to the crew of the British customs ship, the *Gaspee*. After the ship crashed into the shore in Rhode Island, it was boarded by colonists. They wounded some of the crew, looted the ship, and burned it.

Definition: Tea Act and Tea Party, 1773

The Tea Act actually did not raise prices, but it gave the British East India Company a monopoly in America. British tea was now available at a discount price (coupled with the small tax on tea from the Townshend Acts). However, the Americans resented such an action in principle. In addition, the act also upset local merchants who were trying to sell their own tea, as well as colonial middle men. So, led by Samuel Adams of the protest-organization ***The Sons of Liberty***, colonists dressed up like Native Americans and dumped 342 cases of British tea into Boston Harbor.

Definition: Intolerable Acts of 1774

The Intolerable (or Coercive) Acts punished the colonists for the Tea Party. The Acts:

1. Closed Boston Harbor.
2. Decreased the power of the Massachusetts legislature.
3. Made colonists pay for the destroyed tea.
4. Issued a new ***quartering act*** (troops could stay in private homes).
5. The Quebec Act was passed as well which increased the size of Quebec, and the prevalence of Roman Catholicism in the region. The mostly Protestant colonists opposed this.

Definition: Committees of Correspondence

In the early 1770s, Samuel Adams reported about British activity taking place in towns throughout Massachusetts. Virginia would follow suit to create a chain of communication throughout the colonies.

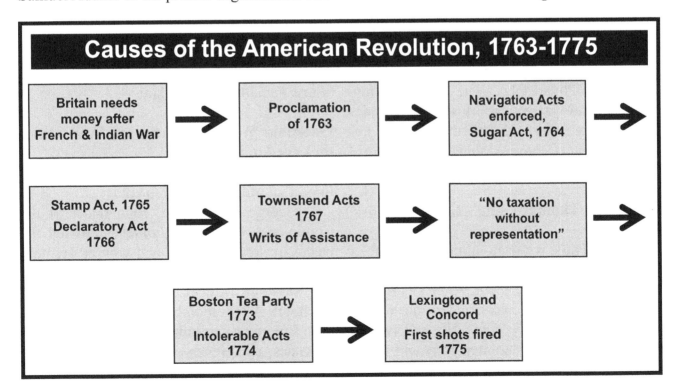

Causes of the American Revolution, 1763-1775

Britain needs money after French & Indian War → Proclamation of 1763 → Navigation Acts enforced, Sugar Act, 1764 →

Stamp Act, 1765 / Declaratory Act 1766 → Townshend Acts 1767 / Writs of Assistance → "No taxation without representation" →

Boston Tea Party 1773 / Intolerable Acts 1774 → Lexington and Concord / First shots fired 1775

Question: Where were the first shots of the Revolutionary War fired?

Answer: Lexington, and soon after, Concord, Massachusetts.

These were two unorganized battles. Lexington was known as "the shot heard around the world." Although Paul Revere was captured in his ride warning of the attacking British, soldiers at Lexington were ready for battle. Still to this day, no one knows who fired first. Colonial *Minutemen* (who assembled within minutes) defended Lexington against the British Regulars. The war officially began, thus dividing colonists between American *Patriots* and British Loyalists or *Tories*.

Definition: Olive Branch Petition, July 1775

This was a last ditch effort to reconcile with King George III. The King was not receptive. To "extend the olive branch" means to ask for peace.

Definition: Continental Congress

There were two separate meetings:

1. 1774, Philadelphia. Colonists protested both Parliament's actions and a lack of representation. Note: They were still loyal to the British Crown at this point.

2. 1775, Philadelphia. The colonists from New England wanted war. Most other colonies wanted more diplomacy. Still, the colonists prepared for war. George Washington was named Commander-in-Chief of the Continental Army.

Definition: Thomas Paine's *Common Sense*, 1776

Thomas Paine wrote an influential pamphlet where he said that it was "*common sense*" for America to be independent. After all, Britain is thousands of miles away, and is substantially smaller. "*Tis time to part.*" His widely read pamphlet challenged the monarchy and led to increased demands for independence.

Definition: Egalitarianism

The spirit of the Revolution was egalitarianism...simply put, a fancy word for equality.

Question: What do I need to know about the Declaration of Independence of July 4, 1776?

Answer:

1. Enlightenment thought: "All men are created equal" with three unalienable rights..."life, liberty, and the pursuit of happiness." Remember, these are Enlightenment ideas stemming from *John Locke* in particular. Much of US history involves groups such as women, African Americans, and Native Americans fighting for these rights. The document used the term "consent of the governed" referring to Locke's belief that legitimate governments, while respecting basic rights and liberties, gain permission from their citizens to exert power.

2. The document included a long list of grievances against King George III.

The document, written by Thomas Jefferson, declared independence, and that the United States was a free nation. Of course, it would mean nothing if the war with Britain was lost. All of the signers would have been tried for treason in that case, including John Hancock, whose signature was the largest.

Question: What Revolutionary War battles do I need to know?

Answer: The following tend to be the most important military events to know:

1. George Washington, commander of the Continental Army of *volunteers*, crossed the Delaware River in 1776 and won at Trenton, New Jersey, and later at Princeton, New Jersey.

2. Saratoga, New York in 1777 was the turning point. A few months after British General John Burgoyne surrendered to American Horatio Gates, the French signed an alliance with the United States. The French gave massive aid

for the independence cause.

3. At Valley Forge, Pennsylvania in 1777-78, Washington held his army together in the winter, and recharged them for battle.

4. The final British defeat was at Yorktown, Virginia in 1781. General Charles Cornwallis surrendered his army to Washington.

Question: What famous foreigners helped the US out?

Answer:

1. Marquis de Lafayette - Young French aristocrat who came over and was like a son to Washington as his assistant.

2. Thaddeus Kosciuszko - Polish engineer who helped move artillery to the high ground at Saratoga.

3. Baron von Steuben - German officer known for his discipline and drilling of soldiers at Valley Forge.

Question: How on Earth did the United States win this thing?

Answer: Although Great Britain was a much stronger force…

1. The US had foreign help from France, Spain, and the Netherlands.

2. The US was fighting a defensive battle on their own soil.

3. Britain left much of its army in Europe because the continent was always in a flux of chaos.

4. The US had higher morale and a desire for independence. It is important to know that the American soldiers were volunteers. There would be no drafting of soldiers until the Civil War.

Definition: Treaty of Paris, 1783

This treaty ended the war, and established the 13 colonies as 13 states. It also secured more US territory east of the Mississippi River. Benjamin Franklin and John Adams were present to make sure the United States kept its land.

Adams left France to become Minister to Britain. Jefferson later became Minister to France.

Definition: Republican Motherhood

This was the idea that women should become educated, and teach their kids to honor civic duty and *republicanism*. The belief was that the republican virtues of the Revolution (liberty, equality, service) should be passed down to the next generation. As the keeper of the home, women were vital for the raising of good citizens. In 1776, Abigail Adams wrote to her husband John with an early plea for women's rights. She asked him to "remember the ladies" in their new code of laws.

Question: Who wrote the Articles of Confederation?

Answer: John Dickinson of Pennsylvania gets most of the credit. But Benjamin Franklin looked over the document.

The Articles were a governing document that gave power to the states, as after being controlled by Britain, there was a reluctance to form a strong central government. The Articles were in effect from 1781-1789 (The Critical Period).

Question: What were some of the weaknesses of the Articles of Confederation?

Answer:

1. Each state could coin its own money.

2. No Executive Branch existed.

3. No regulation of interstate commerce.

4. No national court system.

5. No army.

6. 9 of the 13 states had to agree to pass a law.

7. All 13 states needed to agree to pass an amendment.

8. No efficient taxation system.

Definition: Shays' Rebellion, 1786-87

Daniel Shays' Rebellion was a Massachusetts uprising where farmers protested imprisonment for debt, lack of currency, and high taxes. It showed just how weak the Articles were, as there was no national army to put down the insurrection. The Massachusetts state militia eventually ended the violence, but plans to scrap the Articles intensified.

Definition: Land Ordinance of 1785 and Northwest Ordinance of 1787

These were two of the few accomplishments of the Articles. Both provided for future settlement in the west (today's Midwest). The Land Ordinance divided land into townships containing 36 sections for purchase. The Northwest Ordinance was of more importance, as it *provided statehood* for areas that reached 60,000 inhabitants. *No slavery would be allowed in the Northwest Territory.*

Definition: Annapolis Convention

This was a meeting that decided to have another meeting. Only five states were represented here in Maryland. They determined that the Articles were weak, and further discussion would take place in Philadelphia in 1787.

Definition: Philadelphia Convention

Fifty-five delegates assembled in Philadelphia in 1787. *Their intention was not to make a Constitution*, but rather to *amend* the Articles of Confederation. Of course, they would indeed write a new Constitution here.

Definition: Virginia Plan, New Jersey Plan, Great Compromise of the Convention

In a *republic*, people are elected by the people, to serve the people. The Great Compromise created the modern-day Legislative Branch that makes laws. It was based on:

1. The Virginia Plan - James Madison wanted a bicameral (2 house) legislature based upon population. The greater the population, the more representatives a state would have.

2. The New Jersey Plan - William Paterson wanted representation to be equal so the small states would not be under-represented.

The Great Compromise (or Connecticut Compromise of Roger Sherman) – Created the modern-day bicameral (2 house) legislature where the *House of Representatives* is based upon population, and the *Senate* has equal representation (2 Senators per state). A *census* taken every ten years determines state population and representation. Representatives were the only federal offices voted on by local citizens in the early years of the Republic.

Definition: 3/5th Compromise

But wait a minute! If the House is based on population, how should the United States count slaves?

The Northern states wanted slaves to count for taxation, but not representation.

The Southern states wanted slaves to count for representation but not taxation.

Compromise - Each slave would count for 3/5th of a person for both taxation and representation.

Note: The Transatlantic Slave Trade could continue until 20 years after the Constitution (until 1808).

Definition: Commercial Compromise

The Northern states wanted to regulate interstate commerce and foreign trade. The Southern states feared export taxes, as they exported significant amounts of farm goods.

The compromise gave the federal government the power to regulate interstate commerce and foreign trade, but not the power to tax exports. A tax on imports is referred to as a *tariff*. Sometimes the term *customs duties* is used instead.

Definition: Federalists/Anti-Federalists

Federalists favored the Constitution and were led by James Madison, George Washington, and Alexander Hamilton.

Anti-Federalists were scared that the Constitution might put too much power into the hands of the government, and voiced concerns in their "Anti-Federalist Papers." They were led by James Winthrop, John Hancock, George Clinton, George Mason, and Patrick Henry.

Note: Jefferson (in France), and John Adams (in Great Britain) were not present for the debate.

Question: What was written to persuade New Yorkers and other doubters to ratify the Constitution?

Answer: **The Federalist** (or *The Federalist* Papers) was a series of 85 published essays that argued the need for a strong Constitution.

Alexander Hamilton wrote most of them. John Jay wrote a few on foreign policy. But, James Madison wrote the most famous one, Federalist #10 (see next).

Definition: Federalist #10

James Madison contended that the Constitution would work in a large republic. He believed that a strong union would be able to control tyrannical *factions*, or groups who were out for their own good. He believed that a republic that serves the public good could eliminate smaller factions, and the Constitution would further limit their effects.

Definition: Bill of Rights, 1791

Ultimately the Constitution was ratified (approved) in 1788 when 9 of the 13 states agreed. But the promise for a Bill of Rights was critical. It would become the first 10 Amendments (changes/additions) to the Constitution. The Bill of Rights protected important freedoms such as speech, right to bear arms, due process, prevention of cruel and unusual punishment, and the right to an attorney. The ones you need to know the most are in the No Bull Review Sheet, and will be addressed later in court case explanations.

Note: The Bill of Rights was ratified in 1791, two years after the Constitution went into effect.

Review Questions

"The history of the present King of Great Britain is a history of repeated injuries and usurpations, all having in direct object the establishment of an absolute Tyranny over these States. To prove this, let Facts be submitted to a candid world …

"He has endeavoured to prevent the population of these States; for that purpose obstructing the Laws for Naturalization of Foreigners; refusing to pass others to encourage their migrations hither, and raising the conditions of new Appropriations of Lands.

"He has combined with others to subject us to a jurisdiction foreign to our constitution, and unacknowledged by our laws; giving his Assent to their Acts of pretended Legislation:

"For Quartering large bodies of armed troops among us;

"For protecting them, by a mock Trial, from punishment for any Murders which they should commit on the Inhabitants of these States;

"For cutting off our Trade with all parts of the world;

"For imposing Taxes on us without our Consent:"

– Declaration of Independence, 1776

1. Which of the following directly caused the above list of grievances?
   A) The Battle of Saratoga
   B) British acts following the French and Indian War
   C) The Philadelphia Convention
   D) Growing support in the colonies for a limited monarchy

2. Why were the complaints of the colonists not further voiced before 1760?
   A) Freedom of speech was denied in the colonies
   B) A time period of salutary neglect kept opinions loyal to Britain
   C) Opposition party members were sent west of the Appalachians to French territory
   D) Revolutionaries planned their actions in secret

3. How did Britain view colonial representation in Parliament?
   A) They did not believe colonists to be subjects of the British Crown
   B) They believed the hundreds of colonial diplomats already in Britain were sufficient
   C) They viewed the colonies as a foreign legislative body
   D) They believed the colonists were already virtually represented

Answers and Explanations

1. **B**. A series of acts such as the Sugar Act, Tea Act, and Intolerable Acts, are reflected in the grievances listed in the Declaration of Independence.

2. **B**. Salutary neglect refers to the time period before the French and Indian War where the British government didn't enforce laws to a great extent. The French and Indian War created a debt for which the British government tried to satisfy with higher taxes.

3. **D**. "No taxation without representation" was a large complaint of the colonists. However, the British believed the colonies were indeed "virtually represented" as Parliament was passing laws in the interests of all British subjects … wherever they happened to be in the world.

Short Essay Question Set

Document 1:

"Under their own construction of the general clause, at the end of the enumerated powers, the Congress may grant monopolies in trade and commerce, constitute new crimes, inflict unusual and severe punishments, and extend their powers as far as they think proper; so that the state legislatures have no security for the powers now presumed to remain to them, or the people for their rights."
                                                     - George Mason, 1787

Document 2:

"To be fearful of investing Congress, constituted as that body is, with ample authorities for national purposes, appears to me the very climax of popular absurdity and madness. Could Congress exert them for the detriment of the people without injuring themselves in an equal or greater proportion? Are not their interests inseparably connected with those of their constituents?"
                                                     - George Washington, 1786

•**Describe the historical context surrounding documents 1 and 2**
•**Analyze Document 2 and explain how *audience*, or *purpose*, or *bias*, or *point of view* affects this document's use as a reliable source of evidence**

U.S. Government

For understanding US History, certain government and constitutional procedures are necessary to know. This unit will simplify the major themes, powers, and structures of United States government.

Question: What do the three branches of government do?

Answer: The idea of *separation of powers* came from Enlightenment philosopher, Baron de Montesquieu. He believed that the powers of government should be balanced between the:

1. *Legislative Branch* - Makes the laws. The United States has a bicameral (two house) system composed of the ***House of Representatives*** (435 members) which is based on population, and the ***Senate*** which has 2 members for each state (100 members). The Speaker of the House controls the House of Representatives. The Vice President can preside over the Senate, though rarely does. A President pro tempore is chosen by the Senate instead.

2. *Executive Branch* - Enforces, or executes the laws to ensure people obey them. The President leads this branch. In a state, this would be the Governor. If the President can't perform duties, the Vice President becomes "Acting President."

If the President dies in office, the Vice President becomes the President. After the VP, the next in line for the Presidency would be the Speaker of the House, and President pro tempore of the Senate.

3. *Judicial Branch* - Interprets the laws to make sure they are fair and just. ***They protect the Constitution as the highest law of the land.*** No laws can overrule the Constitution.

The head of this branch is the Supreme Court.

Question: What are the main powers of each branch?

Answer:

1. Legislative Branch's two houses - Makes laws, approves Presidential appointments, overrides vetoes, declares war, regulates interstate trade, and impeaches federal officials including the President.

2. Executive Branch's President - Commander-in-Chief of the military, signs and vetoes laws (strike them down), pardons people to erase their federal crimes, makes treaties, appoints government officials, recommends laws to Congress, and delivers the State of the Union Address.

3. Judicial Branch's Supreme Court - Decides if legislation is in line with the US Constitution. They can settle the disputes of *state vs. state*. The Supreme Court can strike down federal (national government) acts, as well as high state court decisions.

Question: What other offices in government should I know about?

Answer: The President has a cabinet, or group of advisors. Some of these departments are:

1. Secretary of State - Deals with foreign policy.

2. Secretary of Defense - Military affairs.

3. Department of the Treasury - Financial matters.

4. Attorney General - Heads criminal investigations for the Department of Justice.

Question: What are the qualifications to hold major office?

1. House of Representatives - Must be 25

years old, a US citizen for 7 years, and a resident of the state where they are serving. The term is 2 years.

2. Senate - Must be 30 years old, a US citizen for 9 years, and a resident of the state where they are serving. The term is 6 years.

3. President/Vice President - Must be 35 years old, **born in the United States**, and a US citizen for 14 years. The term is 4 years. Today, Representatives and Senators are elected by the people, and the President is chosen by electors (explained later).

Question: How does a Bill Become a Law?

In your textbook there's probably a really complex web of stuff. Most of it you don't need to know until you take a full year government class. Here's a simple 9-word phrase for you: **Passed by House, Passed by Senate, Signed by President**.

In detail:

1. Before a law is passed and signed, it's called a "bill."

2. Bills are drafted in **committees** in both the House and the Senate. There are even subcommittees that study the bills. Each house amends the other one's bill so the potential law voted on is the same. Each house then debates the bill and votes. In the Senate, debate can be unlimited. This is called a **filibuster**. If the bill passes both houses by a **simple majority** (one more than half), it can be signed by the President.

3. Presidents can **veto** (strike down) a bill if they don't approve of it. The Legislative Branch can then override the veto with a 2/3 vote from each house, or make changes to the bill for the President to reconsider.

Note: There are differences between the House and Senate. The House has powers to start all revenue (money) bills, impeach the President (explained later), and they determine who becomes President if the Electoral College is deadlocked.

The Senate can ratify treaties, act as the jury for the impeachment case, and approve Presidential appointments. They are generally known as the *upper house*.

Question: What other items about the law-making process should I know?

Answer:

1. Lobbying - When powerful special interest groups attempt to persuade lawmakers to vote a certain way.

2. Pork-Barrel Legislation - "Pork" benefits only certain districts, usually in the form of public works projects such as bridges or roads. The idea is to bring money into local areas and benefit specific representatives.

3. Logrolling - Trading votes. "I'll vote for your bill, if you vote for mine."

4. Rider - Something added to a bill that has little to do with it. For example, let's say a bill on science research is drafted. A rider is then tacked onto it for television censorship.

Definition: Federalism

Federalism is the division of power between the state and federal governments. According to Article I, Section 8 of the Constitution, the Congress has **delegated** or **enumerated powers** and can do big things like declare war and coin money. According to the Tenth Amendment, states have **reserved powers**. This means they are reserved the right to control other things, such as education, marriage, and driving laws. Some powers are shared, like taxation. These are called **concurrent powers**. The chart on the next page sums up what you need to know about federalism.

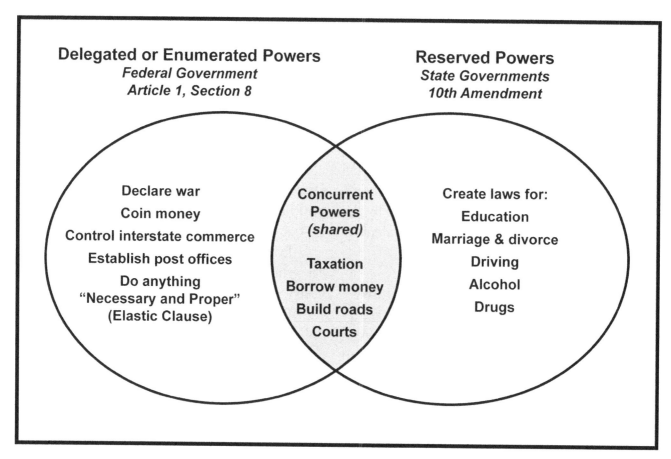

Delegated or Enumerated Powers
Federal Government
Article 1, Section 8

Reserved Powers
State Governments
10th Amendment

Declare war
Coin money
Control interstate commerce
Establish post offices
Do anything
"Necessary and Proper"
(Elastic Clause)

Concurrent Powers (shared)

Taxation
Borrow money
Build roads
Courts

Create laws for:
Education
Marriage & divorce
Driving
Alcohol
Drugs

Note: An incredibly common error is for students to mix up *separation of powers* and *federalism*. Don't do that! *Federalism* means *division of power* between the federal and state governments. The word *federal* is right in the term! *Separation of powers* deals with the three branches *within* the national/federal government.

Definition: Elastic Clause

Congress also has a delegated power to do anything "necessary and proper." This allows the Constitution to grow over time, so it doesn't become a dated document. This power is found in the **Elastic Clause** (Article I, Section 8, Clause 18). Use of the Elastic Clause is indicative of a **loose interpretation** of the Constitution, and gives government more power to legislate (with **implied powers**). So let's say the

government wants to pass a bill on internet reform. There was no internet in 1789, but making such a law is "necessary and proper." **Strict construction/interpretation** would be the opposite, and would limit the government's power.

Definition: Denied Powers

To protect against tyranny, the Founding Fathers denied some powers to both the federal and state governments.

The federal government can't grant titles of nobility, or levy export taxes. They also can't pass **ex-post facto** laws. This means that if you did something legal on Tuesday, and a law was passed on Thursday against what you were doing, you wouldn't be breaking the law for your Tuesday actions. Finally, there is no **Bill of Attainder** permitted for illegal imprisonments without a trial.

States are denied the right to enter into treaties with foreign nations. They also can't coin money or tax imports or exports.

Definition: Electoral College

For the path to the Presidency just remember that <u>P</u>encils <u>N</u>eed <u>E</u>rasers … <u>P</u>rimary + <u>N</u>ominating Convention + <u>E</u>lectoral College.

Primaries, or caucuses, are small elections in the states that determine which candidate from each political party will be chosen in a ***nominating convention***. Those candidates nominated will then run in the November Presidential Election.

Whoever gets the most votes in the ***Electoral College*** wins the November Election. The popular vote is irrelevant, and candidates therefore campaign in "swing states," or those states where the election can go either way. Typical blue (Democrat) and red (Republican) states don't see much campaigning, as the election results are rarely in doubt.

On Election Day, in all 50 states, people vote for electors who have sworn to vote for a candidate. The number of Electoral Votes a state has is equal to the number of Representatives plus two, for the two Senators each state has. You need to know that to win a Presidential Election, a candidate must receive a majority of all possible Electoral Votes. If no candidate gets a majority, then the House of Representatives chooses the President.

Today, there are 538 votes up for grabs. That's 435 Representatives + 100 Senators + Washington, DC gets 3 (23rd Amendment). Because they are the most populous states, California, Texas, New York, and Florida have the most electoral votes on the table.

At the end of the night, all of the secured Electoral Votes are added up. Whoever reaches 270 votes (which is a majority of the 538 possible votes), wins the election.

Definition: Impeachment

Impeachment does not mean to kick out of office! The House of Representatives can impeach certain federal officials, such as the President. This means to charge with a crime. After the House impeaches, the Senate holds a trial and decides if they want to kick the official out of office.

Question: How can the Constitution be changed?

Answer: Through Amendments (changes or additions). An Amendment becomes a part of the Constitution, and is therefore the highest law of the land. There are four methods of passing an amendment, but only one is generally used. After 2/3 of each House approves an Amendment, 3/4 of the state legislatures have to ratify it. Only the Twenty-First Amendment didn't use this method. It instead ratified when 3/4 of the states had a special convention to bring back the sale of alcohol.

Question: How does the Supreme Court work?

Answer: Article III of the Constitution created the Judicial Branch and the Supreme Court. Today, there are 9 justices (which includes the Chief Justice) on the high court.

1. They only hear cases that involve Constitutional issues.

2. They can overturn cases that come out of the lower federal courts and the highest court of each state.

3. To get to the Supreme Court, there's an ***appeals process*** (***appellate jurisdiction***) that goes through the federal court system or the states' courts. Much rarer is ***original jurisdiction***, which means that cases involving ambas-

sadors, foreign ministers, or state vs. state, can go *directly* to the Supreme Court.

4. The Supreme Court is the highest court in the US. It can overturn decisions from both state and federal governments. See *judicial review* on pg. 30.

Definition: Checks and Balances

Each branch looks over the shoulders of the other two to make sure that there are no abuses of power. You need to know certain checks and balances. If the President doesn't like a bill, it can be vetoed to prevent it from becoming a law. The Legislative Branch can then override that veto with a 2/3 vote from each house. The President appoints federal jobs such as Supreme Court justices, and the Senate approves these appointments. The President can make treaties, but the Senate must approve them. The Judicial Branch can strike down actions of both the President and Congress. See the illustration below.

Question: How are Supreme Court Justices appointed?

Answer: They are appointed by the President and confirmed by the Senate. Once appointed and confirmed, they serve for life.

Definition: Unwritten Constitution

This term is used to describe things that happen in United States government procedure, that's not directly in the Constitution. Exam-

	LEGISLATIVE	EXECUTIVE	JUDICIAL
LEGISLATIVE CHECKS		1. Can override vetoes by 2/3 vote 2. Senate can refuse to confirm a Presidential appointment	1. Can change the size of the Supreme Court 2. Can impeach and convict justices (as well as the President)
EXECUTIVE CHECKS	1. Can veto bills 2. Can call Congress into special session		1. Appoints Supreme Court justices 2. Grants pardons and reprieves
JUDICIAL CHECKS	1. Can declare an act of Congress to be unconstitutional (judicial review)	1. Can declare an act of the President to be unconstitutional	

ples include political parties, the President's cabinet, judicial review, and nominating conventions. These are all big parts of American government. It's almost as if they are in the Constitution…but they're not!

There are 27 Amendments. As stated earlier, the Bill of Rights provided the first ten at the same time in 1791. Here are some of the most important ones you should know.

Question: What Amendments do I need to know?

Bill of Rights Amendments (1791)
1st – Freedoms of speech, press, religion, assembly, and right to petition the government.
2nd – Right to bear arms.
4th – Freedom from unreasonable searches and seizures.
5th – Due process rights (right to fair justice, and freedoms from self-incrimination). Also, one cannot be tried twice for the same crime. This is a freedom from "double-jeopardy."
6th – Right to a fair trial and attorney.
10th – Division of power between the states and federal government (called federalism).

Civil War Amendments
13th Amendment (1865) – Abolition of Slavery
14th Amendment (1868) – Equality
15th Amendment (1870) – Universal Male Suffrage

Progressive Era Amendments
16th Amendment (1913) – Income Tax
17th Amendment (1913) – Direct Election of Senators
18th Amendment (1919) – Prohibition
19th Amendment (1920) – Women's Suffrage

Other Important Amendments
22nd Amendment (1951) – Two Term Limit for Presidents
26th Amendment (1971) – Lowered the voting age to 18 in 1971, as Vietnam War soldiers were not old enough to vote

You will also have to know several US Supreme Court decisions. They are described throughout this book. For a listing, see the No Bull Review Sheet on pages 171-173.

The New Republic, 1789-c1823

(c, an abbreviation for the Latin circa, *will be used in this book to approximate time periods)*

The New Republic was a time period from roughly 1789-1823 (or George Washington's Inauguration to James Monroe's Doctrine). The country was fragile. Would the American experiment work? Washington's Presidency was full of walking on foreign policy eggshells. His financial advisor, Alexander Hamilton, presented a new financial plan that included a national bank. To Washington's chagrin, political parties began to emerge, leaving Federalists (Hamiltonians) battling Democratic-Republicans (Jeffersonians). After nearly going to war with France and limiting free speech of the American people, Federalist President John Adams lost the Election of 1800 to Democratic-Republican, Thomas Jefferson. However, Jefferson would legislate like a Federalist. So too at times would his Democratic-Republican successor, James Madison. After the War of 1812 ended in a stalemate, President James Monroe took over and looked to eliminate foreign influences from the Western Hemisphere.

HERE IS WHAT YOU NEED TO KNOW:
Question: What were some of the precedents of George Washington's Presidency?

Answer: A precedent means things borrowed by future Presidents.

1. A two term limit.
2. Neutrality in foreign affairs.
3. Formation of a cabinet to aid him in decisions.
4. A farewell address upon leaving office.

Question: Where were the three capitals of the United States?

Answer:
1. New York City 1789-1790

2. Then, it temporarily moved to Philadelphia (1790-1800), but…

3. After James Madison, Thomas Jefferson, and Alexander Hamilton had a fateful dinner, the capital was moved to Washington, DC. At the dinner, it was agreed that the capital would move south in exchange for state debts being assumed by the federal government. The paying off of Revolutionary War debts favored Northern states, as the South did not owe as much money. The Dinner Compromise, formally called the Compromise of 1790, was also important to the South because slavery could now exist in the nation's capital.

Question: Who was in Washington's first cabinet?

Answer: A cabinet is a collection of advisors.

1. Secretary of State (deals with foreign affairs) - Thomas Jefferson

2. Secretary of the Treasury (deals with financial affairs) - Alexander Hamilton

3. Secretary of War (deals with the military) - Henry Knox

Question: What made up Hamilton's financial plan?

Answer: In short, Hamilton wanted to:

1. Pay off all debts, foreign and domestic, by issuing new bonds to cover old debts. He believed that owing an immense debt would weaken the nation's credit and economic reputation.

2. Support a national bank to monitor and control the money supply. It favored the wealthy, as stockholders controlled the bank. It was passed by virtue of the *Elastic Clause*. The Elastic Clause allows Congress to do anything "necessary and proper." This creates a *loose interpretation* of the Constitution, and gives government more power to legislate (with *implied powers*). *Strict con-*

struction/interpretation would be the opposite, and would limit the government's power.

3. Support taxes on imports and luxury items such as whiskey.

Question: What were the differences between the Hamiltonians and Jeffersonians?

Answer: For most of it, remember that you made safe plans…**SAFE PLANS**

Jefferson = favored **S**tates' rights or **S**trict interpretation of the Constitution, **A**griculture, **F**rance over Great Britain, and the **E**ducated and common man…**SAFE**

Hamilton = favored the **P**ropertied and rich, **L**oose interpretation of the Constitution, an **A**rmy, **N**ational bank, and a **S**trong central government...**PLANS**

Definition: Whiskey Rebellion, 1794

In 1794 "moonshiners" in western Pennsyl-

Differences Between Thomas Jefferson and Alexander Hamilton

Issue	Thomas Jefferson	Alexander Hamilton
Who should have power in government?	The educated/ commoners	The propertied aristocracy
Give most power to the:	States	Federal or Central Gov't. (Strong Federal Gov't.)
Constitutional Interpretation	Strict — Don't give the Federal Government too much power to legislate	Loose — Allow the Federal Government to do whatever is "necessary and proper"
Stance on Army	Against! Gives government too much power	For! Will make the government powerful
National Bank	Con: Favors the rich	Pro: Stabilizes the economy
Favored foreign nation	France — They supported our revolution	Great Britain — the strongest nation; similar heritage
Preferred Economy	Agriculture	Industry and Commerce

NOTE: Hamiltonians became Federalists; Jeffersonians became Democratic-Republicans

vania were defying Hamilton's whiskey tax. They began an armed protest. Washington, as Commander-in-Chief, sent in the army to end the rebellion. This is significant. Compared to Shays' Rebellion which exposed the absence of an army under the Articles of Confederation, this insurrection was peacefully put down by the stronger government that existed under the Constitution.

Definition: Neutrality

Neutrality means to stay out of foreign alliances and conflicts. This was Washington's foreign policy amidst the backdrop of the French Revolution and conflict between Britain and France. The new nation could hardly afford to fight a war. Going one step further would be *isolationism*. Isolation would mean cutting off all ties, including trade. However, Washington is associated with *neutrality*, which he stated in his 1793 **Proclamation of Neutrality.**

Definition: John Jay's Treaty, 1794

John Jay's treaty with Great Britain was unpopular. First, it did not end **impressment**. Impressment was when Britain seized American sailors and forced them into the British navy (described more in-depth later). In addition, the treaty made the US pay pre-Revolutionary War debts to British merchants, and made Britain the favored nation in terms of trade. This upset other countries, notably France. The treaty did promise to remove British troops from the west.

Definition: Citizen Genêt

Genêt was a French ambassador to the United States in the 1790s. He encouraged anti-British sentiment and the attacking of British ships. The government condemned Genêt, and his actions never amounted to much.

Definition: Thomas Pinckney's Treaty, 1795

Thomas Pinckney's treaty with Spain gave the United States navigation of the Mississippi River, and a right to trade in New Orleans.

Definition: Washington's Farewell Address

As he left office, Washington warned about forming alliances with foreign countries. He was also concerned about the rise of political parties at home.

Definition: Election of 1796

John Adams (Federalist) defeated Thomas Jefferson (Democrat-Republican). Jefferson became the Vice President because of a provision in the original Constitution that said the second place finisher would become VP. In a country that now had political parties, Adams' presidency was doomed from the start.

Definition: XYZ Affair, 1797

To smooth things out with the French after Jay's Treaty favored Britain, the United States sent Secretary of State John Marshall and others to France to protect peace. The only problem was, the French wouldn't let the Americans talk to a diplomat named Talleyrand unless a fee of $250,000 was paid. The Americans wouldn't pay, and this incident led to the **Quasi-War**, or **Undeclared War** with France. No battles occurred

Definition: Alien and Sedition Acts, 1798

After the XYZ Affair, panic set in for Adams and the Federalists. The Alien and Sedition Acts were four separate laws that limited free speech against the government, and allowed the President to deport undesirables who were suspected of plotting against the United States. The acts were a black eye for the Adams Administration, and might have led to his losing re-election.

Definition: Kentucky and Virginia Resolutions, 1798-99

Arguing for states' rights and strict interpretation of the constitution, Vice President Thomas Jefferson (Kentucky Resolution) and James Madison (Virginia Resolution) secretly wrote these statements in response to the Alien and Sedition Acts. They wrote that state legislatures *should* have the right to declare these acts of the federal government "null and void." That idea, of course, would go against the very fabric of the Constitution. Unlike similar ideas penned later, these were created as protests against the Federalist Party, rather than an argument for disunion. Here is the timeline of events:

Definition: Election of 1800

The Election of 1800 was a mess. Jefferson had more Electoral Votes than Adams, but he was tied with Aaron Burr. Burr was supposed to be Jefferson's Vice Presidential candidate. But Burr did not step aside, and the election went to the House of Representatives. With recommendations from his old foe Hamilton, Jefferson was chosen President. In 1804, Burr assassinated Hamilton in a duel for unrelated reasons. Burr would later be involved in a failed plot to get part of the country to secede (leave the Union).

Definition: Twelfth Amendment

Because of the chaos stemming from the Election of 1800, this amendment stipulated that the President and Vice President shall run together on the same ticket. This way, it's evident as to which candidate is running for what office.

Definition: Revolution of 1800

The Revolution of 1800 was the nickname for Jefferson's Presidential victory. The Democratic-Republicans, the party thought to represent the average citizen, peacefully took power from the Federalists.

Definition: Louisiana Purchase, 1803

Looking to gain control of New Orleans for agricultural trade on the Mississippi River, President Jefferson found a better deal. He used implied powers to purchase the enormous territory of Louisiana from France's Napoleon Bonaparte, who was looking to leave the area amidst a slave revolt in Haiti. The US paid $15 million in a purchase made *via a treaty ratified by the Senate.* Although the deal would double the size of the country, Jefferson was forced to act like a Federalist to secure it.

Definition: Lewis and Clark

Meriwether Lewis and William Clark explored the new Louisiana Territory, and went as far as the Pacific Ocean, traveling much of the way on the Oregon Trail. They received help from a young Native American, Sacagawea. By the way, she did not speak English! Her husband could translate her language into French.

Question: Where was the first overseas battle for the United States?

Answer: Tripoli

Jefferson sent gunboats to Tripoli (Libya) to defeat the Barbary Pirates that were disrupting American trade in the Mediterranean Sea.

Definition: John Marshall and *Marbury* v. *Madison*

Supreme Court Chief Justice John Marshall increased the power of the federal government. More importantly, he was known for *judicial review,* which is the Supreme Court's power to review a law and determine if it is constitutional or unconstitutional. In *Marbury* v. *Madison*, Marshall and the Court declared part of the Judiciary Act of 1789 unconstitutional. Most of the important parts of the act were kept alive, as it created the structure of the Judicial Branch and explained the appeals process. If you want more information:

John Adams appointed Federalist "midnight judges" in the last days of his Presidency which were created by the Judiciary Act of 1801. He wanted to make these appointments before the Democratic-Republicans took office. Federalist William Marbury never received his job commission from the next Secretary of State, James Madison. He went to the Supreme Court to get a *writ of mandamus* (court order to force Madison to deliver his appointment). Although the Judiciary Act of 1789 said one could obtain a writ, the Constitution said nothing about going directly to the Supreme Court for such a matter. Hence, that part of the law was unconstitutional.

Note: Jefferson hated the Federalist Supreme Court, and attempted to get Federalist judges, like Samuel Chase, impeached and removed from office. He was not successful.

Definition: Embargo Act (1807)

OGRABME! (That's "Embargo" spelled backwards in a famous political cartoon). Jefferson wanted to keep the United States neutral by cutting off trade to Europe. Outlawing exports was an unpopular idea that hurt his Presidency. The Embargo Act would be repealed after widespread protest in the northern states. Here's how it was gradually repealed:

1809 - The Non-Intercourse Act allowed the US to trade with countries other than Britain and France.

1810 - Macon's Bill Number 2 allowed the US to trade with Britain and France if they respected US neutrality.

Question: What were the major causes of the War of 1812 with Britain?

Answer:

1. Impressment of sailors. The British were seizing Americans who were presumed deserters of the British navy, and forcing them into service. Note: Some were indeed deserters, others were not. The notable incident of impressment was the **Chesapeake-Leopard Affair** of 1807. The *Chesapeake* was boarded by the British, and four members of the crew were captured.

2. A quest for more land, particularly Canada.

3. A desire to finally remove Britain from the American northwest.

Question: What should I know about the war itself?

Answer:

1. Washington, DC, including the White House (then called the Executive Mansion or Palace), was burned by the British.

2. Old Ironsides, the USS *Constitution*, fought legendary naval battles.

3. Andrew Jackson became a hero at the Battle of New Orleans, which ironically was fought in 1815 after...

4. The Treaty of Ghent was signed in 1814, which ended the war with no land changes.

5. War Hawks wanted war. Doves wanted peace.

6. President James Madison favored a conscription act (draft), but troops were not drafted into this war.

Question: What were the results of the War of 1812?

Answer:

1. Increased nationalism. While watching a bombardment in Baltimore harbor in 1814, Francis Scott Key wrote his poem, *Defence of Fort M'Henry* (McHenry), that eventually became the US National Anthem.

2. Death of the Federalist Party after the Hartford Convention (which will be explained next).

3. Increased manufacturing.

4. Increased isolationism.

Definition: Hartford Convention, 1814-15

The Federalists assembled in New England to voice their displeasure with the War of 1812 (which

Development of US Political Parties

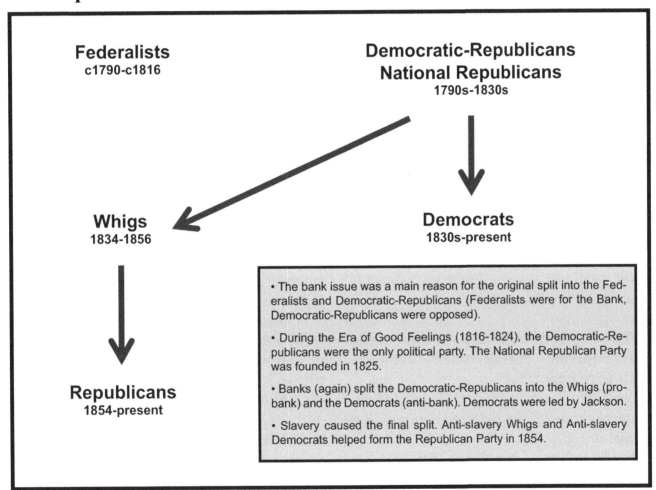

Federalists
c1790-c1816

Democratic-Republicans
National Republicans
1790s-1830s

Whigs
1834-1856

Democrats
1830s-present

Republicans
1854-present

- The bank issue was a main reason for the original split into the Federalists and Democratic-Republicans (Federalists were for the Bank, Democratic-Republicans were opposed).

- During the Era of Good Feelings (1816-1824), the Democratic-Republicans were the only political party. The National Republican Party was founded in 1825.

- Banks (again) split the Democratic-Republicans into the Whigs (pro-bank) and the Democrats (anti-bank). Democrats were led by Jackson.

- Slavery caused the final split. Anti-slavery Whigs and Anti-slavery Democrats helped form the Republican Party in 1854.

was popular elsewhere). They talked about New England secession, and their party broke up. This was the end of the Party of Alexander Hamilton.

Definition: Era of Good Feelings

After the War of 1812 and the disappearance of the Federalist Party, the Republicans (Democratic-Republicans) were the only major political party until c1824. We will refer to the chart on pg. 31 throughout the book to explain political parties during the nineteenth century. As good as the feelings appeared to be, there were still divisions which would boil over into sectionalism (explained later). Economically there was the Panic of 1819 which caused massive unemployment and bank failures. Speculation in the west was a major contributor, as many lost land to foreclosure (or even went to debtors' prison) as a result.

Definition: American System

Kentuckian Henry Clay had a belief that America could self-sufficiently sustain itself, as there was enough agriculture and industry to remain isolated from Europe. High tariffs would protect American jobs, a national bank would control finances, and an internal improvements bill would support infrastructure with new roads and bridges. The full idea never happened, as his internal improvements bill did not become law.

Definition: Adams-Onis Treaty, 1819

This was Secretary of State John Quincy Adams' treaty that led to the purchase of Florida. Andrew Jackson, then in the military, fought in the Seminole Wars in Florida to protect US interests before the treaty.

Question: Besides *Marbury* v. *Madison*, what other Supreme Court decisions of John Marshall were important?

Answer: The following cases all led to a ***strengthening of the federal (national) government***.

1. *McCulloch* v. *Maryland*, 1819 - Because the State of Maryland wanted to get rid of a branch of the Second Bank of the United States, it put a tax on its banknotes. Marshall ruled that a state could not tax a federal entity. He said that the power to tax meant "the power to destroy." The decision affirmed the principle of implied powers, which created the bank.

2. *Gibbons* v. *Ogden*, 1824 - Thomas Gibbons was issued a license from the *federal government* for steamship commerce between New York and New Jersey. Aaron Ogden was issued a similar license from *New York State*. Marshall said that Gibbons had the legitimate license, because the federal government regulated interstate commerce (commerce between different states). Thus, Marshall upheld the supremacy of the federal government.

3. *Cohens* v. *Virginia*, 1821 - Marshall contended that the US Supreme Court could review higher court decisions of the states. Throughout American History, state decisions would be overturned by the Supreme Court. Again, Marshall was extending the federal government's power over the states.

4. *Fletcher* v. *Peck*, 1810 - This was the first time the Supreme Court declared a state law unconstitutional. State legislators in Georgia were bribed into selling a large chunk of land near the Yazoo River (Mississippi). When the next legislature in Georgia came to power, they wanted the land back. Marshall ruled that although the contract was scandalous, it had to be honored. Contracts were binding.

5. *Dartmouth College* v. *Woodward*, 1819 - New Hampshire wanted to change the charter of Dartmouth College which dated back to the days of King George III. Similar to the *Fletcher* case, Marshall stood by the original contract.

Definition: Monroe Doctrine

President Monroe, with the support of Britain, looked to prevent other European nations from establishing new colonies, or meddling in the affairs of countries in the Western Hemisphere. In particular, this was created over concerns that some recent independent countries of Latin America might fall back into the hands of Spain.

Review Questions

"We owe it, therefore, to candor and to the amicable relations existing between the United States and those powers to declare that we should consider any attempt on their part to extend their system to any portion of this hemisphere as dangerous to our peace and safety. With the existing colonies or dependencies of any European power we have not interfered and shall not interfere, but with the Governments who have declared their independence and maintained it, and whose independence we have, on great consideration and on just principles, acknowledged, we could not view any interposition for the purpose of oppressing them, or controlling in any other manner their destiny, by any European power in any other light than as the manifestation of an unfriendly disposition toward the United States."

- Monroe Doctrine, 1823

1. The purpose of the above statement was to
    A) further imperialistic interests in the Pacific
    B) prevent European powers from establishing new colonies in the Western Hemisphere
    C) outline the pretexts for future wars
    D) offer alliances to foreign nations

2. In the time period from 1789-1823, America's foreign policy was most often guided by
    A) the actions and policies of George Washington
    B) a desire for war with France
    C) a quest to obtain overseas colonies
    D) the forming of alliances during the Napoleonic Wars

3. The immediate cause of the above statement was
    A) a need to deprive Britain of its most valuable colonies
    B) a desire to increase the size of the American navy for overseas expansion
    C) a hope to prevent Spain from recolonizing
    D) a need to prevent the French from taking back Louisiana

Answers and Explanations

1. **B**. The purpose of the Monroe Doctrine was to keep European powers from establishing new colonies in the Western Hemisphere. The United States did not want strong nations imperializing in their backyard.

2. **A**. Washington's Proclamation of Neutrality had a great influence on the time period. However, there were still pockets of interventionism and war during that time, such as the War of 1812.

3. **C**. Spain lost many of its colonies to independence movements in the early nineteenth century. The Doctrine looked to prevent Spain from re-colonizing in Latin America. The document is most concerned with Latin American governments maintaining their independence.

Short Essay Question Set

Document 1:

...That if any persons shall unlawfully combine or conspire together, with intent to oppose any measure or measures of the government of the United States, which are or shall be directed by proper authority, or to impede the operation of any law of the United States ... shall be punished by a fine not exceeding five thousand dollars, and by imprisonment during a term not less than six months nor exceeding five years; and further, at the discretion of the court may be holden to find sureties for his good behaviour in such sum, and for such time, as the said court may direct.

The Sedition Act, 1798

Document 2:

That the several states who formed that instrument, being sovereign and independent, have the unquestionable right to judge of its infraction; and that a nullification, by those sovereignties, of all unauthorized acts done under colour of that instrument, is the rightful remedy: That this commonwealth does upon the most deliberate reconsideration declare, that the said alien and sedition laws, are in their opinion, palpable violations of the said constitution...

Kentucky Resolution, 1799

•**Describe the historical context surrounding these documents**
•**Identify and explain the *relationship* between the events and/or ideas found in these documents (Cause and Effect, *or* Similarity/Difference, *or* Turning Point)**

Jacksonian Democracy c1824-c1840

After losing the Election of 1824, the common man, Andrew Jackson, came back with a vengeance to win in 1828. Jackson was a loose cannon, and a powerful President. He enforced a tariff, vetoed the Bank, and removed American Indians to west of the Mississippi River. Although associated with *Jacksonian Democracy*, he was notorious for appointing his friends and campaign supporters to office. Socially, the Age of Jackson included the *Age of Reform (see pg. 40)* where movements such as the Second Great Awakening, transcendentalism, and temperance spread throughout the nation. At the same time, an economic transformation, or market revolution, was happening in the North and West. Transportation and communication were becoming more accessible.

HERE IS WHAT YOU NEED TO KNOW:
Definition: Sectionalism

Sectionalism is the belief that one's loyalty should rest with their section of the country, rather than the nation as a whole. Here are the sectional loyalties you need to know from 1830-1850:

North	South	West
Most populous	Population part slave	Least populous
Supports the Bank	Hates the Bank	Split on Bank Issue
More Industrial	Agricultural	Developing
Pro-Tariff. The tariff promotes industrial growth.	Anti-Tariff. The tariff raises prices, and the South mainly exports.	Split on tariff. Favors both industry and agriculture.
Anti-slavery feeling growing by 1850	Pro-slavery	Split on slavery issue
Leader: Daniel Webster	Leader: John C. Calhoun	Leader: Henry Clay

Definition: Corrupt Bargain

In the Election of 1824, Andrew Jackson of Tennessee led John Quincy Adams in both the electoral and popular vote. But, since William Crawford and Henry Clay also received Electoral Votes, no man received the majority necessary to win. So, the election went to the House of Representatives. In an alleged backroom agreement, Henry Clay offered the House's support to Adams, so long as Clay could become the next Secretary of State. This agreement was later nicknamed by opponents as "The Corrupt Bargain." Clay always denied it. Nonetheless, Adams was a one term President.

Jackson would come back to win the Election of 1828. He was the first President to be from the West.

Question: What are the four main things to know about Andrew Jackson's Presidency?

Answer: **B-I-T-S**

B - **B**ank Veto

I - **I**ndian Removal Act

T - **T**ariff Enforcement

S - **S**poils System (all four will be explained)

Definition: Spoils System

"To the victor belongs the spoils!" Back in the nineteenth century, those who helped a president's campaign expected to receive a nice cushy job in government. Jackson was notorious for such appointments. This practice would end in 1883 after the passage of the Pendleton Act.

Definition: Caucus and Nominating Convention

Originally, there was a *caucus system* where just a few party bosses sat in "smoke-filled rooms" (as they smoked cigars) to choose the candidates who would run in the November Presidential Election. New *nominating conventions* expanded democracy, as now common people were allowed to help nominate a future President. The Anti-Masonic Party had the first one in 1832. During Jackson's time, property requirements to vote began to lift.

Definition: Jacksonian Democracy

This was the belief that government should represent and be controlled by the ***common man***. It was similar to Jefferson's belief in political equality. With few exceptions, Jacksonian Democrats controlled the White House until the Civil War.

Alexis de Tocqueville was a French political writer who visited and wrote about life in the US. In 1835, he authored *Democracy in America*, in which he observed the equality and liberty being experienced by American citizens in the age of Jacksonian Democracy. He also commented on the importance of Christianity in the lives of the American people.

Definition: Kitchen Cabinet

Jackson's "Kitchen Cabinet" was a term coined by his opponents. They used it to describe the way Jackson would seek the opinions of advisors who weren't necessarily in his true cabinet.

Question: What do I need to know about the economic transformation of the early nineteenth century?

Answer: There was a "market revolution" in the early to middle nineteenth century.

1. First there were roads, like the National Road, or Cumberland Road, which went from Maryland to Illinois. Roads with tolls were called ***turnpikes.***

2. The man-made ***Erie Canal*** was completed in upstate New York in 1825, and it linked the Atlantic Ocean to the Midwest by connecting the Hudson River to the Great Lakes. This led to more trade.

3. Railroads emerged by 1830. They were slow, but faster than road travel. The North and South had equal amounts of railroad track mileage until about 1850. After that, the North far exceeded the South.

4. On the water, steamboats were prevalent by 1830, and were based on Robert Fulton's technology.

5. Eli Whitney invented the *cotton gin* in 1793. This led to a greater demand for slaves, as Southern "King Cotton" became more profitable. Whitney also invented the system of *interchangeable parts*. This meant that if a part of a firearm broke, you could just replace that part…instead of the entire weapon.

6. *Samuel Slater* was seen as the "Father of the American Factory System," as he brought English textile machinery to the United States. In New England, the factory system emerged in places such as *Lowell, Massachusetts*. Here, the company provided lodging for workers. The labor force of unmarried women, or *"mill girls,"* eventually gave way to Irish immigrants, many of whom were escaping the potato famine of the 1840s. New England had abundant harbors for trading raw materials and finished goods.

Question: Why did Jackson veto the re-charter of the Bank of the United States in 1832?

Answer: In his 1832 veto message, Jackson said he vetoed the Second Bank of the United States (successor to Hamilton's National Bank) because:

1. Foreigners had too much stock in the bank.
2. The bank favored the rich, and not the common man.

He also did not trust Nicholas Biddle, the head of the bank. Jackson thought he was corrupt.

Question: What is the difference between hard and soft money?

Answer:

Hard Money = gold and silver coins, also known as *specie*.

Soft Money = paper. Paper money can create inflation faster than hard money.

Paper was favored by bankers and people who purchased a lot of land known as *speculators*. It was not typically favored by *the common man*. Note: 60 years later, poor farmers will want inflation on crop prices during the age of Populism in the 1890s.

Question: What was the outcome of the Bank Veto?

Answer:

1. Money was taken out of the bank and put into "pet" banks (state banks loyal to Jackson).

2. The money found its way out of banks, and into people's pockets. Too many paper notes in circulation created inflation.

3. To control the inflation, Jackson issued the *Specie Circular* order in 1836, which stated that federal lands had to be purchased in hard money (gold and silver).

4. That order quickly slowed land purchases while further threatening the stability of currency.

5. The economy spiraled out of control and the Panic of 1837 set in under President Martin Van Buren. Widespread unemployment and business failures were important effects.

The next few decades saw a fight to put the government's money into an *independent treasury*. This meant keeping it in a place that did not function like a powerful bank.

Definition: Whig Party

Supporters of the Bank felt alienated by Jackson's veto. They believed that he was acting like a king. In Britain, those who did not support the King called themselves Whigs. The Whig Party in America was a new conservative creation that was anti-Jackson. *(See pg. 31)*

Definition: Peggy Eaton Affair

Most of Jackson's cabinet resigned because they hated Peggy Eaton, the wife of Jackson's Secretary of War John Henry Eaton. Jackson took her under his wing. Years before, Eaton was accused of adultery, and Jackson felt this was unwarranted. The treatment reminded him of similar accusations against his late wife. John C. Calhoun resigned as Vice President partly over this "Petticoat Affair." Martin Van Buren would succeed him after the Election of 1832.

Definition: Tariff of Abominations, 1828

Review: A tariff raises money by taxing imports. A protective tariff is a tax on imports that inflates foreign prices to protect American jobs. The South had little use for a tariff because they didn't have many industrial jobs, and would have to pay higher prices on all finished goods (tariffs were known to raise domestic prices as well). Also, higher prices on imported textiles could hurt international demand for Southern cotton. The 1828 tariff reached a very high level, leading to its southern nickname, "The Tariff of Abominations."

Definition: *South Carolina Exposition and Protest*, 1828

After the Tariff of Abominations, Vice President John C. Calhoun wrote the *South Carolina Exposition and Protest*. It stated that South Carolina and the Southern states *should* be able to nullify acts of Congress. This was written in the spirit of Jefferson and Madison's *Kentucky and Virginia Resolutions*. Calhoun, however, hinted at secession over the tariff, even at this early date.

Related to the subject, in 1830, Daniel Webster of Massachusetts debated Robert Hayne of South Carolina, attacking the idea of secession and disobeying federal law. Webster championed a firm union. This was the famous *Webster-Hayne Debate*.

Definition: Ordinance of Nullification, 1832

The Tariff of 1828 was replaced by the Tariff of 1832, whose rates the South still found too high. South Carolina held a special convention in which they passed the Ordinance of Nullification. This declared the tariffs of 1828 and 1832 "null and void."

Question: How was conflict avoided after the Ordinance of Nullification?

Answer: As the chief executor of federal laws, President Jackson threatened a *Force Bill* to shove the tariff down the throat of South Carolina. However, before violence would ever occur, Henry Clay brokered a Compromise Tariff in 1833 that promised to gradually reduce tariffs over the next several years. Here is the sequence of events you need to know:

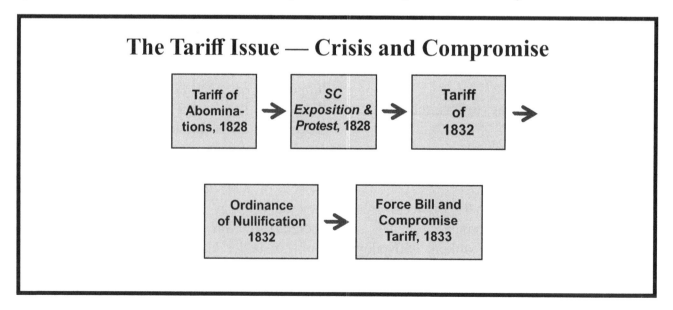

The Tariff Issue — Crisis and Compromise

Tariff of Abominations, 1828 → SC Exposition & Protest, 1828 → Tariff of 1832 →

Ordinance of Nullification 1832 → Force Bill and Compromise Tariff, 1833

Definition: Indian Removal Act of 1830

This was legislation that removed Native Americans from the east, and relocated them west of the Mississippi River (see Trail of Tears below).

Question: How did Jackson clash with the Supreme Court over Native American rights?

Answer: Here are the two cases you need to know:

Cherokee Nation v. *Georgia* (1831) - The Supreme Court ruled that because the Cherokee Indians of Georgia were not a foreign nation, they could not get original jurisdiction (have their case heard directly) at the Supreme Court. But...

Worcester v. *Georgia* (1832) - The Supreme Court ruled that Georgia could not pass legislation regarding Cherokee lands.

Jackson defiantly said of Chief Justice John Marshall, "John Marshall has made his decision, now let him enforce it." Thus, there was a confrontation between the Executive and Judicial branches. But as a strong executive, Jackson held an edge over Marshall.

Definition: Trail of Tears

In the winter of 1837-38, approximately 16,000 Cherokee people were uprooted from Georgia. On the western voyage, thousands died from starvation and cold temperatures. Note: Jackson was out of office by then, as Martin Van Buren had become the new Commander-in-Chief. Still, it was Jackson's removal policy that associated him with this tragedy. During the nineteenth century, the US recognized *reservations*, or areas within the United States where American Indians could govern themselves.

The Age of Reform: Social History c1830-c1850

Definition: Transcendentalism

This was mysticism and philosophy that helped a person find their true inner-self. The movement renounced materialism and conformity, embraced nature, and favored artistic achievement. Key writers were Ralph Waldo Emerson, Henry David Thoreau, and Walt Whitman. Thoreau, who was famous for his introspective writings of isolation at Walden Pond, believed in civil disobedience, or disobeying laws seen as unjust.

Definition: Second Great Awakening (See graphic on pg. 41)

Yes, another Great Awakening. For this one you need to know:

1. It started in the "*burned over district*" in western New York near Rochester, with a man by the name of *Charles Grandison Finney*. The movement was strong from about 1800-1850.

2. It was another religious revival that strongly encouraged faith.

3. There was a belief in a *millennium* (thousand years of peace where Jesus Christ would return to rule over the people).

4. There was a hope for *perfectionism*, or faith in the human ability to eliminate sin, and achieve a better life on Earth through acts of will.

5. It increased the numbers of both Methodists and Baptists.

Movements affected by the Second Great Awakening included abolition, temperance, women's rights, public education, and utopian communities.

Definition: Temperance

Temperance was a movement in the mid-nineteenth century that looked to get rid of the consumption of alcohol. As protectors of the home, women saw alcohol addiction as causes of crime and the destruction of the family. The issue gave an opportunity for women to enter the political world. Years later, the sale of alcohol would be prohibited (Eighteenth Amendment, 1919).

Definition: Seneca Falls Convention, 1848

This was a major women's convention that took place in upstate New York. Elizabeth Cady Stanton and Lucretia Mott were key leaders. They adopted a *Declaration of Sentiments*, and concluded that "all men and women are created equal."

They challenged the *cult of domesticity*, which stated that women were meant to be passive, virtuous, stay in the home, and be subservient to men. Women hoped to leave their *sphere* of the home, and have more political and economic opportunity.

Another woman important to know is *Dorothea Dix*. She fought for the better treatment of mentally ill patients in asylums.

Definition: Horace Mann

Mann was a Massachusetts legislator who favored universal public education as a means to create a population of disciplined, good, young citizens. His plans began in Massachusetts and spread to other states. Under the laws of federalism (division of powers between the state and federal government), education is a reserved, or state power. So, public education was done on a state to state basis. Just try to remember, "Mann, did he love public education!"

Adults also received education, as traveling lecturers, speaking at *lyceums* (educational meetings), talked about everything from science to philosophy. The movement was founded by Josiah Holbrook. Ralph Waldo Emerson was known to speak at lyceum lectures. Furthermore, newspapers continued to increase in circulation and readership during the Jacksonian Era. Many of these brought with them a political bias.

Definition: Hudson River School

The Hudson River School was an art movement dedicated to the painting of nature *landscapes* near the Hudson River in upstate New York. The paintings, which exhibited romanticism, also reflected the exploration and settlement of nineteenth century America.

An important artist of the period to know is John James Audubon. He was a naturalist who painted life-size images in his *The Birds of America* (1827-38).

Definition: Shakers

The Shakers created a deeply religious movement that had elements of socialism. They lived isolated in a community of shared property with separation of the sexes (and no sexual relations). They renounced all aspects of sin.

Definition: Brook Farm/New Harmony

Brook Farm looked to become a *utopian community*. But a utopia was more of a hope than a reality. It aimed to have a perfect, self-sustainable, and isolated society. Brook Farm was founded by transcendentalist and Unitarian minister, *George Ripley*. People worked together for a common good and the survival of the community. Brook Farm had financial problems, and lasted less than a decade.

Robert Owen led the utopian community at New Harmony (Indiana). Founded in 1825, it was an attempt to find social perfection. This experiment was also short-lived.

Definition: Unitarians

Unitarian Christians explained that God existed only within Himself, and not in the Trinity. They increased in number at this time, believing that a doctrine of good deeds and works could lead to salvation.

Definition: Mormons

The Church of Jesus Christ of Latter-day Saints was founded by *Joseph Smith*, who published the Book of Mormon in 1830. After Smith was murdered, *Brigham Young* led the Mormons to Utah where they established a religious community. The movement had thousands of followers who settled in the Utah Territory. Because the religion condoned polygamy (multiple wives), controversy stalled Utah from becoming a state.

The Second Great Awakening influenced the following movements c1840 (WE AUDIT)

W - Women's Rights
E - Education Reform

A - Abolition
U - Utopian Societies
D - Dorothea Dix and...
I - Insane Asylum (and Prison) Reform
T - Temperance

Review Questions

"This act authorizes and encourages transfers of its stock to foreigners and grants them an exemption from all State and national taxation. So far from being "necessary and proper" that the bank should possess this power to make it a safe and efficient agent of the Government in its fiscal operations, it is calculated to convert the Bank of the United States into a foreign bank, to impoverish our people in time of peace, to disseminate a foreign influence through every section of the Republic, and in war to endanger our independence."

– President Andrew Jackson's veto of the Bank

1. What Constitutional issue is President Jackson referring to when he says "necessary and proper"?
   A) Checks and Balances
   B) The Elastic Clause
   C) Reserved Powers
   D) Executive Privilege

2. Which of the following would be offered as evidence to refute Jackson's veto?
   A) Foreigners held a lot of stock in the Bank
   B) The President of the bank, Nicolas Biddle, was a political enemy
   C) The Bank favored the rich
   D) Creation of the Bank was found to be constitutional

3. In this time period, which action of Andrew Jackson caused the greatest level of sectional controversy?
   A) Indian Removal Act
   B) Use of the spoils system
   C) Enforcement of the Tariff of Abominations
   D) Support for the common man to take part in elections

4. What was an immediate effect of the vetoing of the Bank?
   A) Money was quickly put into an independent treasury
   B) The federal government dispensed rebates directly to the people
   C) Funds were given to state banks, who loaned out the money
   D) Foreigners who owned stock in the bank took the action as a threat of war

Answers and Explanations

1. **B**. The elastic clause of the Constitution gives Congress the ability to do things they feel are "necessary and proper." The National Bank was created in the early years of the republic using this clause.

2. **D**. In *McCulloch* v. *Maryland*, the implied powers used to create the Bank were found to be constitutional, and because the federal government was supreme, states could not tax the bank.

3. **C**. The Tariff of Abominations led to rumblings of secession in the 1830s. Despite South Carolina's verbal rejection of the tariff, Henry Clay's Compromise Tariff restored order.

4. **C**. Jackson vetoed the recharter of the Bank of the United States. The money was then sent to "pet" banks, or state banks loyal to Jackson. Those banks lent out large sums of money which led to inflation.

Short Essay Question Set

Document 1:

January 16, 1833

A message was received from the President of the United States, transmitting copies of the proclamation and other documents relating to South Carolina, her ordinance ... Mr. CALHOUN then rose and said, that his object in taking the floor was not to make any remark on the motion which was immediately before the Senate ... It was stated by the Chief Magistrate, in substance, that the movements made by the State of South Carolina were of a character hostile to the Union ... There was not a State in the Union less disposed than South Carolina to put herself in such attitude of hostility.

Source: A Century of Lawmaking for a New Nation: U.S. Congressional Documents and Debates, 1774 - 1875; Register of Debates, Senate, 22nd Congress, 2nd Session. Courtesy of Library of Congress.

Document 2:

My D'r sir, If I can judge from the signs of the times Nullification, and secession, or in the language of truth, disunion, is gaining strength, we must be prepared to act with promptness, and crush the monster in its cradle before it matures to manhood. We must be prepared for the crisis. The moment that we are informed that the Legislature of So Carolina has passed laws to carry her rebellious ordinance into effect, which I expect tomorrow we must be prepared to act.
> - President Andrew Jackson in a letter to Lewis Cass, Washington, December 17, 1832.

Source: Cass, Lewis, and Andrew Jackson. Andrew Jackson to Lewis Cass. 1832. Manuscript/Mixed Material. Retrieved from the Library of Congress' <www.loc.gov/item/maj012938/>.

• **Describe the historical context surrounding documents 1 and 2**
• **Analyze Document 2 and explain how *audience*, or *purpose*, or *bias*, or *point of view* affects this document's use as a reliable source of evidence**

Antebellum/Pre-Civil War, 1820-1860

Economic tension, slavery, political strife, ideological conflict, and ultimately the Election of Abraham Lincoln. All of these events led to Southern secession from the Union in 1860. Throughout the antebellum (pre-Civil War) era, Northerners and Southerners attempted to compromise their differences. However, because of manifest destiny and sectionalism, the Civil War proved inevitable. Throughout this time period, there was a growing movement to end slavery. From literature to violent actions, the abolition movement spread from the North to the West.

HERE IS WHAT YOU NEED TO KNOW:
Definition: Antebellum

Antebellum means the time-period before the Civil War. Again, don't forget the importance of *sectionalism* where loyalty rests with one's own section of the country rather than the nation as a whole. When you think "antebellum period," visualize 1820-1860.

Definition: Compromise of 1820/Missouri Compromise

This was Major Slave Legislation #1 of 3. The goal in the antebellum period was to keep a balance between slave and free states. So, when certain territories were ready for statehood, decisions had to be made. In this compromise:

1. Maine would enter as a free state.
2. Missouri would enter as a slave state, but…
3. After the admission of Missouri, no slavery would be allowed north of the 36° 30' latitude line within the Louisiana Territory.

Henry Clay of Kentucky, "The Great Compromiser," received credit for this legislation.

Question: What should I know about slave life?

Answer: Much of the economy of the South was based on the "peculiar institution" of slavery. Regarding slavery:

1. Slaves worked many jobs including as servants inside homes and as labor on *plantations* (large agricultural estates).
2. Only a very small percentage of people owned slaves before the Civil War. Surprised? Statistics on this vary but about, 6-7% of people, or 25% of families, had slaves in the South. Even smaller were statistics of those who owned many slaves. Most of the Southern population was comprised of poor *yeoman* farmers. The lack of slave-owners is a very important fact to know.
3. Slaves held onto their African culture in music, but combined it with Christianity.
4. Eli Whitney's cotton gin actually increased the need for slaves, as about 2/3 of the world's cotton came from the American South by 1860.
5. The human rights violation of slavery differed from area to area. It is difficult to make generalizations about slave life. On many plantations a harsh *gang labor* (large groups) persisted.

Question: What do I need to know about Texas, The Alamo, etc.?

Answer: Americans had been settling in Texas before 1836. Mexico hoped the Americans would become Mexicans, but later considered the settlements a conflict. Settlers saw their rights limited, and angrily declared independence. This meant a fight. The Alamo was a former mission (religious center) which was turned into a fort by the Texans.

1. In 1836, Americans and Tejanos (Texans of Mexican descent) were defeated at the Alamo by the Mexican army led by President

Santa Anna. All soldiers within were killed, including legendary frontiersman Davy Crockett.

2. "Remember the Alamo" was yelled at the Battle of San Jacinto one month later. There, the Americans won Texas, but...

3. ***President Jackson wouldn't take Texas into the Union because it would disrupt the free/slave state balance.***

4. In 1845, President John Tyler annexed Texas as a state. It became a slave state.

Definition: Manifest Destiny

Manifest Destiny was the belief that the United States was destined to expand and gain all land from "sea to shining sea," or between the Atlantic and Pacific Oceans. The term was coined by John L. O'Sullivan in 1845 when he wrote about it in the *US Magazine and Democratic Review.*

Manifest Destiny

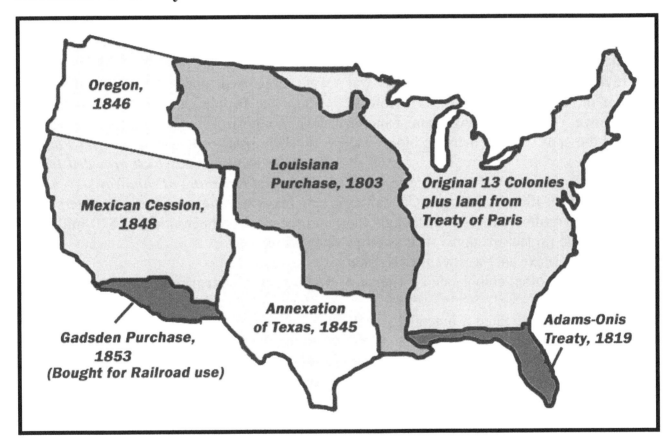

54°-40' or Fight!

In 1842, Secretary of State Daniel Webster negotiated the ***Webster-Ashburton Treaty*** with Britain. After a bloodless conflict on the Maine-Canada border called the ***Aroostook War***, this treaty decided where the border was between certain spots of the United States and British-controlled Canada.

However, Democratic President James K. Polk wanted more land north of Oregon, believing that the border between the US and Canada was at the 54°-40' latitude line. Britain insisted the border was further south. Although Democrats would threaten "54°-40' or fight," negotiations in 1846 compromised the border at 49°, which is still in effect today.

Question: What do I need to know about the Mexican War, 1846-48?

Answer:

1. The United States under President Polk was itching for a fight. They wanted territory, and believed that the border between Mexico and the US was the Rio Grande. Mexico held that the border was further north at the Nueces River.

2. Polk and Congress were convinced that the Mexican Army "shed American blood on American soil," so a war was fought and the United States won. Future US President Zachary Taylor was a military leader in this war (hero of the Battle of Buena Vista). Note: A little-known Whig named Abraham Lincoln doubted the spot where American blood was shed.

3. The US received California and a lot of western territory after the Treaty of Guadalupe Hidalgo was ratified in 1848. Although the treaty aimed to protect freedoms such as property rights for Mexicans, westward expansion into the frontier often complicated ownership claims.

4. The new land created a potential imbalance between slave and free states, and partially led Ralph Waldo Emerson to say that, "Mexico will poison us!"

Definition: Wilmot Proviso, 1846

This was a failed attempt to prevent slavery from expanding into any territories taken over during the Mexican War. David Wilmot was a young Congressman whose bold idea would cause a split between Northern and Southern Democrats. In addition, a *third party* opposed to the expansion of slavery in the west was formed, called the ***Free-Soil Party***. But again, Wilmot's idea never became law.

Definition: Compromise of 1850

This was Major Slave Legislation #2 of 3. Henry Clay constructed the compromise with the help of Stephen Douglas. The goal was to keep a balance between slave and free states. It failed at first as an omnibus (group of laws), but then was passed as individual laws.

1. California needed to become a state after the Gold Rush of 1849. It became a free state.

2. The slave *trade* was abolished (the sale of slaves, not the institution of slavery) in the District of Columbia.

3. The Territories of New Mexico and Utah were organized under ***popular sovereignty*** (where the people can vote on if they want slavery or not).

4. ***With great controversy, a strict Fugitive Slave Act was passed, which provided for the seizure and returning of runaway slaves.***

5. Texas gave up some of its western land, and received compensation of $10 million to pay off its debt.

Definition: Underground Railroad

Harriet Tubman gained fame for helping run this network of safe-houses for slaves who were looking to escape to the North and Canada. This took on increased importance after the Fugitive Slave Act became law.

Definition: Ostend Manifesto, 1854

Named for a secret meeting in Ostend, Belgium, it was a scheme for the United States to purchase Cuba from Spain for $120 million. Inevitably, Cuba would have become a Southern slave state. When free-soilers (term for those who didn't want slavery to expand) in the North learned of this, they greatly protested and the plan was dropped.

Slavery Legislation and Compromises, 1820-1854

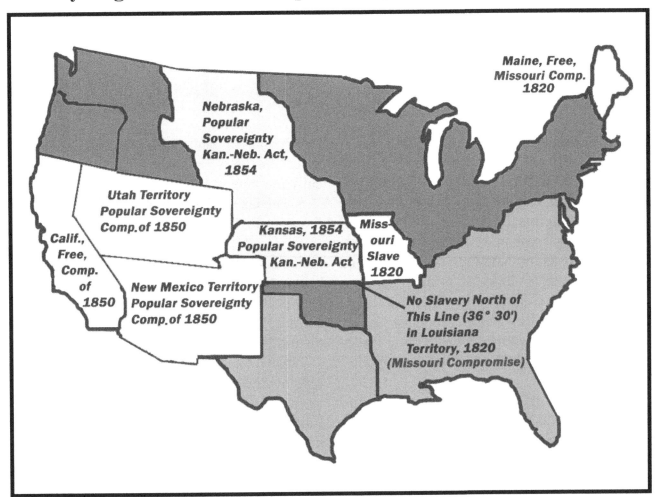

Definition: Kansas-Nebraska Act, 1854

This was Major Slave Legislation #3 of 3. This law was constructed by the "Little Giant," Stephen Douglas (Clay had died by then). Originally, Congress was looking to open up land for settlement, as well as construction of a transcontinental railroad. But slavery became the issue. The act:

1. Reversed the Missouri Compromise.

2. Let the people of Kansas and Nebraska vote on whether or not they wanted to be a slave or free state. Again, that notion is called *popular sovereignty*.

So, the three major slave legislations were: Missouri Compromise of 1820, Compromise of 1850, and the Kansas-Nebraska Act of 1854. See map above.

Definition: Bleeding Kansas

Now that popular sovereignty was law, violent pro-slavery Border Ruffians clashed with Free-Staters (some were referred to as *jayhawkers*). Both converged on Kansas to stuff the ballot box in the slave or no slave vote. The result was massive violence. Bleeding Kansas:

1. Led to millions of dollars in property damage, and dozens dead.

2. Proved to be a mini-Civil War in Kansas.

3. John Brown became a national figure after he killed Border Ruffians at Pottawattamie, Kansas.

Definition: Lecompton Constitution

Kansas ultimately voted for slavery and it was written into the Lecompton Constitution. This new state constitution was approved by President James Buchanan, but it didn't last.

Definition: Republican Party

With sectionalism boiling over on the slave issue, a new political party emerged. The Republican Party combined Northern Democrats, Free-Soilers, Know-Nothings (anti-immigrant party), and former Whigs. Their main goal was to stop the spread of slavery in the west. Some in the party were abolitionists (against slavery altogether). Thus, the political party illustration that appears on page 31 is now complete.

Question: What abolitionist writers and speakers should I know?

Answer: Abolitionism means wanting an end to slavery. From 1836-1845, *"gag rule"* made it impossible to petition for the abolition of slavery in the House of Representatives. However, that did not affect writers and speakers. You need to know:

1. From 1831-1865, William Lloyd Garrison published *The Liberator*, an anti-slavery newspaper. Founder of the *American Anti-Slavery Society*, he was not for total equality, but was an abolitionist. Garrison was ahead of his time, although not well received in the North at first. You should also know that he favored increasing rights for women.

2. *The Slave Narrative of Frederick Douglass*, 1845. Douglass was a free black who detailed his experience as a slave. Frequently a public speaker, Douglass also published an abolitionist newspaper called *The North Star*.

3. *Uncle Tom's Cabin* by Harriet Beecher Stowe, 1852. Stowe, the daughter of an abolitionist, wrote this novel that detailed the horrors of slavery. In 1862, Abraham Lincoln said to her, "So you're the little woman who wrote the book that made this great war."

4. *The Impending Crisis of the South* by Hinton Rowan Helper, 1857. Written by a Southerner, this book criticized slavery as economically inefficient. It was banned in the South.

5. The Grimké Sisters were early women reformers. In 1836, **Angelina Grimké** wrote *An Appeal to the Christian Women of the South*, in which she encouraged women to join the abolitionist cause.

6. Sojourner Truth was a former slave. She traveled the country fighting for abolition and recognition of women's rights.

7. Not a total abolitionist group, but you need to know the ***American Colonization Society***. It looked to return slaves to Africa, or the colony of Liberia. It was supported by people who ranged from Northern abolitionists to Southerners nervous about the presence of free blacks.

Definition: Bleeding Sumner, 1856

Republican Charles Sumner of Massachusetts verbally attacked South Carolina Senator Andrew Butler in a speech, "The Crime Against Kansas." In response, Butler's relative, Preston Brooks, beat Sumner over the head with a cane on the Senate floor. Things got so tense in Congress that legislators carried firearms with them to the chambers each day.

Definition: *Dred Scott* v. *Sandford*, 1857

Dred Scott was a slave who was taken to live in free northern territory. Because he lived on free soil for an extended period of time, he believed he had legal recourse to sue for his freedom. Chief Justice Roger B. Taney (pronounced Taw´-ny), on behalf of the Supreme Court, stated that:

1. Scott was a slave, which meant that he was not protected by the United States Constitution, and couldn't even sue in court.

2. Slave compromises, specifically the Missouri Compromise, were unconstitutional, as according to the Fifth Amendment, people could not be deprived of their property. Slaves were property.

Definition: Lincoln-Douglas Debates, 1858

This refers to the Illinois Senatorial debates between Republican Abraham Lincoln and Democrat Stephen Douglas. Although he lost the election, Lincoln became a national celebrity and a critic of slavery. ***Lincoln was against the spread of slavery, but was not an abolitionist in 1858.***

In his ***Freeport Doctrine***, Douglas favored popular sovereignty over the *Dred Scott* Decision.

Definition: John Brown/Harper's Ferry, 1859

This was a raid on the federal arsenal in Harper's Ferry, Virginia (today West Virginia). Brown and a few followers attempted to fuel a larger slave revolution. It didn't happen. Brown got holed up in a firehouse, and was later captured by the federal army. After being hanged, he was hailed as a martyr in the North, and a terrorist in the South. Other slave rebellions to know:

Stono Rebellion, 1739 - Armed resistance in South Carolina that led to slaves losing their rights (explained in greater detail on pg. 8).

Gabriel Prosser, 1800 - Failed plot in Virginia. Prosser and his followers were executed.

Denmark Vesey, 1822 - Failed plot in South Carolina. Vesey and others were executed.

Nat Turner, 1831 - A violent rebellion in Virginia that led to almost 200 deaths (black and white). Turner and others were executed.

Definition: Presidential Election of 1860

Two years after his defeat in the Senatorial

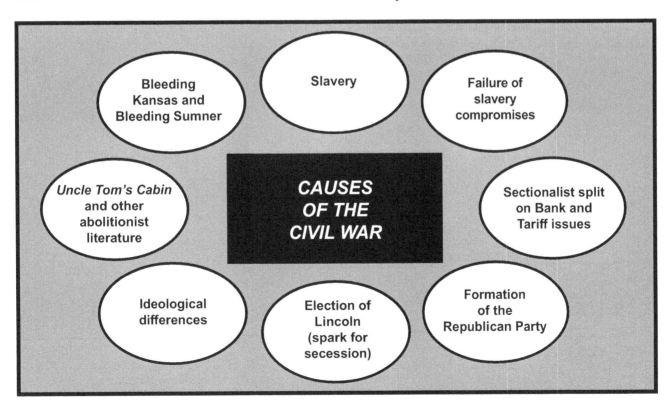

Election of 1858, Republican Abraham Lincoln won the Presidential Election without receiving a majority of the popular vote. He received less than 40%. Stephen Douglas, the Northern Democrat in the race, got 29%. John C. Breckinridge, a Southern Democrat, received 18%, and John Bell of the Constitutional Union Party secured 13%. Lincoln won the Electoral College vote with 180.

Definition: Secession

Secession occurs when states leave the Union (United States). Eleven Southern states left after the Republicans gained control of the White House. South Carolina was the first to leave, followed by the rest of the *Confederacy*.

Question: So in simplest terms, what were the causes of the Civil War?

Answer:

Long Term Causes:

1. Slavery.

2. Sectional differences such as the bank, tariff, and economic lifestyles.

3. Creation of the Republican Party.

4. Ideological differences of opinion socially and politically.

5. Failure of the slave compromises.

Immediate Cause for Secession:

The election of Lincoln in 1860, and the Republican Party controlling the White House. Secession began on December 20, 1860.

Review Questions

"In the opinion of the court, the legislation and histories of the times, and the language used in the Declaration of Independence, show that neither the class of persons who had been imported as slaves nor their descendants, whether they had become free or not, were then acknowledged as a part of the people, nor intended to be included in the general words used in that memorable instrument.

"It is difficult at this day to realize the state of public opinion in relation to that unfortunate race which prevailed in the civilized and enlightened portions of the world at the time of the Declaration of Independence and when the Constitution of the United States was framed and adopted. But the public history of every European nation displays it in a manner too plain to be mistaken."

- Chief Justice Roger B. Taney, 1857

1. The above majority opinion of the Supreme Court reflects the decision of
   A) *Plessy* v. *Ferguson*
   B) *Dred Scott* v. *Sandford*
   C) *Brown* v. *Board of Education*
   D) *Worcester* v. *Georgia*

2. What was one finding of the Supreme Court in the above case?
   A) Native Americans do not have claims to citizenship
   B) The Declaration of Independence applies to each race
   C) Territory received during the Mexican War is not open to slavery
   D) Slave-owners were guaranteed rights to what was considered property

3. The above court decision contrasted the greatest with the writings of
   A) Jefferson Davis
   B) William Lloyd Garrison
   C) Dorothea Dix
   D) John C. Calhoun

Answers and Explanations

1. **B**. This is the decision from the Dred Scott case. Sometimes, students confuse this case with *Plessy* v. *Ferguson*. Plessy involved the discriminatory issue of "separate but equal" in 1896.

2. **D**. Justice Taney gave the opinion that slaves were property, not citizens. They therefore could not sue in court, nor could slave-owners be deprived of such property. Therefore, the Missouri Compromise, which had already been replaced, would have been unconstitutional.

3. **B**. William Lloyd Garrison, author of the abolitionist publication *The Liberator*, would have strongly disagreed with the court's findings.

Short Essay Question Set

Document 1

"… in regard to the abolition of slavery in the District of Columbia. In relation to that, I have my mind very distinctly made up. I should be exceedingly glad to see slavery abolished in the District of Columbia. I believe that Congress possesses the constitutional power to abolish it. Yet as a member of Congress, I should not with my present views, be in favor of endeavoring to abolish slavery in the District of Columbia, unless it would be upon these conditions: First, that the abolition should be gradual. Second, that it should be on a vote of the majority of qualified voters in the District; and third, that compensation should be made to unwilling owners. With these three conditions, I confess I would be exceedingly glad to see Congress abolish slavery in the District of Columbia, and, in the language of Henry Clay, "sweep from our Capital that foul blot upon our nation."

- Abraham Lincoln at Freeport, Illinois, 1858

Document 2

"The next question propounded to me by Mr. Lincoln is, can the people of a Territory in any lawful way, against the wishes of any citizen of the United States, exclude slavery from their limits prior to the formation of a State Constitution? I answer emphatically, as Mr. Lincoln has heard me answer a hundred times from every stump in Illinois, that in my opinion the people of a Territory can, by lawful means, exclude slavery from their limits prior to the formation of a State Constitution. Mr. Lincoln knew that I had answered that question over and over again. He heard me argue the Nebraska bill on that principle all over the State in 1854, in 1855, and in 1856, and he has no excuse for pretending to be in doubt as to my position on that question. It matters not what way the Supreme Court may hereafter decide as to the abstract question whether slavery may or may not go into a Territory under the Constitution, the people have the lawful means to introduce it or exclude it as they please, for the reason that slavery cannot exist a day or an hour anywhere, unless it is supported by local police regulations."

- Stephen Douglas at Freeport, Illinois, 1858

•**Describe the historical context surrounding documents 1 and 2**
•**Analyze Document 2 and explain how *audience*, or *purpose*, or *bias*, or *point of view* affects this document's use as a reliable source of evidence**

The Civil War, 1861-1865

The turning point in American History was the Civil War. Outside of only certain major battles, you need to know about the Emancipation Proclamation, the draft, social movements, the Union and Confederate economy, and the actions of slaves and African American soldiers during the war.

HERE IS WHAT YOU NEED TO KNOW:
Definition: Fort Sumter, 1861

The South attacked first to start the Civil War on April 12, 1861. Ironically, no one was killed in this initial bombardment near Charleston, South Carolina. Two people died the next day in the cannon salute to the fort. A horse died as well.

Question: Who exactly was fighting whom in the Civil War?

Answer:

North = The Union. President Lincoln. Blue uniforms. Major force was the Army of the Potomac (which had multiple leaders, ending with Ulysses S. Grant).

South = The Confederacy. President Jefferson Davis. Gray uniforms. Major force was the Army of Northern Virginia led by Robert E. Lee.

The North had the advantage, as they boasted a larger population, a stronger navy, greater farm acreage, more bank deposits, superior industry, and a greater amount of railroad track.

Question: What was Lincoln's game plan at the beginning of the Civil War?

Answer:

1. Lincoln was *not* fighting to end slavery in 1861. That changed later. In 1861, he was fighting to *maintain the Union*.

2. He wanted to secure the border states, and stop the Confederacy from expanding even further northward.

Definition: Peninsula Campaign

This was the initial war strategy for the North. The Peninsula Campaign aimed to follow the peninsula of Virginia and capture Richmond (the Confederate capital).

Definition: Anaconda Plan and Economies

The longer the war went on, the better it was for the North. Because the South had a lot of cotton to export, they needed to get to Europe to trade. Therefore, the North placed its navy around Southern ports and enforced a *blockade* of all Southern goods coming in and out of the Confederacy. The idea was to strangle the South like an anaconda (big snake) would squeeze its prey. By the end of the war, there was massive inflation and a shortage of common goods in the Confederacy. The North also experienced inflation, however not as bad, as billions of dollars in *greenbacks* (paper money) were put into circulation. Paper money causes inflation (soft money).

Note: The most famous battle of ironclad ships was between the *Monitor* (Union) and the *Merrimack* (Confederacy; also called the *Virginia*). The *Merrimack* was attempting to break the blockade. The battle ended in a draw.

Question: What major battles in the East do I need to know about *before* Gettysburg?

Answer:

1. Bull Run/Manassas Junction, 1861 (the latter is the Confederate name) - First big battle, and place where Stonewall Jackson received his nickname. The Union lost when they couldn't retreat on a road congested with picnic wagons driven by war-spectators.

2. Antietam/Sharpsburg, 1862 - Bloodiest single day in American History with over

23,000 casualties. Lee couldn't move northward through Maryland. No one won, but the Union claimed victory and issued the Emancipation Proclamation (discussed later).

3. It's important to note that in the eastern theater of the war, the Union lost many major battles, including at Fredericksburg and Chancellorsville.

Definition: Emancipation Proclamation

The proclamation was issued by Abraham Lincoln after Antietam in 1862, and went into effect on January 1, 1863. It:

1. Freed the slaves in the rebelling states (the states who wouldn't listen to the Union anyway). Therefore, the Proclamation...

2. Freed 0 slaves!

3. Changed the war aim from "maintaining the Union" to "freeing the slaves."

4. Kept Britain out of the war. Britain had strong ties to the South because of the cotton trade. However, now they couldn't support the Confederacy, as the British had abolished slavery decades before. Early in the war, in the *Trent Affair*, Confederates were captured attempting to negotiate an alliance with the British. There was also controversy over the *Laird Rams*, which were ironclad ships being built in Britain for the Confederacy.

Question: What do I need to know about African American troops?

Answer:

1. At first, slaves were acquired as "contraband" and used by the army for labor.

2. The first official black regiment recognized by the Union Army was the 54th Massachusetts Volunteer Infantry (as seen in the movie *Glory*). There were earlier unofficial black troops.

3. African American soldiers were paid a lower salary than white soldiers for most of the war.

4. About 180,000 black soldiers comprised about 10% of the army by the end of the Civil War.

5. Even the Confederacy had plans for African American regiments by 1865.

Definition: Gettysburg and Pickett's Charge

Lee and the Confederacy went as far north as Pennsylvania. Traveling to the North, they wound up in Gettysburg. In the three day battle (July 1-3, 1863):

1. The Union won, and it was the turning point of the Civil War.

2. George Pickett of the Confederacy led a losing charge across an open field.

3. There were more casualties in the three days at Gettysburg than any other Civil War battle.

4. In November of 1863, Lincoln delivered the *Gettysburg Address* at the battlefield, in which he spoke about freedom, equality, uniting the country, and the sacrifices made by the soldiers. He began the speech, "Four score and seven years ago," alluding to the Declaration of Independence of 1776.

Definition: Copperheads

The Copperheads were Peace Democrats in the North and Midwest who were pro-Union, but against the Civil War. They wore pennies on their lapels in Congress, and were compared to the poisonous snake by their opponents. Clement Vallandigham was a vocal leader. Lincoln *suspended habeas corpus* and had him deported during the war. It is constitutional for a President to do so during such a conflict.

Definition: New York City Draft Riots

The Enrollment Act of 1863 meant that for the first time in history, the United States could draft troops. New York City was a Democratic stronghold where there was immense opposition to the act because:

1. The draft law favored the rich. The act said that one could pay $300, or find a substitute, to get out of the draft (that was a huge amount of money). The common slogan was, "a rich man's war, poor man's fight."

2. There was racial conflict between Irish and African American populations, as they competed for the same jobs and housing in New York City. The Emancipation Proclamation meant that New York's Irish troops would be fighting for African American slaves.

3. There was both anti-war and anti-Republican sentiment in Democratic New York City.

The riot erupted in July, 1863, and led to violence against poor and affluent African Americans, Republican supporters, and rich whites. It should be noted that the South also instituted a draft with the passage of the Conscription Act of 1862. Owning 20 slaves would get one out of the original Southern draft law.

Definition: Election of 1864

Lincoln defeated Democrat George B. McClellan (whom he had fired as Commander of the Army of the Potomac). Lincoln chose Andrew Johnson, a pro-Union Southern Democrat from Tennessee as his running mate to attract Democratic votes in the North and Border States. This decision would later cause much conflict during the Reconstruction Era. Many Lincoln supporters proclaimed, "Don't swap horses in the middle of the stream."

Definition: Total War

War used to be an event where armies would converge on a battlefield. The Civil War changed that. William Tecumseh Sherman waged war on every aspect of society, including civilians and their property. He marched his soldiers from Atlanta to Savannah in 1864 and burned everything in between.

Question: What do I need to know about the Civil War in the West?

Answer: The Union had a little more success in the West. You should know:

1. Battle of Shiloh, 1862 - Saw the Union win on the second day. It gave prominence to the then little-known Ulysses S. Grant.

2. Battle of New Orleans, 1862 - Led by Admiral David Farragut, the Union won an important naval battle.

3. Siege of Vicksburg, 1863 - The Union won, and divided the Confederacy in half by controlling the Mississippi River.

Question: What do I need to know about the Civil War *after* Gettysburg?

Answer:

1. Grant took over command of the Army of the Potomac.

2. Between 1864 to 1865, he chased Lee through Virginia, fighting at the Battle of the Wilderness, Spotsylvania Court House, Petersburg, and ultimately...

3. Lee surrendered to Grant at Appomattox Court House (that's the name of the village) on April 9, 1865.

4. There were generous terms of surrender, and Lee's army returned home. The war ended with over 600,000 lives lost.

Question: What were some of the innovations of the Civil War?

Answer: As the first "modern war," the Civil War saw many new innovations in battle, including:

1. Trench warfare, which became more prevalent after Gettysburg, was commonplace during World War I.

2. The biggest man-made explosion in the US to its day at the Battle of the Crater at

Petersburg, Virginia (Union troops detonated an underground mine).

3. Ironclad ships. These were ships that had metallic sides to them.

4. Great improvements in submarine and torpedo technology.

5. Telegraph wires crisscrossed the country by 1865. They bridged the communications gap between the President and his Generals. Samuel Morse's electrical telegraph released its first long-distance message in 1844. Morse helped develop a code for communicating over such a device.

Definition: John Wilkes Booth

Booth assassinated Abraham Lincoln on April 14, 1865 as part of a larger conspiracy to target members of government. He shot Lincoln at Ford's Theater during a production of *Our American Cousin*. He waited for the part of the show with the loudest laughter, pulled the trigger, and then leaped to the stage, breaking his leg in the process. Yet he managed to escape (he was killed twelve days later). Andrew Johnson became President when Lincoln died the next day.

After the Civil War came the difficult task of rebuilding the South. The Presidents wanted lenient Reconstruction that would peacefully bring Southern states back into the union. The Radical Republican Congress wanted harsh Reconstruction that punished the South and gave immediate constitutional rights to the newly freed slaves. Although Reconstruction laws provided basic civil rights, the enforcement of such legislation would be nearly impossible. After the federal government pulled out its troops, it would be nearly 100 years before African Americans would receive similar civil rights.

Reconstruction, 1865-1877

Definition: Reconstruction

1865-1877 was a time period where the following had to be reconstructed:

1. The South's infrastructure had to be rebuilt.
2. African Americans needed to be given Constitutional rights.
3. The Southern states had to be readmitted into the Union and agree to follow the Constitution.

Question: What was the difference between Presidential and Congressional (Radical) Reconstruction?

Answer: Presidential Reconstruction (from about 1865-1867) was lenient. Democratic President Andrew Johnson did not want to punish the South. He vetoed much Congressional legislation, and offered pardons to former Confederates. Note: Lincoln also wanted to be lenient in an attempt to heal the country. But, John Wilkes Booth took away any hopes of Lincoln bringing peace.

Radical Reconstruction began by 1867. It was harsher and involved military troops enforcing laws in the South.

Definition: 10% Plan/Wade Davis Bill

Lincoln favored a 10% plan. This meant that a state could re-enter the Union after 10% of its voting citizens (from 1860) agreed to take a loyalty oath to the United States Constitution.

Congress favored the Wade-Davis Bill which stipulated that a majority of a state's voting citizens should take the oath. Before the assassination, Lincoln pocket-vetoed this bill (did not sign it, and it automatically became a veto).

Question: What Reconstruction Amendments do I need to know?

Answer: **A** **C**ool **S**ong

Thirteenth - **A**bolition of slavery, 1865.

Fourteenth - Equality of **C**itizenship, equal protection under the law, plus a due process clause for the states, 1868. Note: Native Americans were not included.

Fifteenth - Universal male **S**uffrage (voting), 1870.

Definition: Black Codes

Black Codes appear at various times in history. They existed in the South during early Reconstruction, and denied free blacks Constitutional rights such as freedom of speech and the right to serve on juries. Southern whites feared that if free blacks had rights, they would feel empowered to dismantle the Southern plantation system. Radical Republicans looked to end these unfair codes.

Definition: Radical Republicans

Congressman *Thaddeus Stevens* and Senator *Charles Sumner* were the two most famous Radical Republicans. The Radical Republicans controlled Reconstruction by 1867, and hoped to bring basic rights and freedoms to former slaves. They also wanted to use force to make Reconstruction a harsh reality for the South.

Definition: Freedmen's Bureau

Established in 1865, the Freedmen's Bureau looked to adjust newly-freed blacks to Southern society. The organization aimed to help with housing, education, food, healthcare, and jobs. President Johnson later vetoed a bill in 1866 that would have increased the Bureau's power.

Definition: Civil Rights Act of 1866

Passed over President Johnson's veto, this act hoped to make African Americans equal under the law. However, the law was not enforced very well. The Civil Rights Era, one hundred years later, looked to deliver a more thorough equality.

Definition: Reconstruction Act of 1867

This was a very important component of Reconstruction legislation. Passed over Johnson's veto, the act:

1. Divided the South into 5 districts occupied by Union troops.

2. Forced all former Confederate states to ratify the Fourteenth Amendment.

3. Made the former Confederate states create new state constitutions which would ensure the voting rights of former slaves. The federal government would have to approve the new state constitutions.

The Southern states had to obey these provisions to be readmitted to the Union.

Definition: Ku Klux Klan

There was uneasiness in the South because Reconstruction legislation aimed to help former slaves. The KKK began as a fraternal organization, and escalated into a terrorist one under the guidance of former Confederate General Nathan Bedford Forrest. They targeted blacks through lynching (murder, often by hanging), and other violence. The organization disbanded after the *Enforcement Act* (1870), and *Ku Klux Act* (1871). The Klan would make a comeback in the 1920s (see pg. 88).

Definition: Impeachment of Andrew Johnson

The Radical Republicans hated Johnson, the Democratic President. They looked for any excuse to get rid of him. That excuse came when Johnson fired the Secretary of War, Edwin M. Stanton, thereby violating the *Tenure of Office Act* (according to the law,

he was supposed to consult with Congress first). The House of Representatives impeached Johnson (brought him up on charges). However, the Senate found him not guilty by one vote, and he was never removed from office. He was the first President to ever be impeached.

Definition: Amnesty Act of 1872

This act permitted former Confederate leaders and secessionists to hold office again. It also allowed about 160,000 of them to vote. This helped the Democrats reclaim the South from the Republicans.

Definition: Carpetbaggers

This was the label for Northerners who went to the South for political and/or economic gain during Reconstruction. They were resented by Southerners.

Definition: Scalawags

Scalawags were Southerners loyal to the Republican Party. They often worked alongside carpetbaggers and newly-freed blacks to create new state constitutions. They were greater in number than the carpetbaggers. Remember, traditionally Southerners were Democrats.

Definition: Election of 1876

Samuel J. Tilden (Democrat) was leading Rutherford B. Hayes (Republican) in both popular and Electoral Votes. But alas...20 Electoral Votes were disputed. A 15-member Electoral Commission comprised of 5 Representatives, 5 Senators, and 5 Supreme Court Judges had to decide who would receive the votes. Ultimately, a compromise in 1877 produced the following:

1. The Republicans received all of the Electoral Votes, which gave Hayes the Pres-

idential Election.

2. The Democrats got removal of Union troops from the South, thus ending Reconstruction.

Definition: Home Rule

When the Republicans pulled Union troops out, it meant that the South would rule itself for the first time since the Civil War. Often, this meant not following Reconstruction legislation. This post-Reconstruction time was known as Home Rule. Home Rule pleased **Redeemers**, or those who tried to eradicate Republican influence from the South during Reconstruction. For almost a century, every Southern State would vote Democratic in Presidential Elections. This was called **The Solid South**.

Definition: Sharecropping/Crop Lien

Newly-freed slaves, often working for their former masters, lived an impoverished existence as a sharecropper. Sharecropping meant farming for only a share of harvested crops, with much of the profit going to the landlord for rent. In such a "crop-lien" system, the landlord often provided supplies, but had a lien on the crops yet to be grown. Because of this, sharecroppers experienced extreme "debt peonage," or poverty. The practice continued into the twentieth century.

Definition: Civil Rights Cases, 1883

The Civil Rights Act of 1875 aimed to get rid of racial discrimination within juries and public places such as restaurants and transportation methods. However, in the Civil Rights Cases of 1883, the Supreme Court said that the Fourteenth Amendment only protected against government denials of civil rights, not the actions of private individuals who owned public accommodations.

Definition: Jim Crow Laws

Historians believe that the term Jim Crow came from a Thomas D. Rice minstrel (sarcastic portrayal of black culture) show from the 1830s. There was no real Jim Crow.

The laws were all about "separate but equal." That meant segregating blacks from whites, assuming that their bathrooms, schools, and water fountains were equal (which of course, they often weren't). After the Supreme Court upheld (agreed with) "separate but equal" in the 1896 *Plessy* v. *Ferguson* case, Jim Crow survived until the mid-twentieth century.

Question: After Reconstruction, how did the South prevent free blacks from voting?

Answer: To avoid the Fifteenth Amendment, Southerners used all of the following:

1. Violence at the polls. Southern whites typically voted Democratic. Surely, African Americans would vote Republican. There were no secret ballots back then, and intimidation played a part at the polls. As early as 1875, the **Mississippi Plan** organized such violence against African American voters.

2. A poll tax, or a tax to vote. Before voting, free blacks would have to present a receipt proving they paid their tax. The Twenty-Fourth Amendment would outlaw this practice in 1964.

3. **Literacy Tests**. In order to vote, one had to pass a difficult exam. Whites would not have to take it because of the...

4. **Grandfather Clause**. If your descendants could vote before the Civil War, the literacy test wouldn't disqualify you from voting. Newly-freed blacks' grandfathers had been slaves who

couldn't vote.

Definition: New South

After the Civil War, there was a movement in the South for more industry with less dependence on the plantation system. Some cities like Atlanta industrialized. Most other areas did not add a significant amount of industry.

Definition: Slaughterhouse Cases, 1873

These were cases that put into question the protections of the Fourteenth Amendment. Louisiana created a corporation for the slaughtering of livestock. This corporation put all of the local slaughterhouses out of work. The butchers who lost their jobs believed that the Louisiana creation was a violation to their Fourteenth Amendment right to exercise free trade equally.

The butchers lost, as the Supreme Court stated that although the Amendment looked to protect against racial discrimination, it did not protect the privileges of the business owners. Therefore states could create a slaughterhouse for the health and safety of the public.

Review Questions

"That on the first day of January, in the year of our Lord one thousand eight hundred and sixty-three, all persons held as slaves within any State or designated part of a State, the people whereof shall then be in rebellion against the United States, shall be then, thenceforward, and forever free; and the Executive Government of the United States, including the military and naval authority thereof, will recognize and maintain the freedom of such persons, and will do no act or acts to repress such persons, or any of them, in any efforts they may make for their actual freedom."

- Abraham Lincoln, effective January 1, 1863

1. The purpose of the above proclamation was to
   A) free all slaves in the Union only
   B) free slaves in Confederate controlled areas only
   C) free all slaves in the Union and Confederacy
   D) free only those slaves who aided the Union army

2. Which amendment to the US Constitution was a direct result of the above statement?
   A) Thirteenth Amendment
   B) Fourteenth Amendment
   C) Fifteenth Amendment
   D) Sixteenth Amendment

3. Which of the following would become a continuation of the above statement?
   A) Granting voting rights to former Confederates
   B) Supporting political advantages of Scalawags
   C) Providing citizenship and voting rights to former slaves
   D) Instituting a system of sharecropping

Answers and Explanations

1. **B**. The Emancipation Proclamation didn't free any slaves directly because the order only applied to the states not listening to federal law ... that is, those states rebelling in the Confederacy. Union slave states were unaffected.

2. **A**. The Thirteenth Amendment abolished slavery at the conclusion of the Civil War in 1865.

3. **C**. Freed slaves would receive such rights later during Reconstruction, as the 14th Amendment gave citizenship, while the 15th Amendment provided universal male suffrage.

Short Essay Question Set

Document 1:

Amendment XIII
Section 1.

Neither slavery nor involuntary servitude, except as a punishment for crime whereof the party shall have been duly convicted, shall exist within the United States, or any place subject to their jurisdiction.

Document 2:

...no freedman shall keep or carry fire-arms of any kind, or any ammunition, dirk or bowie knife....

...Any freedman committing riots, routs, affrays, trespasses, malicious mischief, cruel treatment to animals, seditious speeches, insulting gestures, language, or acts, or assaults on any person, disturbance of the peace, exercising the function of a minister of the Gospel without a license from some regularly organized church, vending spirituous or intoxicating liquors, or committing any other misdemeanor, the punishment of which is not specifically provided by law, shall, upon conviction thereof in the county court, be fined not less than ten dollars, and not more than one hundred dollars, and may be imprisoned at the discretion of the court, not exceeding thirty days....

- Mississippi Black Codes, c1865

•**Describe the historical context surrounding these documents**
•**Identify and explain the *relationship* between the events and/or ideas found in these documents (Cause and Effect, *or* Similarity/Difference, *or* Turning Point)**

The Gilded Age, c1870-1890

Mark Twain coined the term, "Gilded Age" to describe the time period between the 1870s-1900. Gilded meant that what appeared to be golden on the outside, was really junk on the inside. It seemed as though everything was great in this era. But it wasn't. There were "robber barons" who grew quite rich in their monopolized industries. Some of the rich rose to power after being rather poor. But in truth, 1% of the population controlled nearly all of the wealth. The laboring class was exploited both as workers and as consumers. Unions attempted to gain rights such as an 8-hour day. Despite the efforts of their strikes, the skilled and unskilled laborers never got the big piece of the pie. To complicate matters, millions of immigrants came to America to work in factories. In response, there was much anti-immigrant sentiment (nativism).

HERE IS WHAT YOU NEED TO KNOW:
Definition: Gilded Age

Coined by Mark Twain, the term refers to the time period from the 1870s until about 1900. Gilded means gold on the outside, and junk on the inside. Life during this time period looked good in terms of industry and invention, but in truth, the common people were suffering.

Definition: Robber Barons/Trusts

Although many considered them *captains of industry* who were beneficial to the country, the term *robber baron* was often used to describe industrialists who controlled monopolies, or *trusts* during the Gilded Age. They included Andrew Carnegie (steel), Cornelius Vanderbilt (railroads), and John D. Rockefeller (oil). Horatio Alger was known for writing *dime novels* about some of these men, like Carnegie, who went from "Rags to Riches" during the Gilded Age.

Trusts formed when one company took over the stock of competing companies in "trust" agreements. This often led to *monopolies*, where one huge corporation controlled almost the entire market. Competition fizzled and prices were often manipulated.

To control most of the steel industry, Carnegie bought out the raw materials and railroad lines associated with production. This is called *vertical integration*. He also looked to buy out similar companies, or merge with them. This is called *horizontal integration*.

Definition: *The Gospel of Wealth*

This was Carnegie's decree that the super-rich should be charitable and give back to society for the common good. However, a fortune should not be squandered, and must be donated to those wise enough to spend it properly.

Definition: Social Darwinism

Playing off Charles Darwin's Theory of Evolution, this was a belief in "survival of the fittest" in the business world. This notion was a defense of monopolies. Note: These same Darwinian principles would be applied decades later during the Age of Imperialism when the United States took over foreign territories.

Edward Bellamy wrote a utopian novel called *Looking Backward 2000-1887*, in which he gave a socialist look at the future. He showed how government reform movements would one day save the world from the evils of the trusts.

Question: What were the scandals of President Ulysses S. Grant's Administration?

Answer: The following scandals took place

at the onset of the Gilded Age:

1. Crédit Mobilier of 1872 was a scandal where the railroad companies and construction suppliers were owned by the same people. The supplier, Crédit Mobilier, was charging inflated prices for construction materials. The government-backed Union Pacific happily paid these prices. Of course, with inflated prices came bribes and kickbacks to the Congressmen involved.

2. The Salary Grab of 1873 was when Congress voted itself a 50% pay raise. Other salary increases were in the same bill. Grant signed this just before his second inauguration.

3. The Whiskey Ring of 1875 was a scandal in which federal whiskey taxes wound up in the pockets of distillers and politicians. Grant's Private Secretary was accused of wrongdoing.

Question: What was Boss Tweed's political machine?

Answer: William M. Tweed was the head of Tammany Hall, a *political machine* in New York City where people voted "early and often" to support the Democratic Party. Tweed's "Ring" basically ran New York City, as members of the Democratic Party controlled all powerful offices there. Tammany Hall also helped immigrants find jobs in exchange for votes. New York was an oasis of **municipal (city) corruption**, as bribery and kickbacks were common. *The New York Times* eventually exposed Tweed with the help of cartoonist Thomas Nast. After being prosecuted by attorney Samuel J. Tilden, Tweed went to prison.

Definition: Pendleton Act, 1883

After President James Garfield was assassinated by an unhappy office-seeker, this act attempted to rid the country of the spoils system (patronage system where a candidate appoints supporters to offices). The act provided for a civil service test to be taken by all government office-seekers.

Definition: Knights of Labor

The Knights of Labor was founded in 1869 as an industrial union led by **Terence Powderly**. With over 700,000 members by 1886, the union fought for an end to child labor, an 8-hour day, and equal pay for equal work. They also allowed African Americans and women to join. The Knights were quite often involved in strikes (though Powderly was against excess striking). A strike is a refusal to work.

Unions sometimes had to deal with *lockouts* where employers did not allow workers to enter their job until agreements were made. Another obstacle for labor at this time was *yellow-dog contracts*, which prevented workers from joining a union if they were to work at a certain job.

Definition: AFL

The American Federation of Labor was founded in 1886 as a **craft union** where people of a similar craft, or job, were grouped together. Their early leader was **Samuel Gompers**. Unlike the Knights of Labor, Gompers urged striking only when necessary. He fought for "**bread and butter**" issues, like an 8-hour day, and higher wages. These were basic financial topics that affected the daily lives of the union members.

The AFL promoted **collective bargaining**, where employees met with employers to compromise and discuss differences of opinion and contracts.

Here's how you can distinguish the two major unions:

BAGS - **B**read Butter Issues / **A**FL / **G**ompers / **S**trike less with collective bargaining

KUPS - **K**nights / **U**nskilled / **P**owderly / **S**trike more...Unskilled spellers can't spell cups.

Definition: IWW

The Industrial Workers of the World (Wobblies) were founded a bit after the Gilded Age in 1905. At times they were led by a vocal socialist, *Eugene V. Debs*. They were the most radical of all unions, and largely comprised of new immigrants.

Definition: Molly Maguires

The "Mollies" were Irish American coal miners in Pennsylvania who belonged to a secret society, and were labeled *anarchists,* who opposed the established government. They sought labor rights in the mines. In the 1870s, Mollies were charged with a number of crimes. With some questionable evidence, several were executed.

Definition: Mugwumps

During the 1880s, the Republican Party was divided. The Stalwarts (or Old Guard) were more conservative than the Half-Breeds, who favored civil service reform. But the Mugwumps were so dissatisfied with their party that they voted for Democrat Grover Cleveland against Republican James G. Blaine in the Election of 1884. Cleveland won.

Definition: Railroad strike of 1877

1877 was the end of Reconstruction, and the beginning of the "Labor Question." The Railroad Strike, or "Great Upheaval" occurred because of a cut to wages after the Panic of 1873. Sympathy strikes (strikes in nearby areas sympathetic to the cause) spread throughout the country from West Virginia to Illinois. President Hayes broke up this strike with federal troops because it was disrupting interstate commerce and the violence was getting out of hand. Note: In the Gilded Age, Presidents tended to side with "Big Business," and not the consumer or worker.

Definition: Haymarket Affair, 1886

In Chicago, a bomb went off in Haymarket Square during a rally near the McCormick Harvesting Machine Company. Police fired weapons in response. Both cops and civilians were killed. This was a landmark event as:

1. Unions were blamed and ultimately associated with socialism and anarchy (anti-establishment).
2. Since many union members were immigrants, there was an increase in nativism (discussed later this chapter).
3. Knights of Labor enrollment decreased.

Definition: Homestead Strike of 1892

This was yet another defeat for unions. Andrew Carnegie's steel plant in Homestead, Pennsylvania began to unionize. The company fought unionization by threatening to hire *scabs*, or non-union replacement workers. Violence erupted between strikers and Pinkerton (private) detectives. Strikers were later arrested and tried for treason.

Definition: Pullman Strike of 1894

Pullman cars were luxury railroad cars. When wages went down at the factory, the workers went on strike. Eugene V. Debs, a socialist, instructed workers of the American Railway Union to halt trains with Pullman cars on them. Much violence and property damage accompanied the strike. President Grover Cleveland said that the strike actions disrupted federal mail. He got a court order (injunction) to end the strike, and Debs went to prison. This was another example of the President siding with employers.

Definition: Panic of 1893 and Coxey's Army of 1894

Every few decades of the nineteenth century (1837, 1857, 1873, and 1893) saw a financial panic.

The one in 1893 led to immense unemployment. Ohio politician Jacob Coxey gathered an "army" of unemployed men who demanded that the government provide jobs in public works (government construction). Coxey marched through the country, and into Washington, DC. There, members of his "army" were arrested for trespassing on the US Capitol lawn.

Definition: Interstate Commerce Act and the Interstate Commerce Commission, 1887

The act created the Interstate Commerce Committee (ICC) that looked to ensure that railroad shipping fees were "reasonable and just." They also made sure that rates were published so price discrimination didn't happen. Of course, in the Gilded Age, nothing was what it seemed. The ICC wasn't too strong in its early years, so little help for the consumer took place.

Before the ICC, farmers pressured Illinois to create legislation to prevent inflated prices for hauling and storing crops. In the 1877 case *Munn* v. *Illinois*, the Supreme Court upheld such "Granger laws" passed by the states which looked to protect farmers. The impact of this decision was greatly reduced by the 1886 *Wabash* case (*Wabash, St. Louis & Pacific Railway Company* v. *Illinois*) when the court said that states could not regulate interstate commerce. Thus, an ICC was needed.

Definition: Sherman Anti-Trust Act, 1890

1. Named for legislator John Sherman, this act attempted to break up monopolies and trusts that exploited consumers.

2. The following is a very common quote: "Any contract or combination in *restraint of trade* is illegal." If you hear "restraint of trade," Sherman is your man.

3. The act did not define "restraint of trade" well, and the law was mostly used *at first to break up unions*. Furthermore, in the 1895

decision of *US* v. *EC Knight Co.*, the Supreme Court said that manufacturing companies (a sugar company in this case) were not monopolies which could be busted. This was because their manufacturing was done *locally*, and therefore did not restrain *interstate* commerce.

Question: What Gilded Age inventions should I know about?

Answer:

1. The incandescent light bulb by Thomas Edison stayed on longer than earlier light bulbs.

2. Henry **Bessemer's Process** found a way to eliminate the impurities in pig iron so it could be mass-produced quicker.

3. In 1869, the Golden Spike was hammered at Promontory Summit, Utah. This completed the Transcontinental Railroad. Railroads were given a lot of land from the federal government (thanks to the Pacific Railway Act of 1862), as the United States had a vested interest in linking the country together. A railroad line across the nation would encourage transportation, settlement, and trade. (More on pg. 68.)

4. In 1883, the Brooklyn Bridge opened in New York City. The largest steel suspension bridge of its time, it connected Brooklyn to Manhattan. In addition to transportation infrastructure, cities expanded sewer systems, clean water, and sanitation at this time to help promote public health.

5. Alexander Graham Bell's telephone would revolutionize communications in the coming centuries.

Question: What were the two Great Waves of immigration?

Answer:

1. Old Immigration - c1845-1860 - First Great Wave. These immigrants were mostly from Western European countries such as Ireland, Britain, and the German states.

2. New Immigration - c1890-1920 - Second Great Wave. These immigrants were mostly from Southern and Eastern European countries such as Italy, Russia, and Poland.

There are two theories on immigration. The first, *the melting pot*, calls for a total assimilation (Americanization) of newcomers. In this theory, immigrants lose their culture as if they have jumped into a crucible (melting pot), thus blending with all other US citizens. The second theory is *cultural pluralism*, or the "salad bowl" idea. In this metaphor, immigrants maintain their cultural identity as they coexist with other Americans.

Question: What was nativism, and how did it affect immigrant *quotas*?

Answer:

Nativism looked to protect the interests of the *native* born. It is a feeling of opposition towards foreigners based on nationalistic sentiment. Nativism existed during the first Great Wave of Immigration, as the ***Know-Nothing Party*** was founded because of anti-Irish-Catholic sentiment. Later in the century, nativism led to:

1. The Chinese Exclusion Act of 1882 which limited Chinese immigration. The Chinese were labeled "coolies" (derogatory slang) by nativists who saw their cheap labor as unwelcome competition in the US.

2. The Gentlemen's Agreement of 1907 in which Japan agreed to limit emigration to the United States. ***Commodore Matthew Perry*** opened up Japan to westernization in the 1850s. After modernizing their economy, many immigrated to the US, but faced segregation and discrimination.

3. In 1917, a literacy test for immigrants was passed over Woodrow Wilson's veto. It was motivated by xenophobia (hatred and fear of foreigners) just before US entry into World War I.

4. The ***Quota Acts*** of the 1920s (specifically the Emergency Quota Act of 1921 and the ***National Origins Act*** of 1924) set limits on immigration, especially from Southern and Eastern Europe. This meant that government policy favored the more assimilated (Americanized) immigrants from Western European nations such as Britain. Immigration from Eastern Europe was greatly curtailed.

The quota acts were partly inspired by a belief in a genetics movement called ***eugenics***. Eugenics attempted to rank the races. On inherited intelligence and desirability, Southern and Eastern European immigrants were ranked lower than Western Europeans. The controversial movement of eugenics lost popularity by the middle of the twentieth century.

Question: What immigration laws of the mid-late twentieth century should I know?

Answer:

1. ***Immigration Act of 1965*** – Replacing earlier quota acts, this law set up a yearly quota of immigration from the Eastern (170,000 immigrants) and Western (120,000 immigrants) Hemispheres. It also made it easier for relatives of immigrants to enter the US. Mostly, this act widened the amount of immigrants coming from areas other than Europe. Most notably, recent immigration has been from places such as Latin America and Asia. Much like the older waves of immigration, people have come from all over the world because of "pull factors" such as jobs and economic opportunity, and have been "pushed" out because of war or religious persecution.

2. In the mid-1980s, the government addressed illegal immigration. The ***Immigration Reform and Control Act of 1986*** targeted those employers who knowingly hired illegal immigrants. Signed by Ronald Reagan, the act also looked to provide a legalization process for those who had been living in the country without proper documentation.

The West, 1860-1890

In the West, the glory of "free land" led to the rise of lawless towns. In addition, settlers continued to expand at the expense of American Indian populations. Wounded Knee became the Trail of Tears for a new generation.

HERE IS WHAT YOU NEED TO KNOW:
Definition: Homestead Act of 1862

Passed during the Civil War, this act provided public land for private use. "Free Land" became the slogan, as about 270 million acres (10% of the US) were claimed and settled under the act. A homestead typically was 160 acres in size.

Homesteaders became *"sodbusters,"* as they had to bust through the thick sod to plant and build homes. Some made homes out of the sod and called it a soddy! Nineteenth century inventions, such as the mechanical reaper, and John Deere's steel plow, led to greater harvests. The federal government even took an interest in supporting agricultural education, as the *Morrill Act of 1862* granted land to states for the creation of colleges focusing on agriculture and mechanical knowledge (as in Texas A&M).

Many African American families looked to escape racism in the South and fled to western states as well. These *"exodusters"* hoped for a better opportunity in Kansas.

Definition: Transcontinental Railroad

This was a railroad that linked the entire country together. The Central Pacific (with the help of Chinese immigrants) built east from Sacramento, California. The Union Pacific built west from Council Bluffs, Iowa. The Golden Spike was hammered at Promontory Summit, Utah on May 10, 1869.

As mentioned earlier, the government provided land to railroad companies in support of this project. The railroads led to the development of cities in the west and created new demands for meat. This caused an expansion of the longhorn cattle industry which was based in Texas. Cowboys herded the cattle to their final destinations.

Question: What famous gunslingers should I know about in the Wild West?

Answer: With western land being claimed so fast, there was little time for the government to provide law enforcement. In case you receive an essay on the west, you might want to throw in…

Billy The Kid - The head of the *Regulators* in the West, he shot a sheriff, escaped a death sentence, and then died on the run.

Jesse James - Part of the *James-Younger Gang*, and a former member of Quantrill's Raiders (Confederate guerrilla warfare soldiers). He robbed stagecoaches and banks. He was shot by a former partner in crime, Robert Ford.

Annie Oakley - Part of *Buffalo Bill Cody's Wild West Show*, she had one of the best shots in the wild west, and performed for thousands.

Wild Bill Hickok - A legendary gunslinger of the Old West, he was shot playing poker while holding Aces and Eights…The Dead Man's Hand.

Wyatt Earp - He made a fortune playing faro (a gambling game of number prediction) in the Old West. Later, he became a man of law. He was triumphant in the legendary gunfight at the OK Corral in Tombstone, Arizona where outlaw Billy Clanton was killed.

Definition: Dawes Severalty Act of 1887

The goal of this act was to assimilate Native Americans and break up reservation tribal lands in favor of individual ownership. The government granted plots of land and United States citizenship to Native Americans who, "adopted the habits of civilized life." This program was mostly detrimental to Native Americans because more white settlers came to the area, and the government would not give full control of the land until 25 years after its issuance. At this time, the government funded boarding schools, such as the Carlisle Indian School in Pennsylvania, which looked to assimilate Native Americans to US culture. Jim Thorpe, the famous US Olympian and football player of the early 1900s, attended Carlisle.

Definition: Buffalo (Bison) Depletion

Buffalo were vital for American Indian survival on the western plains. In 1870 there were millions grazing there. By 1883, there were only a few hundred left. Buffalo hunters, such as Buffalo Bill Cody, were celebrated as American heroes. Trains offered voyages where people could blast guns at the animals from the sides of railroad cars. This left a trail of carcasses littering the Great Plains.

Definition: Little Big Horn, 1876

This was the location of General George Custer's "Last Stand." After gold was reportedly spotted in the Black Hills of Montana, the army went to inspect. Forces including Crazy Horse and Sitting Bull outnumbered the US troops, and killed everyone including Custer. The battle increased Native American morale, and angered the US Government.

Definition: Sand Creek Massacre, Ghost Dance, and Wounded Knee

Despite the first *Treaty of Fort Laramie* (1851) which was supposed to give land to tribes, violations occurred as American settlers moved westward. The Great Plains had its share of conflicts. In 1864, about 200 innocent Cheyenne and Arapaho people were massacred in Sand Creek, Colorado by volunteer cavalrymen.

In the Dakotas in 1890, many Sioux put on Ghost Shirts that they thought would make them invincible to bullets. Following the prophet *Wovoka*, they believed that by doing a dance, they would rid the Dakotas of white expansionists, and bring about peace. However, in the midst of the movement, the US Cavalry showed up near Wounded Knee Creek, SD. In a chaotic and frantic exchange, over 150 American Indians, including Sioux leader Sitting Bull, were killed. The Wounded Knee Massacre became a symbol of Native American discrimination, and oppression.

Definition: Helen Hunt Jackson

In 1881 Jackson wrote *A Century of Dishonor*, a nonfiction work that detailed the horrors of Native American removal in the nineteenth century. She documented how thousands of Native Americans were pushed from their homes without legal protections.

Definition: Turner Thesis

After the closing of the American frontier, Harvard professor Frederick Jackson Turner wrote a thesis in 1893 concluding that the West (frontier) personified the story of America. He displayed the importance of how the frontier line had always sparked individual strength and democracy. He believed that the West was the most important component of the American story.

Also, the frontier offered a "safety valve," meaning free land promised opportunity which diffused economic and social conflict. Adversaries of the thesis believe that Turner overemphasized the importance of the frontier, as other issues such as slavery and industrialization proved to be much larger stories.

Review Questions

The following questions are based on John Gast's *American Progress.*

John Gast, American Progress, 1872
Chromolithograph published by George A. Crofutt
Source: Prints and Photographs Division, Library of Congress

1. Which of the following best reflects the point of view of the artist?
   A) Settlers must not threaten American Indian tribal lands
   B) The Louisiana Purchase was unconstitutional
   C) The spirit of the Second Great Awakening will take over the western lands
   D) The US was destined to settle the land between the Atlantic and Pacific Oceans

2. In 1890, which area of the United States would be most affected by the idea inferred by the artwork?
   A) Texas
   B) California
   C) Kansas
   D) North Dakota

3. This painting can be considered a continuation of which of the following?
   A) Popular Sovereignty
   B) Indian Removal Act
   C) *Worcester* v. *Georgia* decision
   D) Thirteenth Amendment

Answers and Explanations

1. **D**. Many mistake the *American Progress* painting as being from before the Civil War. Although it's later (c1872), a continuation of "manifest destiny" prevails as Americans continued to settle the frontier.

2. **D**. The Dakotas would gain statehood around this time. The other states were settled and admitted to the Union well before 1890.

3. **B**. Settlement in the west continued to have adverse effects on American Indians. Less than two decades after the image was created, the tragedy of Wounded Knee occurred.

Short Essay Question Set

Document 1

Lithograph by J. Ottmann after drawing by J. Keppler. Illus. in: *Puck*, (1889 Jan. 23)

Document 2

Sec. 1. Every contract, combination in the form of trust or otherwise, or conspiracy, in restraint of trade or commerce among the several States, or with foreign nations, is hereby declared to be illegal. Every person who shall make any such contract or engage in any such combination or conspiracy, shall be deemed guilty of a misdemeanor, and, on conviction thereof, shall be punished by fine not exceeding five thousand dollars, or by imprisonment not exceeding one year, or by both said punishments, at the discretion of the court.

- Sherman Anti-Trust Act, 1890

•**Describe the historical context surrounding these documents**
•**Identify and explain the *relationship* between the events and/or ideas found in these documents (Cause and Effect, *or* Similarity/Difference, *or* Turning Point)**

Populism and The Progressive Era, c1892-1920

The Gilded Age alienated the common American. Populism was a movement started by farmers to bring the government back to the people. Although they never elected a President, some of their ideas became a reality during the Progressive Era. The Progressives brought about immense change to the social, political, and economic lives of the American people. New amendments, aid to immigrants, direct participation in politics, and regulation of business were just some of their many reforms. The Progressive Era weakened after World War I when fears of communism swept the nation.

HERE IS WHAT YOU NEED TO KNOW:
Definition: Granger Movement and Farmers' Alliance

Both movements were predecessors to Populism. *The National Grange of the Order of Patrons of Husbandry* defended farmers against big business. The *Farmers' Alliance* organized farmers economically and politically (see pg. 66).

Definition: Populist Party

Also known as the People's Party, they were a short-lived political party comprised mostly of farmers. In 1892, they drafted their platform at Omaha, Nebraska (Omaha Platform) and ran James Weaver for President. He lost.

Question: What did the Populists want?
Answer: Mnemonic Device - **STAR 16**

S - **S**enators to be directly elected.

T - Graduated/Progressive Income **T**ax (the more you make, the more they take).

A - **A**ustralian Ballot (secret ballot).

R - Regulation of the **R**ailroads by the government.

16 - Coinage of silver at a ratio of **16**:1 with gold.

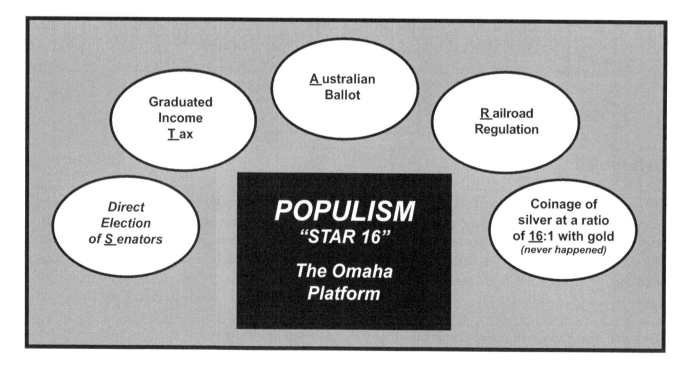

Question: Why did the Populists care so much about the silver issue?

Answer: By 1892, the prices of crops were falling...drastically. So, to make money, farmers **grew more crops!** But when you grow more crops, there's greater supply than demand and...**they lose their value!** So now you have to...*grow even more crops!* This vicious cycle of overproduction and deflation of prices put farmers out of business. They couldn't pay their mortgages. However, mortgages were generally set at a fixed rate and didn't change. If more silver was put into circulation instead of gold, *inflation* would occur. That's because silver is worth less than gold. This inflation would increase the prices of the farm goods, and make that fixed mortgage easier to pay off.

This is very similar to the hard money/soft money battle of the Jacksonian Era (see pg. 37). Flooding the market with silver has the same result as printing more paper money - inflation.

Question: Of what the Populists wanted, what eventually became law?

Answer: Don't underestimate the importance of third parties in American History. They bring attention to new issues. Here is the Populist success rate:

S - **S**enators to be directly elected...***Became the Seventeenth Amendment (1913)***

T - Graduated/Progressive Income **T**ax... *Result of the Sixteenth Amendment (1913)*

A - **A**ustralian Ballot...*Became Law c1900*

R - Regulation of the **R**ailroads by the government...*Became law c1900*

16 - Coinage of silver at a ratio of **16**:1 with gold...**Never happened**. *But to the farmers it was the most important aspect of the Omaha Platform.*

Definition: William Jennings Bryan

Dashing and handsome in 1896, Bryan received the nomination for President from both the Democrats and the Populists. He delivered one of the most famous speeches of all time, ***The Cross of Gold Speech***, where he advocated **bimetallism** (government use of both gold and silver), and the unlimited coinage of silver at a ratio of 16:1 with gold. At the end of the speech, he said that the Republicans were crucifying mankind upon a cross of gold. This meant that, if silver was not mixed with gold in the money supply, the farmer would financially die. Bryan passed away in 1925 shortly after defending creationism in the Scopes Trial (see pg. 88).

Definition: Election of 1896

Republican William McKinley defeated William Jennings Bryan (Democrat and Populist). It was an incredible mass media election, as Republican leader Mark Hanna spent nearly $4 million on McKinley's campaign. Big Business contributed to this fund.

Definition: What exactly was the Progressive Era?

Answer: It was the period between c1890-c1918 that saw many reforms attempting to improve society. The movement looked to:

1. Make new rules for big business.

2. Grant more rights, and bring government closer to the people.

3. Clean up America after the Gilded Age.

Definition: Australian Ballot

It's a secret ballot. Before the Progressive Era, citizens declared their vote choices to their local election officials. This progressive reform looked to change that. The secret ballot was a Populist objective.

Definition: Sixteenth Amendment, 1913

This provided for an income tax. Later it

would become a progressive or graduated income tax that looked to end exploitation of the poor. The progressive tax made wealthy people pay a greater share of taxes, or, "The more you make, the more they take." This was a Populist objective.

How to Remember: Tax has an X in it...so does SiXteenth

Definition: Seventeenth Amendment, 1913

This provided for direct election of Senators. Before this amendment, state legislatures appointed Senators. This change to the Constitution gave citizens a greater say as to who would represent them. This was also a Populist objective.

How to Remember: Seeeeeeventeen... Seeeeeenators (it's the best we could do).

Definitions: Initiative, Referendum, Recall

These are ways to bring lawmaking to the people. These methods are still used today:

Initiative - Some states allow people to introduce bills to the state legislatures.

Referendum - Some states allow people to vote on certain bills.

Recall - Some states allow voters to remove incumbents (those originally elected) from office prematurely. In these cases, there would be a special election to find a replacement (or keep the incumbent).

Definition: Direct Primary

A direct primary is where the major political parties allow citizens to decide who will be nominated for the November Presidential and other local elections. Before primaries and nominating conventions, caucuses composed of men in "smoke-filled rooms" chose the candidates without consulting the people.

So now, for the path to the Presidency just remember that Pencils Need Erasers ... Primary + Nominating Convention + Electoral College.

Question: What Progressive Presidents do I need to know?

Answer: Theodore Roosevelt - (1901-1909). McKinley was assassinated in 1901, and Vice President Roosevelt took over. He was a Republican, but acted more like a Democrat on certain economic issues. He battled trusts, was a friend to labor, and promoted conservation. One of the first people he invited to visit the White House was civil rights leader Booker T. Washington.

Woodrow Wilson - (1913-1921). A true Democrat, Wilson lowered tariffs, increased government control over the economy, and was President during World War I. He wasn't too big on civil rights though. He showed and marveled at D.W. Griffith's *Birth of a Nation* in the White House. The movie portrayed the KKK as heroes defending white women from the advances of African American men.

Also, do not underestimate the importance of Republican **Robert La Follette**. Believed to be one of the most important Senators of all time, the Wisconsin native was instrumental in passing much progressive legislation.

Question: Why was Theodore Roosevelt known as the *trustbuster*?

Answer: Roosevelt wanted to break up trusts that he saw as bad, yet keep the ones that did not exploit the consumer. Ultimately, the big companies busted in the Progressive Era were the **Northern Securities Company** (railroad), and John D. Rockefeller's Standard Oil.

Question: Was Teddy Roosevelt really a friend to labor?

Answer: He was in 1902 in the Anthracite Coal Strike.

In the Gilded Age, Presidents broke up strikes and supported employers. But Theodore Roosevelt sided with workers in this particular strike. He threatened to use force against the owners if they didn't agree to arbitration (fair negotiation with a third party).

Roosevelt said he gave those coal workers a **Square Deal**. His Square Deal platform meant that all middle class consumers should get a piece of the pie, instead of being dominated by big business.

Part of this platform included the Elkins Act of 1903 and the Hepburn Act of 1906. Both strengthened the Interstate Commerce Commission's ability to regulate unfair activities of the railroad industry.

Definition: *The Jungle*

Upton Sinclair hoped to reach Americans through their hearts, instead, he shocked them in their stomachs. *The Jungle* detailed the horrors of the meatpacking industry. Rat feces on meat, melted human flesh, and poisonous fertilizer in the sausage hoppers were just some of the putrid items featured in this work. Sinclair's book ultimately led to the **Meat Inspection Act, and the Pure Food and Drug Act of 1906** which created the Food and Drug Administration (FDA). Still around today, the FDA's job is to make sure that food and drugs are safe for human consumption. *The Jungle* made the meat industry safe for *both* workers and consumers.

Question: Besides Sinclair, what other muckrakers are important to know?

Answer: Muckrakers looked to "rake up muck" (dirt) on society, and foster change through writing. Besides Sinclair, you should know about the following:

1. Jacob Riis - In 1890, he wrote *How The Other Half Lives*, a book detailing the impoverished immigrants who lived in overcrowded *tenement* dwellings of the Lower East side of New York City. When Theodore Roosevelt was governor of New York, the state assembled the Tenement House Commission which looked to improve quality of life in housing. Legislation in 1901 implemented new standards for housing in New York.

2. Ida B. Wells - c1893, she challenged Jim Crow, and promoted anti-lynching laws.

3. Ida Tarbell - *The History of the Standard Oil Company* was published in *McClure's Magazine* in 1904. It described the abuses of the oil monopoly. She received some credit for helping to break up that trust. Think: **Tar**bell...**Oil**.

4. Helen Hunt Jackson - In 1881, she wrote *A Century of Dishonor*. As stated earlier, she challenged the United States Government's treatment of Native Americans.

5. Lincoln Steffens - His 1904 work, *The Shame of the Cities,* detailed corruption in municipalities (cities), and hardships faced by immigrants.

Definition: Conservation

Theodore Roosevelt loved nature. He traveled to North Dakota as a young man to find himself. During his Presidency, he protected about 230 million acres. His goal was to *conserve*, or protect while ensuring proper use of nature for purposes such as recreation. Today, the National Park Service is indebted to him. Another conservationist to know is Gifford Pinchot who supported the "rational use" of nature's resources. Others, such as John Muir, were *preservationists*, who preferred that the government protect nature from both profit and increased usage.

Definition: Election of 1908

Keeping with the two-term legacy of George Washington, Theodore Roosevelt went to

Africa to hunt rather than seek re-election. He threw his weight (no pun intended) behind Republican William Howard Taft. Yes, Taft's the big guy who got stuck in the bathtub. Taft defeated William Jennings Bryan to take the White House.

Definition: Triangle Shirtwaist Fire, 1911

March 25, 1911 saw a horrific fire at a garment factory in New York City. 146 people were killed when locked doors prevented an escape. The exits were locked by employers trying to prevent employee work breaks. The fire led to stricter building and fire codes in cities across the country.

Definition: Ballinger-Pinchot Affair

Gifford Pinchot was the head of the US Forestry Division. He was a prominent conservationist, and a friend of Theodore Roosevelt. During the Taft Administration, Richard Ballinger was Secretary of the Interior, and it appeared like he did not want to conserve. Pinchot attacked him in a letter, believing Ballinger had illegally helped others gain access to Alaskan coal fields. Pinchot was removed from office. The firing angered conservationists, and was an outrage to Roosevelt.

Definition: Election of 1912

Upset over Taft's policies, Roosevelt looked to violate the two-term tradition, and ran for President as the candidate of the *Progressive (Bull Moose) Party*. He was nearly assassinated during the campaign. Luckily an eyeglass case and long speech rolled up in his breast pocket swallowed the bullet.

Taft, a Republican, and Roosevelt, a former Republican, split votes. This made Democrat Woodrow Wilson the victor. Socialist Eugene V. Debs (a founder of the American Railway Union) received 900,000

votes. He got about the same in 1920 when he ran from prison.

Definition: New Nationalism vs. New Freedom

The Election of 1912 saw two progressive candidates who wanted a more active role for the government in economic and social reform. However, they differed a bit in that:

Roosevelt's *The New Nationalism* would bust only bad trusts, while keeping the good ones.

Wilson's *The New Freedom* promised to bust more trusts than Roosevelt would. Wilson also wanted banking reform and lower tariffs.

Definition: Underwood Tariff, 1913

When Democrats were in office, tariffs (taxes on imports) tended to go down as a benefit for consumers. The Underwood Tariff of 1913 brought tariffs to their lowest levels in many decades.

Remember for tariffs: **D** for **D**emocrats, **D** for **D**own. **R** for **R**epublicans, **R** for **R**aise.

Definition: Clayton Anti-Trust Act of 1914

Because the Sherman Anti-Trust Act of 1890 mostly busted unions, a redefinition of the act was in order. This new clarification gave more rights to unions, and opened the door to break up more trusts. It also gave many new specific definitions as to what is "restraint of trade," including such things as price discrimination.

Definition: Federal Reserve Act, 1913

The Federal Reserve Act laid the foundation for our current central banking system, as the Federal Reserve System monitors inflation and determines how the US dollar is circulated.

Definition: Federal Trade Commission, 1914

The FTC ordered corporations to refrain

from unfair business practices such as false advertising. It also looked to stop potential monopolies. This protected consumers.

It must be noted that the Progressive Era increased the size of government *bureaucracies* (agencies with large numbers of workers). The FDA, FTC, Federal Reserve, and other new agencies made the government a much more complex web of offices. It would expand even further in the 1930s during the New Deal.

Definition: Eighteenth Amendment, 1919

The temperance movement of the early nineteenth century finally led to prohibition. Headed by women such as Annie Turner Wittenmyer of the *WCTU* (Women's Christian Temperance Union), prohibition meant that the sale and distribution of alcoholic beverages was illegal. Earlier, there were wet and dry states, as the sale of alcohol was a reserved (state) power. But this amendment changed everything. Note: The **21st** Amendment would repeal the **18th** in 1933. (**18** and **21** were also the last two drinking ages).

Question: What other female reformers of the Progressive Era should I know about?

Answer: Typically, women reformers of the Progressive Era were *middle class and educated*. Many were laboring hard at *settlement houses*. Settlement houses were places that gave shelter, meals, and advice to immigrants. You need to know:

1. Jane Addams - Addams helped establish Hull House in Chicago. Opened in 1889, this settlement house instructed English, and

counseled immigrants on how to cope with America's big city life. A religious movement known as *Social Gospel* emerged, as Christians believed it was their duty to help the poor and fight for better working conditions.

2. Florence Kelley - Similar to Addams, she was instrumental in New York City at the Henry Street Settlement.

3. Susan B. Anthony and Lucy Stone - Leaders of the women's suffrage movement (voting), they were members of NAWSA, the National American Woman Suffrage Association. Carrie Chapman Catt helped with suffrage at the grassroots level c1910.

4. "Mother Jones" (Mary Harris Jones) - Pro-labor reformer who spoke out against child labor, and for the wives of laborers.

5. Pauline Newman and Emma Goldman - Union organizers. Strong women's unions of the time included the Women's Trade Union League and International Ladies' Garment Workers' Union. Constantly fighting for the working class, Goldman spent time in prison for her activism against the World War I draft, and was eventually deported in 1919.

Definition: *Muller* v. *Oregon*, 1908

The Supreme Court's *Muller* decision said that a state can limit a woman's working hours to protect her health and potential maternal functions. The case was a setback for women's equality. This was especially upsetting to them because an earlier case, *Lochner* v. *New York* (1905), stated that the government could not set maximum working hours for bakers.

Definition: Mothers' Pensions

A precursor to modern welfare assistance, these were state government cash payments to single-mothers. Not all states took part, but about 40 did so during the Progressive Era.

Definition: Nineteenth Amendment, 1920

Much like prohibition, women's voting rights were up to the states before 1920. In Wyoming, for example, women had full voting rights. In Nebraska, they could vote in Presidential Elections. In the South, they couldn't vote at all. This amendment gave all women full voting rights in every state of the Union.

Question: What led to the end of the Progressive Era?

Answer: Some historians feel that the reform movement ran its course. But most likely it was the outbreak of World War I and the Red Scare (see pg. 84) which caused a backlash against the reformers, liberals, and perceived socialists associated with the Progressive Era.

Review Questions

"We demand the free and unlimited coinage of silver and gold at the present legal ration of 16 to 1...

"We demand a graduated income tax.

"We believe that the moneys of the country should be kept as much as possible in the hands of the people, and hence we demand that all state and national revenues shall be limited to the necessary expenses of the government, economically and honestly administered.

"Transportation being a means of exchange and a public necessity, the government should own and operate the railroads in the interest of the people."
                                                                    - Omaha Platform, 1892

1. The above text reflects the demands of which third party?
   A) Greenback Party
   B) Populist Party
   C) Bull Moose Party
   D) Anti-Masonic Party

2. Which of the above demands caused the greatest support among America's farmers?
   A) Graduated income tax
   B) Prudent government spending
   C) Free and unlimited coinage of silver
   D) Direct election of senators

3. Which accomplishment of the Progressive Era can be seen as a direct continuation of the platform mentioned above?
   A) Amnesty Act
   B) Sixteenth Amendment
   C) Pure Food and Drug Act
   D) Morrill Act

Answers and Explanations

1. **B**. The Omaha Platform laid out the goals of the Populist Party, a third party whose founders looked to support the interests of rural farmers.

2. **C**. Though the Populists strongly wanted the free and unlimited coinage of silver, this demand was never met during the Progressive Era. They were hoping to raise farm prices.

3. **B**. The Sixteenth Amendment led to a progressive, or graduated income tax. This was one of the demands of the Populists which became law during the Progressive Era.

Short Essay Question Set

Document 1:

"This is no fairy story and no joke; the meat would be shoveled into carts, and the man who did the shoveling would not trouble to lift out a rat even when he saw one – there were things that went into the sausage in comparison with which a poisoned rat was a tidbit. There was no place for the men to wash their hands before they ate their dinner, and so they made a practice of washing them in the water that was to be ladled into the sausage."

- Excerpt from *The Jungle* by Upton Sinclair, 1906

Sinclair, Upton. *The Jungle*. New York: Grosset & Dunlap, 1906.

Document 2:

An Act For preventing the manufacture, sale, or transportation of adulterated or misbranded or poisonous or deleterious foods, drugs, medicines, and liquors, and for regulating traffic therein, and for other purposes.

Be it enacted by the Senate and House of Representatives of the United States of America in Congress assembled, That it shall be unlawful for any person to manufacture within any Territory or the District of Columbia any article of food or drug which is adulterated or misbranded within the meaning of this Act…

- Pure Food and Drug Act, 1906

•**Describe the historical context surrounding these documents**
•**Identify and explain the *relationship* between the events and/or ideas found in these documents (Cause and Effect, *or* Similarity/Difference, *or* Turning Point)**

Imperialism and World War I, 1898-1919

The US was founded with a foreign policy based on neutrality, which was no longer feasible by 1898. The world was changing. Strong nations were taking over weaker ones for political and economic gain. The United States would act no differently. After acquiring territories in the Spanish-American War, the US annexed Hawaii and incited a revolution in Panama to gain access to a canal. Along the way, they also angered the imperialized people of the Philippines and the government of Cuba. The US stayed neutral at the beginning of World War I. However, after the sinking of the *Lusitania*, issuance of the Zimmermann Telegram, and continual unrestricted submarine warfare by Germany, the US had no choice but to get involved in the war. After reading over the Treaty of Versailles, the Senate decided that America should return to a policy of isolationism. Consequently, the treaty was never ratified.

HERE IS WHAT YOU NEED TO KNOW:
Question: How did American foreign policy change c1898?

Answer: George Washington's policies of neutrality were no longer practical by 1898. The United States was looking to expand its growing empire, protect its trading interests, and secure territories around the globe. This meant the US would become *imperialists*, or a nation that looked to take over another country's resources and political life while imposing culture and trade upon them. The US needed markets for products, coaling stations, and sources of raw materials. This policy was an obvious break with both the Enlightenment principles of the Declaration of Independence and Washington's Proclamation of Neutrality.

Question: What were the causes of the Spanish-American War of 1898?

Answer: The two major causes were *The Boat and The Note*...but so were the following:

1. Jingoism - Ultra-nationalistic beliefs in the United States.

2. Support of Cuban uprisings for independence - The United States wanted Cuba to overthrow Spain and rid them from the Western Hemisphere. Violence had been occurring there for decades.

3. *Yellow Journalism* - This mostly stemmed from the competition between Joseph Pulitzer of the New York *World* and William Randolph Hearst of the New York *Journal*. "Yellow" came from the ink used in the newspapers. The term refers to the embellished stories of atrocities committed by the Spanish against the Cubans. The competing papers escalated claims that weren't always true.

The Boat - The USS *Maine*. Recent investigations suggest that this battleship may have sunk on its own. Back then, it was blamed on a Spanish mine explosion.

The Note - The De Lôme Letter was written by a Spanish diplomat. The letter was greatly critical of President McKinley, calling him a weak leader. McKinley ultimately asked Congress to declare war.

Question: What were the results of the Spanish-American War of 1898?

Answer: Secretary of State *John Hay* called this, "a splendid little war" because:

1. The United States received Puerto Rico.

2. The US purchased the Philippines from Spain for $20 million. Note: You will need to know that US rule over the Philippines was quite harsh and led to massive resentment. The military had to put down a rebellion from 1899-

1902. This was the Philippine-American War.

3. The US received Guam.

4. Cuba became independent.

5. Not directly related to the war, but as the battle to secure the Philippines broke out, the US annexed Hawaii. This made businessmen like pineapple mogul Sanford Dole very happy.

Definition: Insular Cases, c1905

Named for the Bureau of Insular Affairs, these were a group of Supreme Court decisions around 1905 that said the US Constitution did not necessarily give full rights to certain territories. Alaska and Hawaii had full Constitutional rights. Places such as the Philippines did not.

Definition: Teller/Platt Amendment

With Spain out of Cuba, the United States fluctuated its foreign policy with the:

Teller Amendment - 1898 - The US said it would respect Cuba to govern itself.

Platt Amendment - 1901 - Just three years later, the US said it could look over Cuba's shoulder as it governed. The US could meddle in Cuban treaties and other domestic issues.

In 1903, the United States leased a 45 square mile area in Cuba known as Guantánamo Bay. It has since been used as a naval base.

Definition: Open Door Policy, 1899

1. The policy was negotiated by Secretary of State John Hay.

2. It said that China was open to all countries who wanted to trade. Of course, China had no say in this, as they were carved into zones controlled by foreigners known as *spheres of influence*.

Generally, the policy was created to protect American trading interests in China. They did not want to lose Chinese trade to other European countries.

Definition: Big Stick Diplomacy

Theodore Roosevelt said to "speak softly and carry a big stick." That meant to go about your business, but when there was a valuable opportunity, or if something looked troublesome, the US would exercise its military might.

Even during peacetime, US military might was put on display. In the final years of Roosevelt's presidency, the gigantic "Great White Fleet" of US naval ships traveled the world displaying American strength.

Question: What do I need to know about the Panama Canal?

Answer: The canal connected the Atlantic and Pacific Oceans. Construction began in 1904. Here is how the US obtained the land:

1. Panama is an isthmus sticking out of Colombia…but back then it was controlled by Colombia.

2. Colombia did not want to honor the Hay-Herrán treaty that would have allowed the US to build a canal there.

3. John Hay told Panama if they wanted independence from Colombia, then America would back it.

4. After the successful Panamanian Revolution, the first order of business was approval of The Hay-Bunau-Varilla Treaty. This treaty granted the US the canal zone.

5. Doctors, such as William Gorgas, aimed to control malaria and yellow fever (spread by mosquitoes) which killed many during the early years of its immense construction.

Definition: Roosevelt Corollary to the Monroe Doctrine, 1904

This was a clarification to the 1823 Monroe Doctrine. The Monroe Doctrine was supposed to keep European nations from re-colonizing Latin America. However, when European nations reappeared in the

Dominican Republic to collect debts, it angered the US. So, this Corollary said that the US would be the police power of the Western Hemisphere. Rather than having the Europeans in the Atlantic, the US would collect debts on their behalf.

Earlier in 1895, Secretary of State **Richard Olney** told Britain that America was in charge of the Western Hemisphere. The British were looking to take land from Venezuela.

Definition: Dollar Diplomacy

Under President Taft, the US looked to invest abroad in China and Latin America.

In addition, private businesses increased investment in Central and South America throughout the twentieth century, as the United Fruit Company harvested bananas, and sold them in the US and abroad.

Question: What caused the US to enter World War I in 1917?

Answer: Similar to the Spanish-American War, it's good to know...*The Boat and The Note*

1. **The Boat** - The *Lusitania*. It was a passenger ship with Americans on board sailing off the coast of Ireland. It was sunk by a German submarine (U-boat) on May 7, 1915. The US warned Germany to refrain from continued submarine warfare. However, the Germans would not stop.

2. **The Note** - *The Zimmermann Telegram*. In 1917, the British intercepted a telegram from German official Arthur Zimmermann. He was writing to Mexico seeking an alliance. He hoped for a Mexican invasion of America where territory lost in the Mexican War would ultimately be reclaimed.

The Germans continued their policy of unrestricted submarine warfare. President Woodrow Wilson asked Congress to declare war on Germany in April of 1917. He was hoping to make the world "safe for democracy."

Definition: National War Labor Board

It would be terrible if workers went on strike during a war. This Labor Board worked out differences between employers and employees during World War I. This was a good thing for unions who sometimes gained labor improvements.

Definition: War Industries Board

This was a government agency that mobilized the domestic economy and oversaw the production of the supplies that were needed for the war effort.

Definition: Espionage (1917) and Sedition Act (1918)

Espionage Act - Threatened long prison sentences for disrupting the armed forces or the draft, which was created by the Selective Service Act of 1917.

Sedition Act - Targeted leftists/socialists who were against the war. The act made it illegal to speak out negatively against the government.

Definition: *Schenck v. United States*, 1919

Charles Schenck was a member of the Socialist Party. He distributed thousands of leaflets containing damaging language against the draft. He was arrested for violating the Espionage Act.

Weren't those leaflets free speech protected by the First Amendment? The Supreme Court said "no." Free speech was not absolute, as he was creating a "clear and present danger." According to Justice Oliver Wendell Holmes, Jr., Schenck's actions were like "shouting fire in a crowded theater."

Question: Who took men's jobs during the war?

Answer: Since men (nicknamed doughboys

abroad) were fighting in Europe, women and immigrants headed to the factories to fill the ranks. Women also helped sell *liberty bonds* to fund the war. In addition, African Americans journeyed north for jobs in the *Great Migration* (see pages 87-88).

Question: What happened with the Treaty of Versailles? Did the US ratify it?

Answer:

1. Democrat President Woodrow Wilson helped draft the Treaty of Versailles. A year earlier, he gave his famous *Fourteen Points* speech where he outlined his peace plans for when the war ended. His fourteenth point was to have a permanent, international peace-keeping organization of nations, or a *League of Nations*.

2. The Senate must ratify treaties by a 2/3 vote, or the provisions in the treaty are not applicable to the United States.

3. The Republican-controlled Senate, led by Henry Cabot Lodge, had *reservations* regarding Article X of the covenant of the League of Nations. This was because it stated that nations in the League had to help other members who were threatened. The Republicans did not want to enter, as it would violate neutrality and perhaps bring European countries into the affairs of the Western Hemisphere.

Wilson collapsed and nearly died campaigning for the treaty. The US would never join the League, nor ratify the Treaty of Versailles.

Definition: Red Scare

After the Bolshevik (Russian) Revolution of 1917, there was a heightened fear of communism in America. Reports of bombings, and influxes of immigrants from Eastern European countries intensified this fear. *Attorney General A. Mitchell Palmer* ordered the arrest of anarchists, some labor leaders, and suspected socialists and communists. These arrests were done with little consideration for due process of law, as many were held for days without being charged with a crime. Collectively, they were known as the "Palmer Raids."

Definition: Moral/Missionary Diplomacy

With regard to Latin America, President Wilson believed that the United States had a moral obligation to only recognize democratic nations which were not oppressive, or against American interests. In Mexico, Wilson refused to recognize the government of Victoriano Huerta, which he considered corrupt.

After Huerta's government dissolved, Wilson recognized the government of Venustiano Carranza. However, this recognition angered the revolutionary *Pancho Villa*. Villa went as far as invading New Mexico in 1916, killing seventeen Americans. He was never caught.

Review Questions

"On the contrary, we succeeded, succeeded largely and nobly, and we did it without any command from any league of nations. When the emergency came we met it, and we were able to meet it because we had built up on this continent the greatest and most powerful nation in the world, built it up under our own policies, in our own way, and one great element of our strength was the fact that we had held aloof and had not thrust ourselves into European quarrels; that we had no selfish interest to serve. We made great sacrifices. We have done splendid work. I believe that we do not require to be told by foreign nations when we shall do work which freedom and civilization require. I think we can move to victory much better under our own command than under the command of others."

- Henry Cabot Lodge, 1919

1. Relevant to the above quote, Henry Cabot Lodge argued
   A) against ratification of the Treaty of Versailles
   B) in favor of making alliances after World War I
   C) for repeal of the Monroe Doctrine
   D) in favor of dividing Germany after World War I

2. What constitutional power was being exercised by Lodge and his followers?
   A) Checks and balances
   B) Control of the military
   C) Judicial review
   D) Future funding of war

3. Lodge's comments can be considered a continuation of which American foreign policy statement?
   A) Macon's Bill #2
   B) Washington's Farewell Address
   C) Roosevelt Corollary to the Monroe Doctrine
   D) Olney Doctrine

Answers and Explanations

1. **A**. Lodge believed that United States entry into the League of Nations would lead to future unwanted conflicts.

2. **A**. Lodge, a Senator, headed a contingent that refused to ratify the Treaty of Versailles. Senate ratification of treaties is a key legislative check on the Executive Branch.

3. **B**. Because Lodge was reluctant to make foreign alliances, his foreign policy was most in line with Washington's Farewell Address which advocated for neutrality.

Short Essay Question Set

Document 1:

"We intend to begin on the first of February unrestricted submarine warfare. We shall endeavor in spite of this to keep the United States of America neutral. In the event of this not succeeding, we make Mexico a proposal or alliance on the following basis: make war together, make peace together, generous financial support and an understanding on our part that Mexico is to reconquer the lost territory in Texas, New Mexico, and Arizona. The settlement in detail is left to you. You will inform the President of the above most secretly as soon as the outbreak of war with the United States of America is certain and add the suggestion that he should, on his own initiative, invite Japan to immediate adherence and at the same time mediate between Japan and ourselves. Please call the President's attention to the fact that the ruthless employment of our submarines now offers the prospect of compelling England in a few months to make peace."

- Arthur Zimmermann, 1917

Document 2:

"We entered this war because violations of right had occurred which touched us to the quick and made the life of our own people impossible unless they were corrected and the world secure once for all against their recurrence. What we demand in this war, therefore, is nothing peculiar to ourselves. It is that the world be made fit and safe to live in; and particularly that it be made safe for every peace-loving nation which, like our own, wishes to live its own life, determine its own institutions, be assured of justice and fair dealing by the other peoples of the world as against force and selfish aggression. All the peoples of the world are in effect partners in this interest, and for our own part we see very clearly that unless justice be done to others it will not be done to us. The programme of the world's peace, therefore, is our programme; and that programme, the only possible programme, as we see it, is this:

I. Open covenants of peace, openly arrived at, after which there shall be no private international understandings of any kind but diplomacy shall proceed always frankly and in the public view.

II. Absolute freedom of navigation upon the seas, outside territorial waters, alike in peace and in war, except as the seas may be closed in whole or in part by international action for the enforcement of international covenants ..."   - Excerpt from Woodrow Wilson's Fourteen Points speech, 1918

•**Describe the historical context surrounding these documents**
•**Identify and explain the *relationship* between the events and/or ideas found in these documents (Cause and Effect, *or* Similarity/Difference, *or* Turning Point)**

The Roaring '20s Boom & Bust, 1920-1932

When people imagine the 1920s, they think *Boom and Bust*. The economy and social behaviors boomed throughout this decade. New changes to both male and female moral attitudes, coupled with excitement for consumerism and mass culture, signaled an end to traditional Victorian morals. However, all was not what it seemed. The KKK was growing in size, most farmers were still poor, and people worked long hours for little pay. A combination of overproduction, bank failures, bad credit, and shady stock market rules precipitated the Great Depression that lasted throughout the 1930s.

HERE IS WHAT YOU NEED TO KNOW:
Question: What was so roaring about the 1920s?

Answer: The stock market was booming, and new social identities were emerging. Some of the social roar included:

1. Mass culture excitement of movies, baseball, and amusement areas such as Coney Island in New York.

2. People like Charles Lindbergh tested the limits of technology. In 1927, he received world-wide acclaim for flying solo from New York to Paris in 33½ hours.

3. A new woman emerged after World War I and the Nineteenth Amendment. (discussed later).

4. The automobile became a common mode of transportation. Henry Ford's *assembly line* mass produced automobiles like the Model T. Everyone on his assembly line did one task until the finished product was completed. The assembly line utilized "scientific management," an idea of Frederick Winslow Taylor. In the 1910s, he looked to increase efficiency in the tasks of industrial production.

The Model T was affordable to the middle class. It should be noted that the car affected the sexual revolution of the 20s, as women and men could now venture out alone. Previously, a chaperone would often go along.

Definition: The Lost Generation

Not everyone was thrilled in 1920. The Lost Generation was popularized by a group of writers who created literary characters that were disillusioned by materialism, and upset by the negative impact World War I had on them. Writers such as T.S. Elliot, Sinclair Lewis, and Ernest Hemingway were a part of this nonconformist movement in literature.

Definition: Flapper

The New Woman of the 20s was armed with more than just the right to vote. Flappers mingled with men and challenged traditional Victorian values. Features of the flappers included:

1. Short dresses.
2. Makeup.
3. The "Bob" hair-style.
4. Smoking.
5. Mingling with men in public, and perhaps delving into the popular dance, *The Charleston*.
6. Sexual activity before marriage, as well as talking about once taboo subjects. *Margaret Sanger* began a campaign for birth control.

Definition: Great Migration

During and after World War I, many African Americans moved from the South to the North. Some came to fill the vacant jobs of the World War I soldiers fighting abroad. Others came with a desire to escape discrimination. Of course, discrimination would be ever-present in the North as well. American artist

Jacob Lawrence detailed the migration in his paintings. This movement of millions of African Americans would continue throughout the twentieth century.

Definition: Marcus Garvey

Garvey was a proponent of black pride, separation, and African nationalism. He also sponsored a Back-to-Africa Movement which looked to bring African Americans to their land of ancestry. Returning to Africa was also suggested by the nineteenth century's American Colonization Society.

Definition: Harlem Renaissance

Harlem, in upper Manhattan in New York City, was home to a flowering of African American culture on stage and in literature. The movement was highlighted by jazz music, like that of Louis Armstrong. Famous writers included Langston Hughes and Zora Neale Hurston.

Question: How successful was the Eighteenth Amendment at enforcing prohibition?

Answer: Not very. The 1919 *Volstead Act* was supposed to enforce prohibition. But people circumvented (went around) the prohibition amendment with:

1. Speakeasies - Places that secretly served alcohol when the cops weren't looking. Or, in some cities...the cops looked the other way after taking bribes.

2. Bathtub gin - Dangerous concoctions of alcohol that were made in people's homes.

3. Bootlegging - Illegal transportation and selling of booze. This type of behavior led to the rise of organized crime. It can be argued that Al Capone would not have been so powerful had it not been for the Eighteenth Amendment.

4. Some people went to Canada to purchase alcohol.

Definition: Scopes Trial, 1925

This was a controversial trial where Tennessee teacher John Scopes broke the law by teaching about Darwin's Theory of Evolution. In the trial, his lawyer, Clarence Darrow, cross-examined the prosecutor, former Presidential candidate William Jennings Bryan. Bryan claimed to be an expert on the Bible. Bryan won the case (popularly called "The Monkey Trial" at the time), but Darrow embarrassed him on the witness stand. The Scopes Trial highlighted the divide between fundamentalists (those who believed in strict and literal religious interpretation) and modernists (those open to more scientific explanation). The conviction was later overturned on a technicality. Bryan died shortly after the trial.

Definition: Sacco-Vanzetti Case

Ferdinando Sacco and Bartolomeo Vanzetti were two Italian American anarchists who were convicted of murdering two men. The trial for murder was seen by many as unfair and containing faulty evidence. Nonetheless, the men were executed in 1927. Many viewed the case as an example of nativism (see pg. 67).

Definition: Second Rise of the KKK

During World War I, *George Creel* headed the *Committee on Public Information* which provided propaganda that was pro-American. With an influx of immigrants coming over from Eastern Europe, there was a new movement in cultural nationalism called *100% Americanism*.

The Klan, which disbanded during Reconstruction, came back strong in the 1920s. Instead of only targeting African Americans, they now rallied against Jews, Catholics, and foreigners who didn't assimilate. By the mid-1920s, there were millions of Klansmen. Despite the violence, there were no signs of any federal anti-lynching legislation. In 1917, the NAACP (see pg. 115) conducted the Silent Protest parade in New York City where an estimated 10,000 people peacefully protested against racial violence, segregation, and lynching.

Definition: Teapot Dome Scandal

The biggest political scandal of the 1920s was the Teapot Dome Scandal during Warren G. Harding's Administration. In the controversy, public oil lands were leased to private speculators. Secretary of the Interior Albert Fall was held accountable for bribery, and sent to prison.

Question: By the time it began in 1929, what were the causes of the Great Depression?

Answer:

1. Overproduction of crops. As seen in the Populist Era, farmers couldn't get high prices for their crops, so they produced more of them. This led to even *lower* farm prices.

2. Speculation (risky and excessive buying) of stocks. Because stocks could be purchased on margin (as little as 10% down with a promise to pay back 90%), they were being bought left and right. Stock prices boomed.

A name you should know is ***Andrew Mellon***. Mellon, Republican Secretary of the Treasury in the 20s, encouraged a bull market, promoted cutting taxes for the rich, and paid off some of the national debt. To remember him, just think: "If you were rich, wouldn't you eat a lot of Mellon?"

3. Buying on credit. Purchasing items on credit loans, similar to modern-day layaway, became prevalent in the 1920s to help people buy all of the new products that consumerism had to offer. Refrigerators, irons, washing machines, vacuum cleaners...everyone wanted them, but not everyone had enough money to purchase immediately. Buying on credit was the solution, but not everyone could pay off their debts. This default on loans would also hurt the chain-stores, or those larger retailers with multiple locations. Such diversified stores became prevalent in the 1920s.

4. Bank failures. Banks don't hold all of your money. They loan it out or invest it. Panic led to bank runs, where people withdrew all of their cash before a failure could occur. This only accelerated bank failures. When banks failed, people lost their entire fortunes (no bank insurance existed until 1933). When people lost their money, they certainly couldn't pay back their stock margin or credit balances.

5. Stock market crash. All of the above helped lead to stocks crashing on Black Thursday, and then again on Black Tuesday in October (24th and 29th) of 1929.

6. The depression that was already going on in Europe didn't help matters either, as foreign trade took a big hit by 1929.

Question: Did President Herbert Hoover do anything to help out during the Depression?

Answer: Yes he did, but only to some degree.

The common misconception is that he did nothing, and Franklin Delano Roosevelt did everything. Hoover did some work projects, like the Hoover (originally called Boulder) Dam. He also set up the ***Reconstruction Finance Corporation*** which provided about $2 billion to bail out states, banks, and corporations. But, Hoover was still blamed for the depression, as "Hoovervilles" (shantytowns) sprung up all over the country. His actions were considered "too little, too late," as many of them came months, or even years after the crash.

Hoover signed the ***Smoot-Hawley Tariff***. Though it was supposed to assist farmers competing with imported crops, by the time Hoover signed the law, it was the highest tariff since the 1828 Tariff of Abominations. It taxed imports so high that it decreased foreign trade. Europe's inability to export to America further depressed the economy abroad.

Definition: Dust Bowl of the 1930s

Over-farming and Mother Nature combined to turn the soil to dust all over the western prairies. Parts of Kansas, Colorado, and especially Oklahoma were heavily hit, and many "Okies" moved to California. A famous photograph of a migrant farmer with her kids clinging to her was taken by Dorothea Lange during this long-term disaster. The Dust Bowl was famously portrayed in John Steinbeck's novel, *The Grapes of Wrath*.

Definition: Bonus Army

Thousands of World War I veterans assembled in Washington, DC and camped out in tents and huts in the summer of 1932. The veterans wanted to get their 1945 bonuses early, as the Depression made it difficult to find employment. Thus, they were hoping to lobby Congress to pass the Patman Bonus Bill. The Senate never passed it.

After finally being told to disperse, the US Army, led by Douglas MacArthur, moved in with tear gas, and set fire to the veterans' tents and huts. The fiasco was a black eye for Hoover, and may have been a contributing factor in his re-election loss in 1932.

Review Questions

"If today you can take a thing like evolution and make it a crime to teach it in the public school, tomorrow you can make it a crime to teach it in the private schools, and the next year you can make it a crime to teach it to the hustings or in the church. At the next session you may ban books and the newspapers."

– Clarence Darrow, Scopes Trial, 1925

"Science is a magnificent force, but it is not a teacher of morals. It can perfect machinery, but it adds no moral restraints to protect society from the misuse of the machine. It can also build gigantic intellectual ships, but it constructs no moral rudders for the control of storm tossed human vessel. It not only fails to supply the spiritual element needed but some of its unproven hypotheses rob the ship of its compass and thus endangers its cargo."

– William Jennings Bryan, prepared statement, Scopes Trial, 1925

1. The above quotes display the divide between
    A) modernists and fundamentalists
    B) Democrats and Republicans
    C) teachers and scientists
    D) students and religion

2. Which component of the Constitution is Darrow most concerned about?
    A) Judicial review
    B) Checks and balances
    C) First Amendment rights
    D) Federalism

3. Charles Darwin's theories were also used during the early twentieth century to justify
    A) United States imperialism abroad
    B) legislation regulating the food industry
    C) legalizing the Australian ballot
    D) completion of the transcontinental railroad

Answers and Explanations

1. **A.** The selection concerns the debate between fundamentalists who believe in strict and literal religious interpretations, and modernists who are more open to scientific explanation.

2. **C.** In the selection, Darrow is concerned not only about freedom of religion, but freedom of speech as well. Both are components of the First Amendment.

3. **A.** Survival of the fittest, or Social Darwinism, was used to justify American conquests abroad. Social Darwinism was also used in the Gilded Age to justify the great wealth of monopolists.

Short Essay Question Set

Document 1:

The following are excerpts from a nineteenth century song called, *The Drunkard's Lone Child.*

We were so happy - till father drank rum:
Then all our sorrows and troubles begun:
Mother grew paler, and wept every day:
Baby and I were too hungry to play ...

... Oh! If some temperance men only could find
Poor wretched Father, and speak very kind;
If they could stop him from drinking: why, then I would feel very happy again!
Is it too late? Men of temperance, please try:
For, little Bessie will soon starve and die:

Source: *The drunkard's lone child. H. De Marsan, Publisher, ... 60 Chatham Street, N. Y. Monographic. Online Text. Retrieved from the Library of Congress,* <www.loc.gov/item/amss.sb10103b/>

Document 2:

Be it enacted by the Senate and House of Representatives of the United States of America in Congress assembled, That the short title of this Act shall be the "National Prohibition Act."

The term "War Prohibition Act" used in this Act shall mean the provisions of any Act or Acts prohibiting the sale and manufacture of intoxicating liquors until the conclusion of the present war ... The words "beer, wine, or other intoxicating malt or vinous liquors" in the War Prohibition Act shall be hereafter construed to mean any such beverages which contain one-half of 1 per centum or more of alcohol by volume. (1919)

•**Describe the historical context surrounding these documents**
•**Identify and explain the *relationship* between the events and/or ideas found in these documents (Cause and Effect, *or* Similarity/Difference, *or* Turning Point)**

The New Deal of the 1930s

Herbert Hoover was blamed for the Great Depression. Voters wanted a more hands-on approach to the crisis, and elected Franklin Delano Roosevelt in 1932. Roosevelt promised a "New Deal" for America, and would be in office until his death during his fourth term in 1945. Roosevelt felt that it was the government's responsibility to help its citizens. The key focuses of the New Deal were creating jobs, reforming banks, limiting farm production, and regulating industry. However, not everyone agreed with Roosevelt's plans. Some, like the Supreme Court, thought he was overstepping his powers. Others, such as Huey Long of Louisiana, didn't think the government was going far enough. The New Deal created an *alphabet soup* of programs that are a lot of fun to memorize.

HERE IS WHAT YOU NEED TO KNOW:
Definition: Election of 1932

Democrat Franklin Delano Roosevelt (FDR) defeated Republican Herbert Hoover in a landslide. Roosevelt campaigned with the promise of a "New Deal" for all Americans. The New Deal would differ from Hoover's approach, as Roosevelt planned to get the government involved in every aspect of the economy. His campaign song and slogan was "*Happy Days are Here Again*," which is what the organist played the night he was nominated.

Elected four times, FDR would attract farmers, women, and African Americans to the Democratic Party. His wife, Eleanor, was very active as a First Lady. She wrote and delivered speeches advocating for her husband. She was also an advocate for women and a proponent of civil rights.

Definition: RRR

Relief, Recovery, Reform...those were the three R's of the New Deal. Relief meant to provide a quick end to people's suffering. Recovery meant to get the economy back on its feet. Reform meant to pass legislation to make sure that a depression of that magnitude never happened again.

Definition: Fireside Chats

Roosevelt used the new media of radio to communicate the issues of the economy to all Americans. He called the citizens his "friends," and was a fatherly figure to many in a time of need.

Definition: John Maynard Keynes and Deficit Spending

Keynesian economics means deficit spending...to spend more money than you have. It was the theory of British economist John Maynard Keynes. The New Deal wanted to spend, spend, spend...so it could fix, fix, fix. This stimulation of the economy is called *pump priming.* By creating jobs, more people would have money to put into the economy. To increase revenue, the government can sell bonds and raise taxes.

Definition: The Hundred Days

Much of Roosevelt's sponsored legislation came in the first one hundred days of his term. Roosevelt's "brain trust" of advisors helped him create his policies. The "Hundred Days" benchmark is still used today to evaluate Presidents during their first few months in office.

Question: How did Roosevelt look to fix the banking crisis?

Answer:

1. Two days after his inauguration, FDR called for a National Banking Holiday whereby

all banks would be closed for four days as a cooling off period. The sound banks could then reopen with government permission.

2. The Emergency Banking Act of 1933 allowed the President to watch over banking transactions, and reopen solvent (stable) banks.

3. The Glass-Steagall Banking Act of 1933 created the *Federal Deposit Insurance Corporation* (FDIC) which insured all bank depositors up to $5,000.

Definition: SEC, 1934

The Security and Exchange Commission (still around today) was created to establish fair rules for stock trading. It also punished those who didn't play by the rules.

Definition: AAA, 1933

The Agricultural Adjustment Act was the solution to remedy the overproduction of crops of the 1920s. This act paid farmers to limit their crop productions. Yes, it paid farmers *not* to grow. The hope was that if the supply of farm products decreased, demand would increase, and so too would prices.

Question: How did Roosevelt look to fix the problem of unemployment?

Answer:

1. PWA, 1933 - The Public Works Administration, headed by Harold Ickes, looked to construct highways and buildings.

2. CCC, 1933 - The Civilian Conservation Corps paid about 3 million young men to dig ditches, improve natural landscapes, develop parks, and build roads.

3. TVA, 1933 - The Tennessee Valley Authority brought jobs and cheap power to the Southeastern

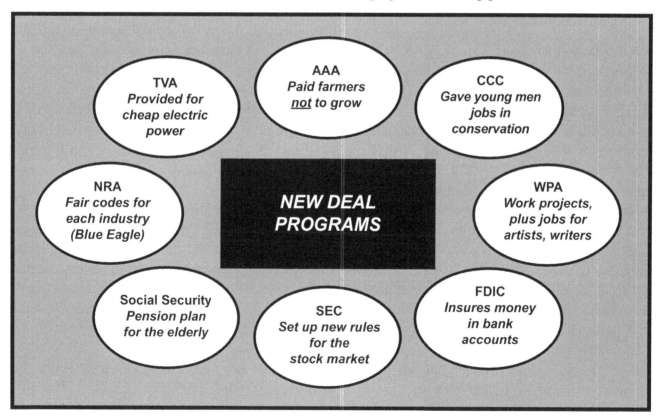

regions near the Tennessee River. Much of the area did not have electricity at the time.

4. WPA, 1935 - The Works Progress Administration was created as part of the Second New Deal (explained later). It looked to employ artists and writers, as well as other laborers for building projects. Slave narratives were written to tell the stories of those former slaves still alive. Opponents of the WPA called it "boondoggling," or wasteful spending for jobs not needed.

Definition: NIRA and NRA, 1933

The National Industrial Recovery Act created the National Recovery Administration which allowed the President to set codes of fair practice (prices, materials, maximum working hours, etc.) for industries. The hope was to ensure *fair competition* among businesses. Businesses that successfully followed the codes were supposed to place a *blue eagle* in their window for all to see. The blue eagle became a symbol of patriotism.

Section 7a of the law gave collective bargaining to workers, and led to increased unionization.

Question: How did the Supreme Court tear apart the New Deal?

Answer: Congress and FDR supported the New Deal. The Supreme Court found parts of it unconstitutional. You should know these two cases:

1. *Schechter Poultry Corp.* v. *US* (1935) - The Supreme Court found that the President was in effect creating laws unconstitutionally, and NIRA was struck down. Congress creates laws, not the President.

2. *US* v. *Butler* (1936) - The Supreme Court found that the AAA was a violation of federalism (division of powers between the states and federal government). Like NIRA, AAA was destroyed by the Supreme Court.

Definition: Court Packing Scheme

Since Justices are appointed for life, FDR tried to get around the Supreme Court any way he could. Congress has the right to increase the size of the Supreme Court. If they do so, the President, or FDR in this case, could then appoint liberal justices who supported his programs. His plan was to appoint six new justices to counterbalance existing justices over 70½ years of age. The packing scheme never happened, as it was quickly targeted by opponents to be a violation of power.

Definition: Second New Deal

The Second New Deal focused mostly on "recovery and reform." Most important were:

1. WPA - Works Progress Administration (see 4 left column).

2. Social Security Act, 1935 - Based on **Dr. Francis Townsend's** pension plan, this act, still around today, promised economic security for the elderly. However, because of the modern "graying" of the post-World War II Baby Boomer generation, today's Social Security has hit some financial obstacles.

3. Wagner Act, 1935 - reworded the NIRA to guarantee the right to unionize. This replaced Section 7a of the NIRA which was declared unconstitutional. It created the National Labor Relations Board (NLRB) to ensure that working rights were not violated. This led to an increase in the unionization of unskilled laborers. In 1935, **John L. Lewis**, the head of the United Mine Workers, formed the **Congress of Industrial Organizations (CIO)**, which rivaled the AFL until merging with them in 1955.

4. Fair Labor Standards Act (FLSA), 1938 - set a minimum wage of 25 cents per hour, a maximum work week of 44 hours, and got rid of oppressive child labor.

Question: What are some arguments that support the New Deal as a success?

Answer: Debating the New Deal could always be an essay. Here's how you can present the pro side:

1. The New Deal restored optimism.

2. It put millions of people back to work in a time of crisis.

3. Although it expanded the federal government, it never broke away from democracy.

4. The government attempted to provide for the people rather than wait for the economy to take care of itself.

5. Some New Deal programs such as TVA, SEC, FDIC, and Social Security are still around today.

Question: What are some arguments that attack the New Deal as a failure?

Answer: *Father Charles Coughlin* used the radio in opposition of the New Deal. He wanted to nationalize the banks. *Huey Long* was a Democrat from Louisiana who thought the New Deal didn't go far enough. But to those who did not want to share wealth:

1. The New Deal made the government bureaucracy too big...even bigger than what came out of the Progressive Era.

2. There was still vast unemployment (World War II was what would get the US out of the Great Depression for good).

3. The government was exercising way too much power and bordering on dictatorship.

Review Questions

"I want to talk for a few minutes with the people of the United States about banking - with the comparatively few who understand the mechanics of banking but more particularly with the overwhelming majority who use banks for the making of deposits and the drawing of checks. I want to tell you what has been done in the last few days, why it was done, and what the next steps are going to be …

"First of all let me state the simple fact that when you deposit money in a bank the bank does not put the money into a safe deposit vault. It invests your money in many different forms of credit-bonds, commercial paper, mortgages and many other kinds of loans."

– Franklin Delano Roosevelt, 1933

1. The above statement was from Franklin Roosevelt's
   A) Inauguration Address
   B) Quarantine Speech
   C) Fireside Chat
   D) Campaign Speech

2. Which effect of the New Deal was a reflection of the above statement?
   A) AAA
   B) NIRA
   C) FDIC
   D) TVA

3. What short-term effect was Roosevelt hoping to achieve with his speech?
   A) Restoration of confidence in the banking system
   B) The return of money which depositors lost at the beginning of the Depression
   C) A repeal the Emergency Banking Act
   D) Creation of pensions for the elderly

4. Compared to Roosevelt, President Hoover hoped
   A) to completely prevent the government from interfering with capitalism
   B) moderate government action would solve economic problems
   C) to share wealth among all Americans
   D) public works projects and creation of government jobs could be avoided

Answers and Explanations

1. **C**. Franklin D. Roosevelt's radio addresses to the public during the Great Depression were known as the Fireside Chats.

2. **C**. The Federal Deposit Insurance Corporation was created to insure bank deposits.

3. **A**. In the Fireside Chats, Roosevelt looked to alleviate the fears of the public and restore confidence.

4. **B**. Hoover set up the Reconstruction Finance Corporation and work projects such as the Hoover Dam. However, he did not go as far as Roosevelt regarding his attempts to solve the economic problems of the Great Depression.

Short Essay Question Set

Document 1:

"This is the end of this business of centralization, and I want you to go back and tell the President that we're not going to let this government centralize everything. It's come to an end. As for your young men, you call them together and tell them to get out of Washington."

- Justice Louis Brandeis, after the NIRA was found unanimously unconstitutional

Document 2:

"We have, therefore, reached the point as a nation where we must take action to save the Constitution from the Court and the Court from itself. We must find a way to take an appeal from the Supreme Court to the Constitution itself. We want a Supreme Court which will do justice under the Constitution and not over it. In our courts we want a government of laws and not of men.

"I want - as all Americans want - an independent judiciary as proposed by the framers of the Constitution. That means a Supreme Court that will enforce the Constitution as written, that will refuse to amend the Constitution by the arbitrary exercise of judicial power - in other words by judicial say-so. It does not mean a judiciary so independent that it can deny the existence of facts which are universally recognized."

- President Franklin Roosevelt, Fireside Chat, 1937

•**Describe the historical context surrounding documents 1 and 2**
•**Analyze Document 2 and explain how *audience*, or *purpose*, or *bias*, or *point of view* affects this document's use as a reliable source of evidence**

World War II, 1941-1945

Much like it did during the early years of World War I, the United States maintained neutrality at the beginning of Europe's Second Great War. However, after the Japanese attacked Pearl Harbor in 1941, the US was at war on two fronts...Europe and the Pacific. The same Americans who suffered through the Depression now had to save the world from fascism and aggression. After D-Day, the US and its allies were able to gain control of Europe. By island-hopping and dropping the atomic bomb, President Truman accepted an unconditional surrender from Japan. On the US Home Front, almost every citizen was able to contribute to the war effort. The Japanese Americans on the west coast, however, were denied civil liberties and were forced to live in internment camps in unpopulated rural areas. The Supreme Court approved these measures.

HERE IS WHAT YOU NEED TO KNOW:
Question: What issues before 1941 should I know about?

Answer: In between the World Wars, the United States was neutral. At the *Washington Naval Conference* of 1921, major powers agreed to limit naval arms. In 1924, the Dawes Plan was created, as US investors looked to help Germany pay off its World War I reparations to Britain and France. Those two nations would then give the money back to the US to pay off their war debt. The Kellogg-Briand Pact of 1928 renounced war as a form of national policy. In the 1932 Stimson Doctrine, the US refused to recognize aggressive Japanese takeovers in China. Here are some other things about the period just before World War II you should know:

1. Good Neighbor Policy - FDR improved relations with countries in Latin America because it was necessary to acquire allies in a dangerous pre-war world. Some wartime manufacturing took place in neighboring countries.

2. Roosevelt hinted at intervention when he gave his famous 1937 "quarantine speech" which spoke sternly against aggressive nations (without naming any of them). However, despite the rhetoric, the US did not directly intervene. The Neutrality Acts of 1935, 1937, and 1939 kept the US neutral, mostly in terms of arms shipments to foreign countries.

3. "Cash and Carry" was a 1939 policy proclaiming that the US would aid Britain and France. This was only if they came to the US on their own ships, paid in cash, and then left with the weapons.

4. The Selective Service Act of 1940 was the *first ever peacetime draft* in American History.

5. The Destroyers for Bases Deal of 1940 avoided upsetting those who favored neutrality. FDR *traded* older large ships (destroyers) in exchange for British bases in the Caribbean. Giving or selling them could have been viewed as a breach of neutrality.

Definition: Lend-Lease Act of 1941

To the dismay of isolationists, this act allowed the United States to sell unlimited weapons to the Allies. Much of the buying was done on credit. Over $50 billion in supplies were sent overseas to allies (Britain, Soviet Union, France, and China).

Definition: Pearl Harbor, December 7, 1941

Reacting to a US oil embargo against Japan, the Japanese attacked Pearl Harbor, Hawaii by air. The sneak-attack resulted in 2,300 American soldiers killed, many of whom were aboard the USS *Arizona*.

After FDR's "Day of Infamy" speech, Congress declared war on Japan. Shortly after, Germany declared war on the US. The United States, Britain, France, and the Soviet Union were called the Allies. They fought the Axis Powers, which consisted of Adolf Hitler's Germany, Benito Mussolini's Italy, and Emperor Hirohito's Japan.

Question: What military events in Europe should I know about?

Answer:

1. The Allies began fighting in northern Africa and then went north to liberate Italy.

2. D-Day, June 6, 1944, was the largest battle and the turning point of the war. The invasion of Normandy created a second front in Europe and led to the liberation of France. General Dwight D. Eisenhower was the Allied Commander.

3. The Battle of the Bulge during the winter of 1944-45 was the deadliest battle of the war for the Americans. However, Germany could not permanently break Allied lines.

4. Adolf Hitler of Germany committed suicide on April 30, 1945 in an underground bunker. V-E (Victory in Europe) Day was proclaimed on May 8th after Germany surrendered.

Definition: Yalta Conference, 1945

This was a meeting between FDR, Joseph Stalin of the Soviet Union, and Winston Chruchill of Britain. The Yalta Conference gave the Soviet Union control over much of Eastern Europe. Though the Soviets promised free elections, these promises were empty, as nations were turned into satellites. It can be said that Yalta was the start of the Cold War.

At the conference, it was also agreed that the Soviets would enter the war against Japan, and Germany would be divided into zones of occupation. This Conference, held in the Soviet Union, occurred in the final days of FDR's life. When he died soon after, Vice President Harry Truman took over.

Other conferences to know about:

1. Tehran, 1943 - Here the Allies planned the end of the war strategy to defeat the Nazis.

2. Potsdam, 1945 - The Allies discussed the fate of Germany after they surrendered.

Question: What do I need to know about the War in the Pacific (Japan)?

Answer:

1. Douglas MacArthur was the commander.

2. The US followed a strategy of *island hopping* before reaching mainland Japan. Some of the islands attacked were Midway, Iwo Jima, and Okinawa.

3. Truman decided a mainland invasion of Japan would be too costly in terms of casualties, so he put in the order for the *Enola Gay* to drop *Little Boy* (the Atomic Bomb). On August 6, 1945 Hiroshima was bombed resulting in the deaths of about 140,000 people. Nagasaki was bombed three days later leading to an estimated 70,000 deaths.

4. Japan surrendered on August 15, 1945. V-J (Victory in Japan) Day would be on September 2nd.

Question: What are some arguments supporting the dropping of the atomic bomb?

Answer: The dropping of the atomic bomb could always appear on essays. Here's how you can present the pro side:

1. The bomb put a speedy end to the worst war in world history.

2. It showed the world, and especially the Soviets, that the US was a great superpower.

3. The Americans suffered terrible casualties in the Battle of Okinawa in 1945. A mainland invasion of Japan could have led to over one

million casualties.

4. The Manhattan Project (bomb plan) cost about $2 billion. The bomb was a display of America's scientific investment.

5. The Japanese refused to unconditionally surrender. Adhering to the *bushido code*, *kamikaze* pilots would sooner die crashing into American ships than surrender.

6. The Japanese people were warned with leaflets describing the potential use of a new weapon. Still, there was no surrender.

Question: What are some arguments against dropping the atomic bomb?

Answer: Here's how you can present the con side:

1. The Japanese were all but defeated. Even General Dwight Eisenhower believed the war could be won through conventional means.

2. Use of the weapon would lead to an arms race with the Soviet Union, and escalate the bitter Cold War.

3. The bomb was dropped on civilians. Hiroshima was not a military base, it was a city. The same could be said about the bombing of Nagasaki.

4. Again, the Manhattan Project cost about $2 billion. Just out of the Great Depression, that was a lot of money to invest.

5. The environmental destruction was immense. No one knew for how long the water and soil would be poisoned.

6. The cancers and illness that would result from the bombing would be experienced by the people for decades to come. The dropping of the bomb was therefore immoral, and cruel and unusual punishment.

Question: What should I know about the American Home Front during World War II?

Answer:

1. Manufacturing boomed during the war. When the troops went overseas, women stepped into the factories. They were nicknamed *"Rosie the Riveter"* as the war progressed (a rivet is a bolt on a ship or plane).

2. Besides women, some Native Americans left their reservations to work in defense plants. They were also "code-talkers" in the war overseas. Communications in Navajo were never broken by the Japanese for the simple reason that no Native Americans lived in Japan.

3. Unions agreed not to strike so materials could continually be produced.

4. *Rationing* of meat, gasoline, and iron was critical to ensure that the troops had enough supplies overseas. *Victory gardens* were created locally by citizens to ensure a surplus of agricultural goods.

5. The war was paid for by a combination of increased income taxes and the sale of war bonds. Advertising campaigns encouraged Americans to purchase the bonds. The war cost about $288 billion, with over 400,000 military lives lost.

Question: What happened to Japanese Americans during World War II?

Answer:

1. Concerned about potential Japanese American sabotage to the war effort, FDR signed Executive Order 9066 in 1942. It permitted the US Government to transform the west coast into a military zone.

2. About 120,000 Japanese Americans on the west coast were relocated and forced to live in *internment camps* spaced around the country. These citizens suffered property and wage losses. Most of the camps were in isolated areas. Remember, the President can suspend habeas corpus in a time of war.

Definition: *Korematsu* v. *United States,* 1944

Believing relocation was unconstitutional,

Fred Korematsu refused to report to an internment camp. His criminal case went to the Supreme Court. The Court did not agree with him. The 1944 *Korematsu* decision stated that the Fourteenth Amendment, though guaranteeing equality in regular instances, could be denied in a time of war. Thus, Executive Order 9066 was constitutional. The federal government eventually acknowledged the regret of internment, and gave all survivors $20,000 in 1988. Korematsu's record was wiped clean.

Definition: Zoot Suit Riots and Braceros

A "zoot suit" was popular attire for young Mexican Americans living in Los Angeles. However, some servicemen who were stationed in the area expressed anti-Mexican sentiment towards young *pachucos*, or those who wore the zoot suits. The servicemen believed the clothing was unpatriotic. In 1943, a race riot broke out where many of those wearing the zoot suits were beaten and had their clothing removed. The police looked the other way in many cases.

Many Mexican Americans served proudly in the military. In addition, to help fill the labor ranks in the United States, many workers from Mexico took advantage of the ***bracero program***. This program offered temporary labor to Mexican workers wishing to come to the United States during World War II. Many of these jobs were agricultural. The program lasted after the war until 1964.

Question: What were the domestic results of World War II?

Answer:

1. Soldiers returned and made babies. This was known as the Baby Boom.

2. The Twenty-Second Amendment prevented another President from seeking a third term. FDR was elected to four terms because of the critical situations at home and abroad.

3. World War II vets took advantage of the G.I. Bill (Servicemen's Readjustment Act), which offered payments for college and vocational training, and good loans on homes and business ventures.

4. After the War, there was a mass-exodus from the cities and a move to suburbia. President Dwight Eisenhower signed the ***Federal-Aid Highway Act in 1956***. This provided for the modern-day interstate highway system. Suburban America found itself buying up new products such as cars, toys, and kitchen appliances. This consumption was partially fueled by new advertising campaigns.

5. The 1950s saw a lot of ***conformity*** (9-5 jobs, and raising of families) in the suburbs. Such conformity upset people known as the Beatniks. The ***Beat Generation*** looked to experiment sexually or with drugs. They also rejected materialism, and sometimes practiced Eastern religions. The Beatnik book to know is ***Jack Kerouac's*** *On The Road*. In terms of art, ***Jackson Pollock*** was anything but conformist. One of the most famous abstract expressionists of all time, he was known for dripping and splattering paint onto canvases.

6. Going against conformity was ***rock 'n' roll*** music of the 1950s. Artists such as Elvis Presley combined African American blues, country, and jazz to help create a new musical sound.

7. There was also a move to the ***Sun Belt***, as cheap land was readily available in the South and Southwest. As the twentieth century came to a close, less people were moving to northern areas such as the ***Rust Belt***, or places such as Pennsylvania and Ohio that thrived during the earlier steel boom.

8. Rosie the Riveter generally went back to the home, as women raised families in the

conservative 1950s.

9. Passed over Truman's veto, the ***Taft-Hartley Act of 1947*** hurt unions badly, as certain types of strikes were prohibited. Also, the act ended the ***closed shop*** (closed shops meant that one had to be in a union to work in a particular industry). Think of it as Taft-"*Hurt*"ley, because it *hurt* unions.

Question: How did foreign policy change as a result of World War II?

Answer:

1. The US and Soviet Union became superpowers, and the Cold War began.

2. Germany was divided into occupational zones controlled by the Soviet Union in the East, and Allies (Britain, France, and the United States) in the West.

3. The ***United Nations*** was formed as an organization that sought *collective security*. The US, Soviet Union, France, Britain, and China would be the Five Permanent Nations with veto power. The UN grew out of the ***Atlantic Charter*** of 1941, where Winston Churchill of Britain, and FDR agreed to stabilize the world with peace when the war ended. Unlike the League of Nations, the UN can assemble peacekeeping troops. Also, unlike the League, the US joined the UN.

4. Despite US aid for the non-Communist Nationalist Party, The People's Republic of China fell to Mao Zedong and the Communist Party in 1949. This event would greatly influence Cold War foreign policy in Asia.

Definition: Nuremberg and Tokyo Trials

Because of immigration restriction, the US could not help out millions of Jews suffering in Europe during the Holocaust. Late in the war, the government created the War Refugee Board, which looked to rescue Jews and prevent them from winding up in Nazi-controlled areas. It is estimated that the Board rescued up to 200,000 Jews.

After the war ended, the world looked for accountability regarding the Holocaust. In the first of a series of trials in Nuremberg, Germany, 22 Nazis were charged with war crimes. 12 were sentenced to death. Hundreds of Nazi officers associated with concentration or extermination camps were never tried for crimes against humanity. Supreme Court Justice Robert Jackson was a Chief Prosecutor.

Japanese leaders were also put on trial for atrocities committed during World War II. At the Tokyo Trials of 1946-8, defendants were charged with war crimes and crimes against humanity. Seven were executed. Many Japanese officials were executed in other trials outside of Tokyo.

Following these trials, the UN (in a committee chaired by Eleanor Roosevelt) adopted the ***Universal Declaration of Human Rights*** which outlined specific liberties and rights that everyone should possess. In Article 1, it states that people are born free and equal in dignity and rights. Furthermore, the Declaration outlaws slavery and torture, while promoting public trials.

Review Questions

"Now, therefore, by virtue of the authority vested in me as President of the United States, and Commander in Chief of the Army and Navy, I hereby authorize and direct the Secretary of War, and the Military Commanders whom he may from time to time designate, whenever he or any designated Commander deems such action necessary or desirable, to prescribe military areas in such places and of such extent as he or the appropriate Military Commander may determine, from which any or all persons may be excluded, and with respect to which, the right of any person to enter, remain in, or leave shall be subject to whatever restrictions the Secretary of War or the appropriate Military Commander may impose in his discretion. The Secretary of War is hereby authorized to provide for residents of any such area who are excluded therefrom, such transportation, food, shelter, and other accommodations as may be necessary, in the judgment of the Secretary of War or the said Military Commander, and until other arrangements are made, to accomplish the purpose of this order."

– Franklin D. Roosevelt, Executive Order 9066, 1942

1. The purpose of the above Executive Order was to authorize the government to
   A) create military areas for the relocation of certain citizens
   B) limit the civil liberties of Mexican Americans living on the West Coast
   C) aid in the support of the military draft during World War II
   D) search and confiscate private property in all areas of the country

2. Which Supreme Court case challenged the actions taken in the above document?
   A) *Dennis* v. *US*
   B) *Schenck* v. *US*
   C) *Plessy* v. *Ferguson*
   D) *Korematsu* v. *US*

3. Which military event preceded the issuance of the above order?
   A) D-Day
   B) Yalta Conference
   C) Pearl Harbor
   D) Battle of Okinawa

Answers and Explanations

1. **A**. Executive Order 9066 expanded President Roosevelt's powers during wartime and led to the creation of military areas for the relocation of Japanese Americans.

2. **D**. Fred Korematsu challenged relocation to internment camps. However, the Supreme Court ruled that in times of war, civil liberties could be limited.

3. **C**. After the Japanese bombed Pearl Harbor on December 7, 1941, concern over domestic sabotage from Japanese Americans helped lead to the relocation of citizens.

Short Essay Question Set

Document 1:

AN ACT
To provide Federal Government aid for the readjustment in civilian life of returning World War II veterans. Be it enacted by the Senate and House of Representatives of the United States of America in Congress assembled, That this Act may be cited as the "Servicemen's Readjustment Act of 1944".

SEC. 501. (a) Any application made by a veteran under this title for the guaranty of a loan to be used in purchasing residential property or in constructing a dwelling on unimproved property owned by him to be occupied as his home may be approved by the Administrator of Veterans' Affairs...

Document 2:

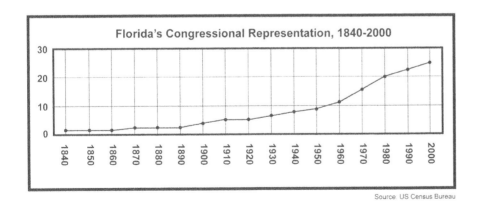

Source: US Census Bureau

• **Describe the historical context surrounding documents 1 and 2**
• **Identify and explain the *relationship* between the events and/or ideas found in these documents (Cause and Effect, *or* Similarity/Difference, *or* Turning Point)**

The Cold War, Korea, Vietnam, 1945-1991

After World War II, the United States and Soviet Union remained the only superpowers in the world. Although the two countries never directly fought, they antagonized each other throughout the Cold War. A space race, blockade of Berlin, spy plane controversy, and near nuclear war over Cuba, were just some of the issues during these tense decades. America's policy to contain communism led to conflicts in both Korea and Vietnam. The War in Vietnam proved to be incredibly unpopular among the young generation of Americans, and led to a harsh backlash against the government.

HERE IS WHAT YOU NEED TO KNOW:
Question: Why was it called a Cold War?

Answer: No, it's not because it's cold in Russia. The Cold War was fought (or not fought) between the US and the Soviet Union from 1945-1991. Although they never directly attacked one another, there were puppet wars at times, such as Korea and Vietnam. One could argue that it's called a Cold War because bullets are hot and none were fired at each other. You might also say that the US and Soviet Union displayed cold feelings towards one another. Whatever the reason, Americans lived in fear of a nuclear war for many years.

Question: What were the differences between the US and USSR?

Answer: United States: Political system is democracy, and economic system is capitalism.

Soviet Union (USSR): Combined elements of a dictatorship, command economy, and socialism to establish power over the people.

The US wanted to: 1) contain communism, 2) strengthen Eastern European countries and open them up for trade, and 3) reunite Germany.

The Soviet Union wanted to: 1) spread communism, 2) control Eastern European satellite nations, and 3) keep Germany divided.

Definition: Containment

US diplomat George Kennan coined this term that meant preventing the spread of communism. This was typically done by forming alliances with weaker countries to fend off communist aggression. Containment is the opposite of appeasement (giving in to what the aggressor wants).

Containment is also the most important term of the Cold War. Why did the US go to Korea? Containment. Why did the US go to Vietnam? Containment. Why did the US spend so much money on the military? Containment. Below is a foreign policy timeline for United States history.

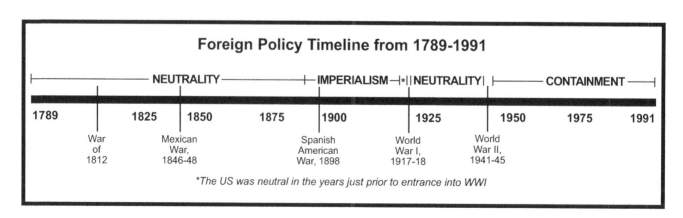

106

Definition: Truman Doctrine, 1947

The doctrine gave military aid (no troops) to countries resisting communism. Greece and Turkey took advantage of the aid.

Definition: Marshall Plan, 1947

This was Secretary of State George Marshall's strategy to give economic aid to countries that were not communist. The idea was to make countries stronger and less susceptible to communist takeovers. About $12.5 billion was given to nations all over Europe. Remember: M for Money, M for Mar$hall.

Definition: Berlin Airlift, 1948

Soviet leader Joseph Stalin, wanting to keep Germany divided, blockaded highways and railroads going into West Berlin (the non-communist side). He hoped this would make West Berlin dependent upon him and his satellites for supplies. However, the US and Britain sent 277,000 flights loaded with food and necessities for the German people. Many thought the airlift might lead to war between the US and the Soviet Union. But, as with everything else in the Cold War, direct conflict was avoided. The blockade was lifted in 1949.

Definition: NATO vs. Warsaw Pact

Think of these two as the gangs of the Cold War. NATO (North Atlantic Treaty Organization) was founded in 1949 and supported democracy. The Warsaw Pact, consisting of the Soviet Union and their satellites, was founded in 1955 and was referred to more commonly as the Communist Bloc.

Definition: Senator Joseph McCarthy and Communist witch-hunts

McCarthy was a Republican Senator from Wisconsin in the 1950s. *McCarthyism* was a witch-hunt that looked to sniff out communists both in government and general American society. It was similar to the Red Scare of A. Mitchell Palmer after World War I. Many Hollywood entertainment figures were targets.

In addition to McCarthy, there was HUAC (The House Un-American Activities Committee) which also looked to arrest suspected communists. The most famous government official targeted by HUAC was Alger Hiss. He was found guilty of perjury after he denied being a communist spy.

The government was watching average citizens as well. In the 1951 case of *Dennis v. US*, the Supreme Court ruled that speech advocating for an overthrow of the government was not protected by the First Amendment. Eugene Dennis of the American Communist Party had violated the Smith Act of 1940, which made such talk a crime.

Definition: Julius and Ethel Rosenberg

Accused of selling nuclear secrets to the Soviets, the Rosenbergs' 1951 court case kept the country on edge. They pled the Fifth Amendment (remained silent), and were convicted. They were later executed in 1953, becoming the first civilians ever to be put to death for treason.

Definition: Sputnik, 1957

In 1957, the Soviets successfully launched a satellite named Sputnik into space. Not only did this make Americans nervous about Soviet technology, but it gave the US a feeling of inferiority. The result of Sputnik's launch was an increase in spending on American education and science. In 1969, the US would win the space race to the moon.

Definition: U-2, 1960

It's not the rock band. But, if you look at some of their cover art, you will see a plane. The U-2

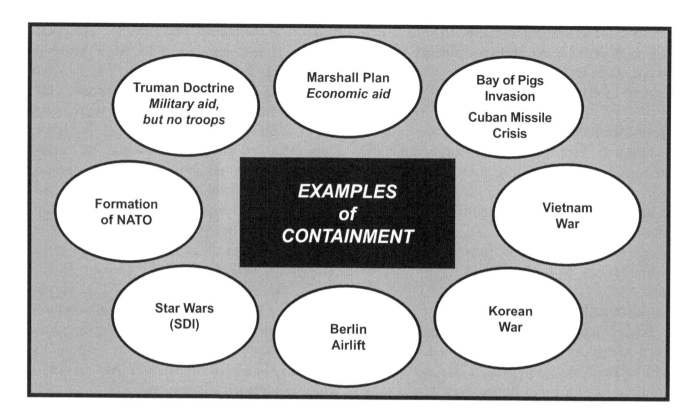

was a spy plane that was shot out of the Soviet sky in 1960. Although the US initially denied a spy plane was flying behind the iron curtain (metaphor for the Communist Bloc's border), the evidence was clear. Francis Gary Powers, the pilot, was held captive. The incident proved that distrust between the superpowers was real, and other spies were likely attempting to infiltrate both borders.

Definition: H-Bomb

The H-Bomb, or Hydrogen Bomb, worked on fusion. It was 1,000 times more powerful than the Atomic Bomb that worked on fission. The fear of a nuclear war was the underlying story of the Cold War, as it led to "duck and cover" drills, as well as the creation of bomb shelters.

Definition: Brinkmanship

This meant going to the brink of war, but coming just short of fighting. The escalation of brinkmanship peaked from 1961-1962 under President John F. Kennedy.

Definition: The New Frontier

John Fitzgerald Kennedy would only be President for a few years, but they would be important ones in the Cold War. His Presidential Election of 1960 promised a New Frontier. Kennedy supported civil rights and helping the poor. He started the **Peace Corps** which sent volunteers to developing nations. Kennedy's **Alliance for Progress** gave economic aid to help develop Latin American countries. This of course had another goal...to prevent Latin America from turning to communism.

Definition: Berlin Wall

In 1961, Nikita Khrushchev's Soviet Union built a wall that would formally divide communist East Berlin from non-communist West Berlin. Kennedy traveled to the wall to deliver his famous *Ich Bin Ein Berliner* (I am a Berliner) speech. He told the people of Berlin that the rest of the world was behind them. It is disputed that what Kennedy said translated to "I am a doughnut" (a Berliner is also a jelly doughnut). In 1987 President Ronald Reagan traveled to Berlin to give his famous, "tear down this wall" speech as a challenge to Soviet leader Mikhail Gorbachev. The wall came down in 1989.

Definition: Bay of Pigs Invasion, April 17, 1961

Fidel Castro helped overthrow dictator Fulgencio Batista at the end of the Cuban Revolution in 1959. Castro soon took over Cuba's economy and ruled firmly over the people. He eliminated all opposition. President John F. Kennedy saw Castro as a threat to political and economic security in the region. Therefore, the US supported a rebellion led by Cuban exiles. They were defeated at the Bay of Pigs in Cuba. Not only did the US sponsor the failed rebellion, but the event strengthened the legitimacy of Castro. Castro would soon become one of the Soviet Union's most important communist allies.

Remember: The US helped free Cuba from the Spanish back in 1898. But, the Platt Amendment of 1901 said that the US could meddle in Cuban affairs. Bad relations caught up with the US by the 1960s.

Definition: Cuban Missile Crisis, October of 1962

The closest the United States and Soviet Union ever came to nuclear war was during these two weeks of October. After the Bay of Pigs Invasion, Cuban and Soviet relations were quite good. So good, in fact, that the Soviets moved missiles into Cuba that could be used to destroy American cities. When US intelligence learned of this, Kennedy took it as a threat of war. His solution was to:

1. Blockade (quarantine) Cuba by surrounding it with US naval ships to prevent the delivery of additional Soviet weapons.
2. Threaten force if Khrushchev did not remove the missiles.

Cooler heads prevailed, and Khrushchev removed the missiles. In return, the US agreed not to invade Cuba. Furthermore, the US removed missiles of their own from Turkey.

Latin America had become an area of concern during the Cold War. In 1954, the CIA (Central Intelligence Agency) led a coup in Guatemala to remove Jacobo Arbenz Guzmán, a perceived communist sympathizer. In 1965, President Johnson sent troops to the Dominican Republic to neutralize a suspected communist threat.

Definition: Détente

This means an easing of Cold War tensions. The Cuban Missile Crisis scared the heck out of everyone. The 1970s saw friendlier diplomacy between the two superpowers. President Richard Nixon and Soviet leader Leonid Brezhnev were sometimes seen smiling together. The key détente event to know is:

SALT - Strategic Arms Limitation Talks. This was a series of meetings that limited the number of nuclear weapons each country had in their arsenal. Of course, this was all a charade, as no one knew for sure how many weapons each country had stockpiled.

About a decade before détente, JFK signed the Limited Nuclear Test Ban Treaty which prohibited the testing of nuclear weapons underwater, in the atmosphere, or in outer space. This was signed in the wake of the fear caused by the Cuban Missile Crisis.

Definition: Star Wars/Strategic Defense Initiative

President Ronald Reagan abandoned détente. His Strategic Defense Initiative was an elaborate

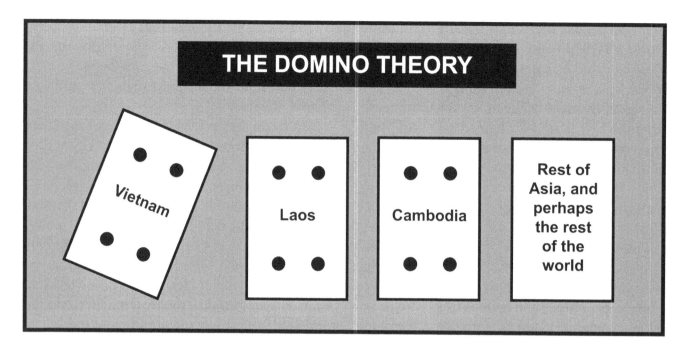

THE DOMINO THEORY

Vietnam

Laos

Cambodia

Rest of Asia, and perhaps the rest of the world

and expensive technological endeavor that looked to zap missiles out of the sky. The plan sounded like science fiction, so it was nicknamed *Star Wars*.

Amidst the containment strategy, the Soviet Union began to collapse internally during the 1980s. Mikhail Gorbachev's policies of Glasnost (openness) and Perestroika (economic restructuring) provided a new outlook for the Soviet Union. With communism falling all over Europe, a failed August coup in 1991 sealed the fate of the Soviet Union. The Cold War was over.

KOREA AND VIETNAM
Question: What do I need to know about the Korean War?

Answer:

1. Because Truman had integrated the army in 1948, African Americans and whites fought *side-by-side* for the first time in Korea (blacks had been in separate regiments since the Civil War, most notable were the distinguished ***Tuskegee Airmen*** pilots of World War II).

Note that Truman's stance on civil rights affected the Presidential Election of 1948. Southern Democrats abandoned their party and formed the segregationist States' Rights Democratic Party, or ***Dixiecrat Party***, and ran Strom Thurmond of SC for President. Truman still won the election. As President, he promised a ***Fair Deal***, which meant social improvement, civil rights, and expanding education and healthcare. Remember: "Tru" was "Fair."

2. Korea was an undeclared war. The UN voted to send in troops after communist North Korea crossed the 38th parallel and attacked non-communist South Korea in 1950.

3. Harry Truman fired Douglas MacArthur from command. MacArthur challenged Truman's decisions publicly. Truman, as Commander-in-Chief, could fire him.

4. The war ended in 1953 during Dwight Eisenhower's Administration. Massive American aid poured into South Korea for decades. The 38th parallel is still the dividing line today, as the two countries are buffered by a demilitarized zone (DMZ). 33,746 Americans were killed in Korea.

Definition: Domino Theory
First appearing during the Eisenhower

Administration, this was the belief that if one nation in Asia fell to communism, the rest of the nations would also fall...like dominos. It was important to stop that first country from becoming communist.

Definition: Eisenhower Doctrine, 1957

In addition to the Domino Theory, Eisenhower offered anti-communist support outside of Asia. The Eisenhower Doctrine offered aid and threatened force against communist threats in the Middle East. Besides containment, Eisenhower was looking to protect American oil interests in the region. The statement was issued after the *Suez Crisis*, where the Soviet Union threatened force against Britain, France, and Israel for their attempts to gain the Suez Canal from Egypt (who the Soviets supported). After a UN ceasefire was called, Egypt secured the canal.

Definition: Military-Industrial Complex

When Eisenhower left office, he warned of the military-industrial complex. The term refers to the money-relationships between legislators, the Pentagon (military), and industry. This web of money, weapons, and the people who make foreign policy could lead to corruption.

Definition: Kennedy's Flexible Response

Kennedy called for a *flexible response*, as he not only looked at non-military political measures to resolve a crisis, but also an increase in the amount of military options that could be used. This meant not only increasing funding for the military, but supporting the Special Forces, or Green Berets. Under Kennedy, there would be a variety of military tactics used in places such as Cuba and Vietnam.

Kennedy's flexible response differed from Eisenhower's "New Look" policy which urged spending on planes and nuclear weapons (rather than the army and navy) to support aggressive containment strategies. Eisenhower's strategy promised "massive retaliation" to threats against the United States.

Definition: Gulf of Tonkin Resolution

In 1954, the French saw their Vietnamese city of Dien Bien Phu fall to the communists, and their leader Ho Chi Minh. Under Eisenhower and Kennedy, there was a gradual escalation of a US military presence in Southern Vietnam. When JFK was assassinated in 1963, Vice President Lyndon B. Johnson became President.

In 1964, at the Gulf of Tonkin in Vietnam, American ships were fired on (many believe the severity of this was likely embellished). After the event, Congress approved the Resolution which gave Johnson a "blank check" to use the military as he saw fit in Vietnam. This meant a large escalation of American forces.

Definition: Vietcong

The Vietcong were communist guerrilla soldiers in *South* Vietnam. Vietnam was divided at the 17th parallel. As with Korea, the communists were supposed to be in the North... not the South.

Question: Militarily, what do I need to know about the Vietnam War?

Answer:

1. Much of the war was fought on dangerous terrain in a jungle.

2. Napalm was an explosive chemical that was used extensively in Vietnam. Agent Orange was a chemical used to remove leaves from the trees where guerrilla soldiers were positioned. Years later, this chemical was known to cause cancer in many Vietnam veterans.

3. The Tet (lunar New Year) Offensive of 1968 was a massive thrust southward by the communists

in the North. Although the United States pushed back the attack, it had a catastrophic effect on American morale, while increasing support for the communists within Vietnam.

4. In 1973, President Richard Nixon ended US involvement with the **Paris Peace Accords.** Vietnam became communist shortly after the US pulled out.

Question: What do I need to know about the anti-war movement?

Answer:

1. In the 1950s, there were Beatniks (who experimented with drugs and sex while condemning war and materialism) such as Jack Kerouac, who wrote the book, *On the Road*. By the 1960s, the Beatnik movement had inspired a new **counterculture** of people preaching peace and love instead of war. So-called **hippies** were part of this movement, and protested the war and the military draft.

2. Folk musicians such as Bob Dylan sang for peace. Others sang against the military draft that affected thousands of young males. Phil Ochs sang against the draft in his song *Draft Dodger Rag*. Other folk musicians to know were Pete Seeger and Tom Paxton. Arlo Guthrie famously protested the draft with his song *Alice's Restaurant*. The negative energy surrounding Johnson led him to abandon plans to seek a second full term in 1968.

3. At Kent State University in 1970, a war protest turned violent when the Ohio National Guard fired on students, killing four. Students were protesting the spread of the war to Cambodia. Most protesters against the war were young, and the males were subject to the draft. In 1971, the Twenty-Sixth Amendment lowered the voting age to 18, thus giving the younger generation a say in government. It was said that young people were old enough to fight in Vietnam, but not old enough to vote.

4. Students became a vocal part of the *New Left*, many of whom were anti-imperialism, supported extensions of rights, and rejected elements of bureaucracy and capitalism. Gaining strength in the 1960s, the **Students for a Democratic Society (SDS)** protested against the Vietnam War. By the end of the decade, part of the society grew violent and evolved into a radical anti-government group called the Weather Underground, or *Weathermen*.

Definition: Vietnamization

Richard Nixon's plan to *gradually remove US troops* from Vietnam was called Vietnamization. He hoped to turn the war over to Vietnamese soldiers. The US began pulling out for good in 1973. There were 58,220 military fatal casualties during the duration of the war. Many soldiers were Prisoners of War (POW) or Missing in Action (MIA).

Definition: Nixon Doctrine, 1969

Nixon's policy stated that the United States would not provide extensive manpower in future Asian wars, but would still give military and economic aid when aggressors threatened nations in need. The US, however, would still carry out their current treaty agreements.

After the Vietnam War, the United States was cautious to enter conflicts around the world where human rights violations were occurring. As will be discussed later, NATO did send troops to Bosnia to intervene during a time of ethnic cleansing.

Review Questions

"Aside from the demoralizing effect on the world at large and the possibilities of disturbances arising as a result of the desperation of the people concerned, the consequences to the economy of the United States should be apparent to all. It is logical that the United States should do whatever it is able to do to assist in the return of normal economic health in the world, without which there can be no political stability and no assured peace. Our policy is directed not against any country or doctrine but against hunger, poverty, desperation and chaos. Its purpose should be the revival of a working economy in the world so as to permit the emergence of political and social conditions in which free institutions can exist. Such assistance, I am convinced, must not be on a piecemeal basis as various crises develop. Any assistance that this Government may render in the future should provide a cure rather than a mere palliative. Any government that is willing to assist in the task of recovery will find full co-operation I am sure, on the part of the United States Government. Any government which maneuvers to block the recovery of other countries cannot expect help from us. Furthermore, governments, political parties, or groups which seek to perpetuate human misery in order to profit therefrom politically or otherwise will encounter the opposition of the United States."

– George Marshall, 1947

1. In his speech, George Marshall advocates for which of the following?
    A) Donating troops to countries resisting communism
    B) Providing military supplies to developing nations
    C) Making European economies stronger and more stable
    D) Creating public works projects to relieve unemployment

2. Marshall's policy was associated with which foreign policy?
    A) Appeasement
    B) Neutrality
    C) Imperialism
    D) Containment

3. A year after Marshall's speech, which event would heighten tensions during the Cold War?
    A) Cuban Missile Crisis
    B) Berlin Airlift
    C) U-2 spy plane incident
    D) Launching of Sputnik

Answers and Explanations

1. **C**. The Marshall Plan looked to strengthen European nations susceptible to communist influence. To do this, massive economic aid was sent across the Atlantic.

2. **D**. Containment is a foreign policy that looked to stop the spread of communism.

3. **B**. In 1948, the Berlin Airlift occurred. This involved enormous amounts of supplies being dropped from airplanes in response to Joseph Stalin's blockade of West Berlin.

Short Essay Question Set

Document 1:

"To ensure the peaceful development of nations, free from coercion, the United States has taken a leading part in establishing the United Nations, The United Nations is designed to make possible lasting freedom and independence for all its members. We shall not realize our objectives, however, unless we are willing to help free peoples to maintain their free institutions and their national integrity against aggressive movements that seek to impose upon them totalitarian regimes. This is no more than a frank recognition that totalitarian regimes imposed on free peoples, by direct or indirect aggression, undermine the foundations of international peace and hence the security of the United States."

- President Harry S Truman speaking in 1947 regarding escalating tensions in Greece

Document 2:

"It would be a mistake for others to look upon Berlin, because of its location, as a tempting target. The United States is there; the United Kingdom and France are there; the pledge of NATO is there - and the people of Berlin are there. It is as secure, in that sense, as the rest of us - for we cannot separate its safety from our own."

- President John F. Kennedy, speaking in 1961 to the public regarding escalating tensions in West Berlin

•**Describe the historical context surrounding documents 1 and 2**
•**Analyze Document 2 and explain how *audience*, or *purpose*, or *bias*, or *point of view* affects this document's use as a reliable source of evidence.**

Civil Rights

Jim Crow, or segregation laws, had been in effect for almost a century. In 1954, things changed when the Supreme Court unanimously declared "separate but equal" in schools to be unconstitutional in the *Brown* v. *Board of Education* decision. The goals of civil rights leaders differed. Some, like Martin Luther King Jr., wanted a harmonious blending of the races in society. Others, such as Malcolm X, called for black separation. Despite the Civil Rights Act of 1964 which declared discrimination illegal, civil rights leaders continued their struggle for liberty.

HERE IS WHAT YOU NEED TO KNOW:
Question: Which twentieth century civil rights leaders should I know about?

Answer:

1. Booker T. Washington - c1900 - Believed that African Americans should gradually gain their rights. In what was later deemed the ***Atlanta Compromise***, he told a mostly white audience that African Americans could continue to accept social segregation if that meant gradual economic gains and continued education. He became the first head of the Tuskegee Institute in 1881. At the Institute, students gained the skills necessary to succeed as part of the labor force.

2. W.E.B Du Bois - c1910 - Disagreed with Washington's gradual rights ideology. He sponsored the ***Niagara Movement***, which called for desegregation and absolute equality. Remember: **WEB** = **W**ants **E**quality for **B**lacks.

Du Bois helped found the NAACP (National Association for the Advancement of Colored People) which still fights today for civil rights and an end to racial discrimination. Du Bois also helped found their magazine, *The Crisis*, which is still published today. Du Bois believed the "talented tenth" of African Americans should become leaders within their communities, and be provided the opportunity to reach their full potential in American society.

3. Marcus Garvey - c1920 - Leader of the Back to Africa (colonization) Movement that encouraged blacks to return to the land of their ancestry. (See pg. 88.)

4. Rosa Parks - In 1955, Parks refused to give up her seat to a white person on a bus in Montgomery, Alabama. Her arrest inspired blacks to boycott the bus system and protest segregation. The ***Montgomery Bus Boycott*** ended just over one year later when the Supreme Court declared segregation on buses unconstitutional.

5. Martin Luther King, Jr. - c1960 - Becoming a national figure in the Montgomery Bus Boycott, he was outspoken for civil rights. He supported civil disobedience, and passive resistance. He delivered the *I Have a Dream* speech in 1963 (discussed later).

6. Stokely Carmichael - c1965 - As a leader of the Black Panthers and Black Power movement, he called for immediate civil rights and for blacks to separate into their own communities. The Black Panther Party was co-founded by Huey Newton and Bobby Seale.

7. Malcolm X - c1962 - A member of the Nation of Islam, he preached black supremacy, and separation of blacks and whites.

8. Freedom Riders - 1961 - Young white and black civil rights advocates rode buses together into the segregated South. They were greeted with violence in Montgomery, Alabama. In Mississippi, riders were arrested for intentionally breaking segregation laws.

9. SNCC (Student Nonviolent Coordinating Committee), and CORE (Congress of Racial Equality) had many college student members. They were involved in many

activities including the Freedom Rides, and *sit-ins* where African Americans sat inside segregated restaurants, an action which was locally illegal before the Civil Rights Act of 1964 (see pg. 117). Fannie Lou Hamer was a civil rights activist and member of SNCC who fought to register African American voters.

Definition: Jackie Robinson

On April 15, 1947 Jackie Robinson made his debut for the Brooklyn Dodgers, becoming the first African American to play in a Major League Baseball game in over sixty years (there were a few African Americans in the game in the 1880s). This triggered a movement to integrate other sports as well.

Definition: *Plessy* v. *Ferguson,* 1896

To understand segregation, let's go back to 1896. Homer Plessy was part African American, but sat in a white's only railroad car. He was challenging the Separate Car Act of Louisiana which segregated blacks from whites on trains. The Supreme Court decided that "separate but equal" did not violate the protections of the Fourteenth Amendment. "Separate but equal" meant that African Americans and whites could be separate, so long as their facilities were the same (which they typically weren't). In the Jim Crow South, that meant separate bathrooms, schools, drinking fountains, and restaurants until about 1954.

Definition: *Brown* v. *Board of Education of Topeka, Kansas,* 1954

In a landmark case (or really, five cases in one) for ending segregation in schools, a 9-0 decision of the *Warren Court* (named for Chief Justice Earl Warren) declared that "separate but equal" was inherently unequal, as it violated the Equal Protection Clause of the Fourteenth Amendment. Thurgood Marshall,

later a Supreme Court justice, argued on behalf of Linda Brown and other African American children who were denied integration. The NAACP was instrumental in constructing this case. Although segregation was declared unconstitutional, schools in the South were still voluntarily segregated for years. Such a separation which is not legally enforced is called *de facto segregation.*

Definition: *Baker* v. *Carr,* 1962

Reapportionment is the way that states redraw their voting districts based on population changes.

Charles Baker lived in Tennessee. He believed the state was overdue for redrawing legislative district lines, and their lack of action was in violation of the state constitution. Baker wanted a greater number of districts in urban areas, where more people lived. Because he believed his vote counted less, he thought his *equal protection rights of the Fourteenth Amendment* were being violated. The Supreme Court agreed, and stated that the federal courts could hear cases and force states to redraw their district lines.

Also of note is *Wesberry* v. *Sanders* (1964), where the Supreme Court ruled that districts had to be of similar populations, adhering to the principle of *"one person, one vote"* seen in the Baker case.

Definition: What other court cases of the Warren Court (1953-1969) are important to know?

Answer: Generally speaking, Earl Warren's Court gave *more rights to the accused*. Details are included for essay purposes:

1. *Miranda* v. *Arizona,* 1966 - Ernesto Miranda admitted to charges of rape and kidnapping after a lengthy interrogation. Because he did not know that he had a right to remain silent, the Supreme Court ruled that Miranda did

not receive fair due process. Since his Fifth Amendment rights were violated, he had to be retried. The controversy of the Warren Court's decision has changed the way police apprehend criminals. Now, a priority is the reading of "Miranda rights" upon arrest. Miranda was later retried and convicted.

2. *Gideon* v. *Wainwright*, 1963 - Clarence Gideon was accused of breaking into a billiards establishment in Florida. At his trial, he was denied the right to an attorney (he could not afford a lawyer) because Florida only appointed lawyers for capital (murder) offenses. He was found guilty. The Warren Court later ruled that Gideon's rights were violated. His Sixth Amendment rights to a fair trial should have applied to the state of Florida because of the Fourteenth Amendment's due process clause. He was retried and acquitted (found not guilty). Another case, *Escobedo* v. *Illinois* involved a similar issue.

3. *Mapp* v. *Ohio*, 1961 - Dollree Mapp's house was searched in Ohio as the police were looking for a fugitive. Instead, they found indecent pornographic material that violated the law. Without a proper search warrant, the police seized the evidence and Mapp was convicted. The Supreme Court heard Mapp's appeal, and ruled that the evidence was not admissible in court. This was because the protections of the Fourth Amendment (unreasonable searches and seizures) applied to the states through the Fourteenth Amendment's due process clause.

Definition: Little Rock Nine, 1957

After the *Brown* decision, controversy rocked Central High School in Little Rock, Arkansas. The nation's media focused on the controversy here when nine students attempting to go to school were met by mobs of protesters. Governor Orval Faubus called in the Arkansas Guard to support segregation. However, President Eisenhower had the final say as Commander-in-Chief of the Army and the chief executer of laws. Ultimately, federal troops enforced integration.

Definition: I Have a Dream Speech, 1963

Martin Luther King, Jr., President of the Southern Christian Leadership Conference, delivered this landmark speech on August 28, 1963 in Washington, DC. Things to know about the speech:

1. He gave it in front of the Lincoln Memorial, as Lincoln was nicknamed the Great Emancipator.

2. He drew upon the Declaration of Independence, saying that African Americans had been written a "bad check" when it came to the distribution of rights from 1776.

3. He mainly spoke about the hope to see a world free of discrimination, where people of all races could live in harmony.

4. King preached *passive resistance*, or nonviolence. Furthermore, he and his followers practiced *civil disobedience*, or refusing to obey an unjust law. King defended civil disobedience action against segregation in his famous *Letter from Birmingham Jail*.

Definition: Civil Rights Act of 1964

Signed by President Johnson after a lengthy Senate filibuster (delay in vote), this act ended all major forms of discrimination and segregation. It made discrimination based on gender, race, religion, or national origin illegal. Still, civil rights were not absolute in Alabama. In 1965, SNCC and Southern Christian Leadership Conference members marched from Selma to Montgomery demanding African American voter registration rights. Along the way, they were met with tear gas and violence from Alabama State Troopers.

That year, the *Voting Rights Act of 1965* was passed. This reiterated the wording of the Fifteenth Amendment and prevented discrimination at the polls. Poll taxes had been abolished in 1964 with the *Twenty-Fourth Amendment*.

Definition: Kerner Commission

In 1967, race riots broke out in Detroit. Riots had occurred in other Northern cities a year before. President Lyndon Johnson appointed Illinois Governor Otto Kerner, Jr. to get to the bottom of the issues causing the riots. Kerner's Commission offered the opinion that a "separate but unequal" black and white nation was emerging, and measures should be taken to prevent further violence. In 1968, rioting would indeed occur all over the North after the assassination of Martin Luther King, Jr.

Definition: George Wallace

George Wallace was a pro-segregation Governor of Alabama. He personally attempted to stop African American students from attending class at the University of Alabama. He was unsuccessful. Wallace ran for President four times, three as a Democrat (never getting the nomination). In 1968 he ran for the far-right American Independent Party. Think: He wanted to put a "wall" up between the races.

Question: How were American Indians and Mexican Americans inspired by the Civil Rights Movement?

Answer: American Indians began AIM, or the American Indian Movement. It looks to protect traditional American Indian culture while also combating racism. AIM is interested in creating jobs, helping to decrease poverty, and obtaining fair treaties. The movement also brought attention to hate crimes against American Indians.

AIM staged protests that received media attention. One in 1973, led by Russell Means, occupied the site of the Wounded Knee Massacre. In some late twentieth century court case settlements, Native Americans received land claims from both state and federal governments.

Similarly, during the Civil Rights Era, those of Mexican descent were inspired by the Chicano Movement. Often led by young student-protesters, advocates looked for education reform and racial justice. Inspiring others, the movement established a powerful voting bloc and celebrated Latino culture in music and art. One art example was the *Chicano Mural Movement* which detailed culture on city walls. Around this time, *César Chávez* (explained later) emerged to help protect the rights of migrant farm workers, many of whom were of Latin American descent. Regarding rights, the Supreme Court under Earl Warren ruled unanimously in *Hernandez v. Texas (1954)* that Mexican-Americans have equal protection under the Fourteenth Amendment.

Definition: Stonewall Riots, 1969

A key event strengthening the gay rights movement, this event took place at a bar in Greenwich Village in NYC called the Stonewall Inn. In many locations, openly homosexual conduct in public was a crime punishable by law. When police raided the bar, gay patrons resisted arrest, and quickly the location became a magnet for protest over the next few days. The event led to the creation of gay rights activist organizations, and rallied the LGBT community.

For Women's Rights and the Equal Rights Amendment, see pages 120-121.

History 1960-Present

Although the Presidency of Richard Nixon saw an easing of Cold War tensions, there was an increase in tension of his own. His resignation after the Watergate Scandal remains one of the rare events in American History. For his successors, the 1970s saw inflation, unemployment, and high oil prices. In the 1980s, President Ronald Reagan lowered taxes for the wealthy and cut social programs. In the 1990s, President Bill Clinton approved NAFTA, and sent troops into Bosnia. Clinton would also become the second President to be impeached. In the first decade of the 2000s, the War on Terror led to two foreign conflicts in the Middle East.

HERE IS WHAT YOU NEED TO KNOW:
Definition: Election of 1960 and Television

Richard Nixon used television to save his spot as a Vice Presidential Candidate in 1952. He went on TV to address accusations that he had an illegal money fund as a Senator. Nixon gave his heartwarming *"Checkers Speech"* in which he denied any wrongdoing. In the speech he talked about his dog, Checkers, a campaign contribution whom he was keeping because his kids loved it so much. The speech was a success, and television saved his spot on Eisenhower's ticket.

Television was not good for Nixon in 1960 during his Presidential debates with Democrat John F. Kennedy. To many, Nixon appeared to have verbally won the four debates, but the charisma and charm of the youthful Kennedy may have been more appealing to the voters watching on television. Kennedy won the election. See the Cold War chapter for more on Kennedy.

Question: What should I know about Lyndon B. Johnson's (Democrat) Presidency? (1963-69)

Answer:

1. Inheriting the Presidency after Kennedy was assassinated, Johnson escalated the War in Vietnam via the Gulf of Tonkin Resolution. See Cold War chapter.

2. *The Great Society* was a plan to help the poor, minorities, and the disadvantaged. Johnson declared a *War on Poverty*, and looked to increase education opportunities for all. Of course, this would mean an increase in government spending.

In the Election of 1964, Johnson defeated Republican *Barry Goldwater*. Goldwater looked to reduce the government's role concerning social programs such as aid to the poor and Social Security. Johnson won the election in part to a television commercial ("Daisy Ad") which portrayed Goldwater as a supporter of using nuclear weapons in military operations.

3. The monumental Civil Rights Act of 1964 made all forms of segregation and discrimination illegal.

4. In 1965, Medicare became law. This guarantees health insurance to people over 65 and those with certain disabilities.

5. Johnson did not run for a second full Presidential term as the War in Vietnam tarnished his legacy. After he left office, *The Pentagon Papers*, meant to be secret, were reported by the *New York Times* in 1971. The papers showed how for years the government escalated the conflict while misleading the public. Freedom of the press prevailed, as the Supreme Court in *NY Times* v. *US* (1971) stated that the *Times* had the right to publish the Pentagon Papers, as such publication was not a threat to national security.

Question: What should I know about Richard Nixon's (Republican) Presidency? (1969-74)

Answer:

In 1968, Nixon defeated Johnson's Vice President, Democrat Hubert Humphrey. Humphrey won the Democratic nomination after fellow candidate Robert F. Kennedy was assassinated. You should know:

1. Nixon exercised détente diplomacy (easing of the tensions between the US and communist powers that existed during the Cold War).

2. He pulled out of Vietnam in 1973.

3. Extending "ping pong diplomacy" (the US and China had previously set up a series of ping pong matches between the two nations), Nixon visited communist China and Mao Zedong. Some believe this was the beginning of China's industrial boom of today.

4. Congress passed the **War Powers Act**, stating that although the President is Commander-in-Chief, he can't use extensive overseas force (for more than 60 days, followed by a 30-day withdrawal period) without the consent of Congress.

5. Nixon battled inflation in the 1970s. In addition, energy prices skyrocketed after OPEC's oil embargo (see pg. 122).

6. Nixon's Presidency would mostly be remembered for the Watergate Scandal (explained next).

Definition: Watergate Scandal

In the 1972 Presidential Election campaign, there was a break-in at the Democratic headquarters at the Watergate Hotel in Washington, DC. Nixon claimed he knew nothing about it, but taped conversations proved otherwise. In **United States v. Nixon** (1974), the Supreme Court ordered President Richard Nixon to release the notorious tapes from the scandal. Nixon was hoping to be protected by *executive privilege*, or the ability of the President to keep classified such confidential information. After Vice President Spiro Agnew resigned following his pleading no-contest to income-tax evasion, Nixon would do the same in 1974 to avoid impeachment for obstructing justice. He remains the only President ever to resign.

Definition: Equal Rights Amendment

First proposed in 1923, this amendment that ensured equal rights for women under the law passed both the House and Senate in 1972. The states never ratified it, and it expired in 1982. You need to know:

Betty Friedan was a feminist who wrote *The Feminine Mystique*. She supported equal rights for women, and was the first president of the National Organization for Women (NOW). She wanted women to be "Frieeee" (Friedan).

Phyllis Schlafly was opposed to modern feminism. She was outspoken against the ERA (Equal Rights Amendment), believing it would hurt the traditional family and put women into situations such as the military draft.

Around the same time, in 1973, the Supreme Court supported a woman's right to choose to have an abortion in the landmark court case of **Roe v. Wade**. The court ruled that a woman's privacy was protected by the Fourth Amendment, as well as the Ninth Amendment's reservation of rights for the people, and the Fourteenth Amendment's protection of personal liberty.

Today, women can't be barred from a job based on their gender, nor can states have age requirements that favor men. For example, a state can't have two different legal working ages for men and women. **Title IX** of the Education Amendments of 1972 prevents gender discrimination in educational activities such as sports.

Despite the Equal Pay Act of 1963 (which prohibits discrimination of wages based on gender), studies show a "gender wage gap" where women tend to be paid less than men who have similar jobs. In recent decades, strict sexual harassment laws have ensured that women are not discriminated against in the workplace.

Question: Besides Friedan and Schlafly, what other famous names should I know about for this era?

1. *Rachel Carson's* book, *Silent Spring* is important to know. The 1962 book gets a lot of credit for helping to launch the environmental movement that led to the ban of certain pesticides, including DDT. In later years, you should know that the *Clean Air Act of 1970* looked to reduce air pollution and auto emissions, and the Water Pollution Control Act of 1972 aimed to rid rivers and lakes of pollution.

The Endangered Species Act of 1973 looks to protect and recover both species in peril and their ecosystems. In 1970, the Environmental Protection Agency (EPA) was created to protect human health and the environment.

2. Andy Warhol - He was a filmmaker, author, and artist. He was most famous for "pop art," where images of pop culture were used in works of art. One of his most famous creations was *Campbell's Soup Cans* in 1962.

3. Ralph Nader - For decades he was a consumer advocate. In 1965, he wrote his most famous book, *Unsafe at Any Speed*, in which he challenged the automotive industry to make safer cars.

4. Benjamin Spock - He was a pediatrician who wrote *The Common Sense Book of Baby and Child Care*, a bestselling book about raising children. Though it was published in 1946, new editions were printed into the 1990s.

5. From the 1960s-1980s, *César Chávez* of the *United Farm Workers* called for boycotts to help farm laborers get better pay and safer working conditions in industries such as grapes and lettuce. (Think: "César" Salad!)

Definition: Affirmative Action

Affirmative action is a government policy which ensures that women and minorities have equal opportunity for jobs, school admissions, and other benefits. Although it was created to prevent discrimination in hiring practices, it has come under fire for "reverse discrimination" against those who aren't minorities.

In the 1978 court case *Regents of the University of California* v. *Bakke*, Allan Bakke claimed he was denied admission to medical school because he was white. The school had a plan in place that set quotas for minority students who could get lower grades, yet be admitted. In a 5-4 decision, the Supreme Court ruled that although the school can consider race as part of the admissions process, a *strict racial quota* violated the Fourteenth Amendment and the Civil Rights Act. Bakke was later admitted.

Question: What should I know about Gerald Ford's (Republican) Presidency? (1974-77)

Answer:

1. After Spiro Agnew resigned, Ford was appointed to the Vice Presidency prior to Nixon's resignation. When Nixon stepped down, Ford became the first non-elected President (that is, not elected as a President or VP).

2. After taking office, he pardoned (forgiveness of a crime) Nixon. Although this was controversial, Ford believed it was best not to prosecute Nixon so the country could heal.

Question: What should I know about Jimmy Carter's (Democrat) Presidency? (1977-81)

Answer:

1. As a peanut farmer and Governor of Georgia, Carter was a Washington outsider.

2. He battled *stagflation*...high inflation, slow growth, and high unemployment.

3. Carter negotiated the Camp David Accords of 1978, where Egypt agreed to recognize Israel as a nation in exchange for Israel returning the Sinai Peninsula.

4. In 1979, Iranian students stormed the American Embassy in Tehran, Iran. For 444 days, Americans were held hostage, decreasing morale in the United States, especially after an attempted rescue failed. The hostages were finally released on Ronald Reagan's inauguration day. The crisis coincided with the Iranian Revolution where US ally Mohammad Reza Pahlavi - the Shah of Iran - was overthrown and Ayatollah Khomeini took power.

5. In 1973 (when Nixon was President), Arab members of OPEC (Organization of the Petroleum Exporting Countries) proclaimed an oil embargo against the United States to protest American military support for Israel. This resulted in an energy crisis in the early 1970s where rationing of gasoline took place. As Iran became unstable in 1979, OPEC once again sent the price of oil skyrocketing. High energy prices and fuel shortages only added to Carter's economic problems.

6. In 1979, there was a partial nuclear meltdown at the *Three Mile Island Nuclear Generating Station* in Pennsylvania. The event led many to question whether nuclear power should be used as an alternative energy source.

Definition: Christian Right

In reaction to liberal social issues such as the Equal Rights Amendment and legalized abortion, a strong conservative voice emerged known as the Christian Right (representing the *Religious Right*). Conservatives looked to reinforce the importance of religious teachings and place greater importance on family values. Groups such as Jerry Falwell's *Moral Majority* gathered strong support for the Republican Party throughout the 1980s.

The Religious Right emerged as part of a "new conservatism" movement which looked to decrease the size of government, lower taxes, and reform social welfare programs. They helped the Republican Party win three straight Presidential Elections from 1980-1988.

Question: What should I know about Ronald Reagan's (Republican) Presidency? (1981-89)

Answer:

1. Reagan increased spending on the military with programs such as the Strategic Defense Initiative, or Star Wars (mentioned earlier). The Soviet Union began to fall apart during his Presidency. Reagan was also forceful. As stated earlier, he gave the "tear down this wall" speech in front of the Berlin Wall in 1987.

2. In his economic policy of *Reaganomics*, he supported wealthy businesses so that profits would "trickle down" to all classes. This was related to the *supply-side economics* theory where less government regulation and tax breaks would lead to more investment and job creation. He also cut certain programs to decrease the government's workforce. One budget hard-hit was the Environmental Protection Agency.

3. Like Carter, Reagan was a Washington outsider. He was a former actor and Governor of California.

4. In the 1985 Iran-Contra Affair, senior military officials sold arms to Iran in an attempt to get hostages rescued. In addition, the money from the sale of the weapons was given to Nicaraguan anti-communist rebels known as

Contras. Both of the above actions were against American policy.

5. Reagan fired over 11,000 workers from the Professional Air Traffic Controllers Organization (PATCO) when members of the union refused to go back to work amidst a strike in 1981. Reagan viewed the strike as a threat to airline safety, and replacement workers were hired. The failure of the strike was a setback for labor unions.

Question: What should I know about George H. W. Bush's (Republican) Presidency? (1989-93)

Answer:

1. He was Commander-in-Chief for Operation Desert Storm during the Persian Gulf War in Iraq, where American forces liberated Kuwait from Saddam Hussein. The US looked to stabilize oil markets in the region.

2. There was a deep economic recession that hurt his re-election campaign.

3. In 1989, the *Exxon Valdez* oil tanker ran aground in Prince William Sound, Alaska, leading to a much-publicized environmental disaster.

Definition: Americans with Disabilities Act (ADA) of 1990

This law protects those with disabilities the same way that the Civil Rights Act of 1964 was meant to protect women and minorities. The act protects those who are qualified for employment, and provides handicapped accommodations in public places, restrooms, and on public transportation.

Question: What should I know about Bill Clinton's (Democrat) Presidency? (1993-2001)

Answer: Clinton won in 1992 without a majority of the popular vote, as billionaire H. Ross Perot was a strong third-party candidate who helped split the vote.

1. He favored health-care reform.

2. The economy recovered into prosperity.

3. The Brady Bill (1993) led to more background checks for owning firearms.

4. He sent **NATO troops into Bosnia**, attempting to end ethnic cleansing and human rights violations.

5. He negotiated The North American Free Trade Agreement *(NAFTA)* that lifted certain tariffs between the US, Mexico, and Canada.

6. In 1993, the official policy towards sexual orientation in the military became "***don't ask, don't tell***" *(DADT)*. It allowed gay and lesbian soldiers to serve, as long as they kept their sexual orientation a secret.

7. It's important to note that Republicans surged in 1994 after their **Contract With America** campaign promised lower taxes, a balanced budget, and less government regulation if they were elected to a majority in the House. The Republicans were successful, and thus controlled the House of Representatives.

8. Clinton was impeached by Speaker *Newt Gingrich* and the Republican-controlled House of Representatives for *obstruction of justice*. He lied about doing something naughty with an intern in the White House. He was not convicted by the Senate.

Definition: Defense of Marriage Act (DOMA)

This 1996 law defined marriage as between a man and a woman. Section 3 of this act banned same-sex couples from receiving over one thousand federal benefits such as health insurance and retirement savings. Section 3 was declared unconstitutional in *US* v. *Windsor* in 2013.

Question: How has the US become involved in a Global Economy?

The term globalization has been used to describe the interconnected trade and communication networks that have linked the world together. Besides NAFTA (see above), much development in globalization has taken place in the last few decades. Those who support globalization look at the benefits of having a world community. They hope to improve lives in developing countries with increased industry and jobs, and the spread of new products. In addition, prices tend to decrease with freer trade and overseas labor. Those against globalization point to the loss of their nation's factories and jobs (freer migration laws can create an influx of workers), which they believe has weakened the domestic economy. For example, many *multinational corporations* (those who have major operations in multiple countries) have outsourced jobs to India and China, thereby leading to the closing of factories in developed nations such as the United States. As seen with the financial crisis of c2008, global markets can experience shockwaves during economic downturns. For example, a weak global economy can severely decrease demand for Chinese exports.

Question: What should I know about George W. Bush's (Republican) Presidency? (2001-09)

Answer:

1. Despite losing the popular vote to Al Gore in 2000, he won the electoral vote in a disputed election where the Democrats contended that not every vote was properly counted. In *Bush v. Gore,* the Supreme Court ordered a stop to the manual recounting of votes in Florida.

2. Bush led military efforts in the *War on Terror* to remove the Taliban (fundamentalist Islamic government) from Afghanistan. The Taliban supported the terrorist group al-Qaeda, which was behind the September 11, 2001 attacks on the US. Osama bin Laden organized the crashing of hijacked planes into NY's World Trade Center, and the Pentagon in Washington, DC. A final plane crashed in an open field in Pennsylvania after heroic actions by passengers. Nearly 3,000 died in the attacks.

3. In 2003, the United States invaded Iraq and removed Saddam Hussein from power. Hussein was seen as a dangerous threat in the region, and was believed to have *weapons of mass destruction* (though extensive weaponry wasn't found). In the aftermath of Hussein's removal and execution, the US battled insurgents, or violent resisters to American forces and the established Iraqi government. The final withdrawal of US troops occurred in 2011.

4. The War on Terror necessitated the creation of the *Department of Homeland Security.* This agency looks to keep Americans safe from terrorist activity.

5. Bush signed the *Patriot Act*, which gave law enforcement more power to search, gather information, deport, or detain suspected terrorists. The act allowed electronic surveillance of phones and email. Critics of the act believed it violated Fourth Amendment protections against unreasonable searches and seizures.

6. He left office amidst a financial crisis. Contributing factors included bank failures, a crash of the housing market, credit/mortgage loans unable to be paid, and rapidly declining stock markets both at home and abroad. The government quickly intervened with a package to help stimulate the economy. There were also bailouts of failing financial giants. The national debt (much of which was owed to China and Japan) increased as a result.

Question: What should I know about Barack Obama's (Democrat) Presidency? (2009-2017)

Answer:

1. Obama was the first African American to

win the Presidency.

2. Taking the Presidency during a recession, he promoted stimulus bills that aimed to fix the economy. However, additional spending led to a large increase in the national debt.

3. He promoted universal healthcare. Passed in 2010, the ***Patient Protection and Affordable Care Act***, also known as the ***Affordable Care Act***, is commonly known as President Barack Obama's *Obamacare*. The act looks to lower health care costs and make health insurance more affordable. Important aspects of the law were upheld by the Supreme Court in 2012 in *National Federation of Independent Business* v. *Sebelius*.

4. He supported an end to ***"don't ask, don't tell"*** in the military. As a result, anyone, regardless of sexual orientation, could openly serve in the military without fear of being discharged. In the 2015 case of *Obergefell* v. *Hodges*, the Supreme Court ruled that the Fourteenth Amendment prevents states from refusing to license and recognize same-sex marriages.

5. In 2010, the Supreme Court decided *Citizens United* v. *Federal Election Commission*. They ruled that money given in political contests by groups such as unions and corporations was protected by the First Amendment. The decision led to an increase in independent expenditures by "Super PACs" who can put large sums of money into elections, just not directly to the candidate.

6. In 2014, a US-led coalition began airstrikes against the extremist Islamic State of Iraq and Syria, or ISIS. Amidst the war-torn background of Syria and Iraq, ISIS gained control over large areas in the region. They became associated with violence, human rights violations, and terror threats in both the Middle East and Western World.

7. Ten years after the 9/11 attacks, al-Qaeda's Osama bin Laden was killed by American forces in Pakistan.

Definition: Election of 2016

Washington outsider and billionaire Donald Trump (Republican) defeated former First Lady, Senator, and Secretary of State, Hillary Clinton (Democrat). Clinton became the first woman to receive the nomination of a major party, and fifth person to win the popular vote, but lose the Electoral Vote. Trump campaigned to "Make America Great Again," favoring regulation cuts, tax reform, stronger borders, and healthcare reform. The campaign saw prolific use of social media to help mobilize voters on both sides.

Review Questions

"**Section 1**. Equality of rights under the law shall not be denied or abridged by the United States or by any State on account of sex.

"**Section 2**. The Congress shall have the power to enforce, by appropriate legislation, the provisions of this article.

"**Section 3**. This amendment shall take effect two years after the date of ratification."
- Proposed Equal Rights Amendment

1. Which of the following people would have been the greatest advocate for the above proposed Amendment?
   A) Betty Friedan
   B) Rachel Carson
   C) Phyllis Schlafly
   D) Ida B. Wells

2. A century earlier, the above ideas would have received the most support from
   A) Industrial Workers of the World union members
   B) justices in the *Muller* v. *Oregon* decision
   C) participants at the Seneca Falls Convention
   D) framers of the Constitution

3. Which piece of legislation can be considered a continuation of the proposed amendment?
   A) Title IX
   B) Defense of Marriage Act
   C) Brady Bill
   D) Patriot Act

Answers and Explanations

1. **A**. Betty Friedan was an outspoken supporter of women's rights and the Equal Rights Amendment.

2. **C**. The Seneca Falls Convention of 1848 adopted a Declaration of Sentiments stating that all men and women were created equal.

3. **A**. Title IX of the Education Amendments of 1972 prevented discrimination to women in education activities, such as organized sports.

Short Essay Question Set

Document 1:

AN ACT
To enforce the constitutional right to vote, to confer jurisdiction upon the district courts of the United States to provide injunctive relief against discrimination in public accommodations, to authorize the Attorney General to institute suits to protect constitutional rights in public facilities and public education, to extend the Commission on Civil Rights, to prevent discrimination in federally assisted programs, to establish a Commission on Equal Employment Opportunity, and for other purposes.

Be it enacted by the Senate and House of Representatives of the United States of America in Congress assembled, That this Act may be cited as the "Civil Rights Act of 1964".

Document 2:

AN ACT
To enforce the fifteenth amendment to the Constitution of the United States, and for other purposes.
Be it enacted by the Senate and House of Representatives of the United States of America in Congress assembled, That this Act shall be known as the "Voting Rights Act of 1965."

SEC. 2. No voting qualification or prerequisite to voting, or standard, practice, or procedure shall be imposed or applied by any State or political subdivision to deny or abridge the right of any citizen of the United States to vote on account of race or color.

•**Describe the historical context surrounding documents 1 and 2**
•**Identify and explain the *relationship* between the events and/or ideas found in these documents (Cause and Effect, *or* Similarity/Difference, *or* Turning Point)**

The US History and Government Regents Exam Explained

The contents of this book reflect the updates made to the exam as of Fall, 2019. The new Regents is based on a new framework and is separated into three parts. Each of which we will address and provide practice for. There will be a multiple choice section where questions are based on a stimulus (document, primary source, secondary source, map, etc.). Part II will ask you to analyze two sets of documents. Part III will offer a Civic Literacy Essay where you will need to analyze six documents, and supplement with outside information. Let's take a deeper look!

Part I - 28 Multiple Choice Questions Based on a Stimulus

You will be given a cartoon, primary source, secondary source, photograph, map, chart, or other source. There will be a series of questions that follow. You will be tested on content and skills represented by "Task Models." The following are some of the skills you need to consider:
- Evaluation, classification, and identification of a stimulus
- Understanding continuity and change over time
- Identifying point of view, purpose, context, bias, format of source, location of source, and a source's audience
- Supporting or refuting a claim based on knowledge
- Understanding a plausible claim that logically flows from what is presented
- Understanding the significance of turning points
- Identifying significance of events, actions, ideas, or developments as part of continuity in history
- Identifying causes and effects
- Understanding the impact of time and place
- Identifying similarities and differences on one or two documents
- Extracting relevant information from a visual stimulus such as a cartoon, photograph, or chart.
- Identifying a course of action taken by historical figures, groups, or governments
- Identifying how historical events are related chronologically
- Identifying a problem, and also identifying a response to the problem
- Using evidence from sources to support or refute a claim or argument.
- Identifying disciplinary issues, and connecting issues to civic activism

Part II - Stimulus-Based Short-Essay Questions

Set 1: You must describe the historical context surrounding two documents. Next, you must identify and explain the relationship between the events and/or ideas found in the documents. This relationship could be cause and effect, similarity and difference, or a turning point. *Analysis depth is key for full credit.*

What is Historical Context? – It is important to connect history to the bigger picture by describing historical context accurately, and explaining how that context influenced the development or process of history. Furthermore, you should grasp the significance of such historical development. For instance, the counterculture movement not only coincided with the Vietnam War, but also the Civil Rights Era. For the second part of the question, go to *page 139 for concrete examples of turning points/continuity and change, comparison, and cause/effect.* Notice how vital outside information is for this task!

Set 2: Again, you must describe the historical context surrounding two documents. Next, you must (for one document) analyze and explain how audience, purpose, bias, or point of view affects the document's use as a *reliable source* of evidence. The ***Point of view*** would reflect the attitude/opinion of the writer based on their background or opinion. They could have a ***bias***, or partial favoring. The ***audience*** refers to the people who are being targeted by the writing. This targeting is usually done with a purpose. The ***purpose*** is the reason behind the writing. Perhaps the purpose is to sway public opinion, or disrupt the status quo.

You need to understand ***reliability***, or how accurate and useful the information in the source is. Perhaps a document is somewhat reliable, as opposed to reliable or unreliable. ***You must explain why!*** The Cross of Gold speech would be reliable when addressing concerns of farmers c1896. However, if you were evaluating the profits of industry, the author's point of view/bias would make the speech far less reliable.

See each chapter of No Bull Review for practice questions for both Part I and Part II of the exam

Part III - Civic Literacy Document-Based Essay

The Civic Literacy Essay involves formulating arguments based on documents regarding constitutional or civic issues. As you did with the Short Essay Questions, you should take into consideration the point of view or bias. You will need to describe the ***historical circumstances surrounding the issue,*** explain ***efforts to address the constitutional or civic issue*** by individuals, groups, and/or governments, and discuss either the ***extent to which these efforts were successful,*** or ***the impact of the efforts.***

The following contains general information which could help you write a Civic Literacy Essay. The test will give you a series of six documents. It is your job to analyze the documents to reflect the tasks mentioned above.

Your score on the essay will be largely based on you answering "yes" to the following questions:
1. Did I **analyze** the documents to answer the questions? (DO NOT SUMMARIZE)
2. Did I utilize *at least four* of the documents?
3. Did I answer the bullets SPECIFICALLY as to what is asked?
4. Did I support the theme with relevant details and facts?
5. Is my **outside information** impressive?
6. Did I set up my essay with an introduction and conclusion, and have statements that go beyond restating what was given to me?

• **Tip #1: First, the Document Questions**
The Civic Literacy Essay has important questions after the documents. They are worth BIG points. So, make sure you TAKE YOUR TIME with them. We know, it's hot outside and you want to go swimming (unless you are taking this test in January, in which case we would recommend an indoor pool). The pool can wait! If you see 2 lines, write 3 lines! Answer in full sentences. Give all you know! Our recommendation would be to first scan the document. Notice who is speaking, what the year is, and what the focus of the document is. Then, read the question and further analyze the document.

• Tip #2: Organize and Analyze the Documents

Organize the documents by topic so you know which ones will fit in the same paragraph when you write. Some will be more relevant to efforts by government or people, others could help you evaluate the success. To get the highest score in the prototypes released in the first year of the test, relevant information was needed from **at least four documents**. In addition, the question is looking for **efforts** (plural), so more than one effort needs to be analyzed within the documents.

• Tip #3: Outside Information

No Bull, you need to have a lot of outside information. As you go through each document, jot down notes in the margins. Your documents should be drowning in ink by the end of the hour! Give anything...ANYTHING... relevant that is not in the documents. For example, consider a document that deals with the rights of farmers. In the margin write down "Populism," "Cross of Gold," "Omaha Platform." Any note about William Jennings Bryan would be a great addition of outside information. Your teacher might suggest that you cite your Outside Information as (O.I.) as well as your documents (Doc 1) (Doc 2). Be warned ...your teachers are pretty smart! Don't write down...Alaska is big and cold. (O.I.) That's not the outside info they are looking for!

• Tip #4: DON'T SUMMARIZE! Describe, Explain, Discuss

If you just copy over the documents, you'll have a really long and TERRIBLE essay. The documents are there to *guide* your argument. **If they are asking about the efforts** brought on by Reconstruction, **and you just summarize** the Fifteenth Amendment without focusing on the question, you are NOT doing it correctly! If they say:

Describe - It means to illustrate or tell about it.

Explain - It means to make understandable and provide reasons, developments, causes, or relationships. If they ask you to explain efforts to address an issue, then show that you understand how Amendments to the Constitution looked to bring about change.

Discuss - It means to make observations using facts, reasoning, argument and presentation of detail.

A big piece of advice we can give is to answer their questions with analysis (or detailed examination). If you just summarize documents without focusing on the question, *the essay will not reach its full potential!*

Now let's take a look at two practice-style Civic Literacy Essays

Historical Context: African American Rights in the Nineteenth Century.
Throughout United States history, many constitutional and civic issues have been debated by Americans. These debates have resulted in efforts by individuals, groups, and governments to address these issues. These efforts have achieved varying degrees of success. One of these constitutional and civic issues is African American rights in the Nineteenth Century.

Task: Read and analyze the documents. Using information from the documents and your knowledge of United States history, write an essay in which you

> •**Describe the historical circumstances surrounding this constitutional or civic issue**
> •**Explain efforts by individuals, groups, and/or governments to address this constitutional or civic issue**
> •**Discuss the extent to which these efforts were successful**

Document 1
The following is an excerpt from the Slave Narrative of Frederick Douglass.

"The allowance of the slave children was given to their mothers, or the old women having the care of them. The children unable to work in the field had neither shoes, stockings, jackets, nor trousers, given to them; their clothing consisted of two coarse linen shirts per year. When these failed them, they went naked until the next allowance-day. Children from seven to ten years old, of both sexes, almost naked, might be seen at all seasons of the year… Mr. Severe was rightly named: he was a cruel man. I have seen him whip a woman, causing the blood to run half an hour at the time; and this, too, in the midst of her crying children, pleading for their mother's release. He seemed to take pleasure in manifesting his fiendish barbarity."

Source: Douglass, Frederick. *Narrative of the Life of Frederick Douglass, an American Slave*, Boston: Published at the Anti-Slave Office, 1845. 10-11.

1. What was *one* effect the institution of slavery had on the author?

_____

_____

Document 2
The following is an excerpt from Roger B. Taney's Majority Opinion of *Dred Scott* v. *Sandford*.

"In the opinion of the court, the legislation and histories of the times, and the language used in the Declaration of Independence, show that neither the class of persons who had been imported as slaves nor their descendants, whether they had become free or not, were then acknowledged as a part of the people, nor intended to be included in the general words used in that memorable instrument.

"It is difficult at this day to realize the state of public opinion in relation to that unfortunate race which prevailed in the civilized and enlightened portions of the world at the time of the Declaration of Independence and when the Constitution of the United States was framed and adopted. But the public history of every European nation displays it in a manner too plain to be mistaken.

2. What was *one* reason why Justice Taney believed slaves should be denied rights?

_____

_____

Document 3
The Emancipation Proclamation

"That on the first day of January, in the year of our Lord one thousand eight hundred and sixty-three, all persons held as slaves within any State or designated part of a State, the people whereof shall then be in rebellion against the United States, shall be then, thenceforward, and forever free; and the Executive Government of the United States, including the military and naval authority thereof, will recognize and maintain the freedom of such persons, and will do no act or acts to repress such persons, or any of them, in any efforts they may make for their actual freedom." - Abraham Lincoln, effective January 1, 1863

3. What is *one* effect that the above proclamation had on United States history?

_____

_____

Document 4a
The Thirteenth Amendment to the US Constitution

Section 1.

Neither slavery nor involuntary servitude, except as a punishment for crime whereof the party shall have been duly convicted, shall exist within the United States, or any place subject to their jurisdiction.

Document 4b
The Fourteenth Amendment to the US Constitution

Section 1.

All persons born or naturalized in the United States, and subject to the jurisdiction thereof, are citizens of the United States and of the state wherein they reside. No state shall make or enforce any law which shall abridge the privileges or immunities of citizens of the United States; nor shall any state deprive any person of life, liberty, or property, without due process of law; nor deny to any person within its jurisdiction the equal protection of the laws.

4. Based on these documents, explain *one* way the amended US Constitution affected African Americans.

_____

_____

Document 5
Dissenting Opinion of Justice John Marshall Harlan in the *Plessy* v. *Ferguson* case

"By the Louisiana statute the validity of which is here involved, all railway companies (other than street railroad companies) carrying passengers in that State are required to have separate but equal accommodations for white and colored persons by providing two or more passenger coaches for each passenger train, or by dividing the passenger coaches by a partition so as to secure separate accommodations.

"Under this statute, no colored person is permitted to occupy a seat in a coach assigned to white persons, nor any white person to occupy a seat in a coach assigned to colored persons. The managers of the railroad are not allowed to exercise any discretion in the premises, but are required to assign each passenger to some coach or compartment set apart for the exclusive use of his race. If a passenger insists upon going into a coach or compartment not set apart for persons of his race, he is subject to be fined or to be imprisoned in the parish jail. Penalties are prescribed for the refusal or neglect of the officers, directors, conductors and employees of railroad companies to comply with the provisions of the act."

5. Based on the document, what is *one* challenge Justice Harlan might have offered to the court's decision?

_____

_____

Document 6a
Fifteenth Amendment to the US Constitution

Section 1.

The right of citizens of the United States to vote shall not be denied or abridged by the United States or by any state on account of race, color, or previous condition of servitude.

Document 6b
Louisiana voting law c1900

Sec. 3. He (the elector) shall be able to read and write, and shall demonstrate his ability to do so when he applies for registration, by making, under oath administered by the registration officer or his deputy, written application therefor, in the English language, or his mother tongue, which application shall contain the essential facts necessary to show that he is entitled to register and vote, and shall be entirely written, dated and signed by him, in the presence of the registration officer or his deputy, without assistance or suggestion from any person or any memorandum whatever, except the form of application...

6. According to the documents, what is *one* result of the Fifteenth Amendment?

_____

_____

Get a guided look at this essay on page 138

Historical Context: Immigrant Rights and Adjustment to Life in the US c1880-c1920.
Throughout United States history, many constitutional and civic issues have been debated by Americans. These debates have resulted in efforts by individuals, groups, and governments to address these issues. These efforts have achieved varying degrees of success. One of these constitutional and civic issues is immigrant rights and adjustment to life in the United States c1880-c1900.

Task: Read and analyze the documents. Using information from the documents and your knowledge of United States history, write an essay in which you

•**Describe the historical circumstances surrounding this constitutional or civic issue**
•**Explain efforts by individuals, groups, and/or governments to address this constitutional or civic issue**
•**Discuss the impact of the efforts on the United States and/or American Society**

Document 1
US Census Region of Birth of Foreign-Born Americans

Year	Total	Europe	Asia	Africa	Oceania	Latin Amer	N. America	Not reported
*1990	19,767,316	4,350,403	4,979,037	363,819	104,145	8,407,837	753,917	808,158
*1980	14,079,906	5,149,572	2,539,777	199,723	77,577	4,372,487	853,427	887,343
*1970	9,619,302	5,740,891	824,887	80,143	41,258	1,803,970	812,421	315,732
*1960	9,738,091	7,256,311	490,996	35,355	34,730	908,309	952,500	59,890
1930	14,204,149	11,784,010	275,665	18,326	17,343	791,840	1,310,369	6,596
1920	13,920,692	11,916,048	237,950	16,126	14,626	588,843	1,138,174	8,925
1910	13,515,886	11,810,115	191,484	3,992	11,450	279,514	1,209,717	9,614
1900	10,341,276	8,881,548	120,248	2,538	8,820	137,458	1,179,922	10,742
1890	9,249,547	8,030,347	113,383	2,207	9,353	107,307	980,938	6,012
1880	6,679,943	5,751,823	107,630	2,204	6,859	90,073	717,286	4,068
1870	5,567,229	4,941,049	64,565	2,657	4,028	57,871	493,467	3,592
1860	4,138,697	3,807,062	36,796	526	2,140	38,315	249,970	3,888
1850	2,244,602	2,031,867	1,135	551	588	20,773	147,711	41,977

*Indicates sample data

Source: census.gov

1. Based on the document, explain *one* way immigration impacted US society.

_____

_____

Document 2a
Chinese Exclusion Act of 1882

Whereas in the opinion of the Government of the United States the coming of Chinese laborers to this country endangers the good order of certain localities within the territory thereof: Therefore, Be it enacted by the Senate and House of Representatives of the United States of America in Congress assembled, That from and after the expiration of ninety days next after the passage of this act, and until the expiration of ten years next after the passage of this act, the coming of Chinese laborers to the United States be, and the same is hereby, suspended; and during such suspension it shall not be lawful for any Chinese laborer to come, or having so come after the expiration of said ninety days to remain within the United States.

Document 2b
Immigration Act of 1924

Sec. 5. When used in this Act the term "quota immigrant" means any immigrant who is not a non-quota immigrant. An alien who is not particularly specified in this Act as a non-quota immigrant or a non-immigrant shall not be admitted as a non-quota immigrant or a non-immigrant by reason of relationship to any individual who is so specified or by reason of being excepted from the operation of any other law regulating or forbidding immigration.

2. What effect did the above documents have on immigration to the United States?

_____

_____

Document 3a
Excerpt from *How The Other Half Lives*, by Jacob Riis

Thousands were living in cellars. There were three hundred underground lodging-houses in the city when the Health Department was organized … The wretched pile harbored no less than forty families, and the annual rate of deaths to the population was officially stated to be 75 in 1,000. These tenements were an extreme type of very many, for the big barracks had by this time spread east and west...

Source: Riis, Jacob. *How the Other Half Lives.* New York: Charles Scribner's Sons, 1890. 13.

Document 3b
The Tenement House Law of the City of New York, 1901

Section 2: Every tenement house hereafter erected exceeding fifty-seven feet, or exceeding five stories or parts of stories, in height above the curb level, shall be a fireproof tenement house...

Section 81: Any shaft used or intended to be used to light or ventilate rooms used or intended to be used for living purposes, and which may be hereafter placed in a now existing tenement house, shall not be less in area than twenty-five square feet, nor less than four feet in width in any part.

3. According to the above documents, what is *one* way in which the government responded to a crisis?

_____

_____

Document 4
A Description of Hull House c1900

The clubs associated with Hull House are many. The Jane Club is a working-girls' club in which the members maintain independence, talking up their residence in the club-house, and surrounding themselves with such order, cleanliness, and beauty as their fathers and mothers were never able to attain. The Hull House Woman's Club is one of four hundred members, formed for literary and social purposes …

The Italian orchestra is an interesting organization which is making a reputation for itself. The playground is a thing of undeniable beneficence. The penny savings-bank is an admirable concern, the Hull House postal station a convenience. The visiting kindergarten, the Visiting Nurse Association, and the Hull House nursery and the sterilized-milk stations are all practical demonstrations of the spirit of Hull House.

Source: Prattie, Elia W."Women of the Hour." Harper's Bazar, XXXVIII, July 1904, pg 1006.

4. What is *one* contribution to society provided by the settlement house mentioned above?

_____

_____

Document 5
Jane Addams speaks of immigrants in government

We do much loose talking in regard to American immigration; we use the phrase, "the scum of Europe," and other unwarranted words without realizing that the unsuccessful man, the undeveloped peasant, may be much more valuable to us here than the more highly developed, but also more highly specialized, town dweller, who may much less readily acquire the characteristics which the new environment demands.

If successful struggle ends in the survival of the few, in blatant and tangible success for the few only, government will have to reckon most largely with the men who have been beaten in the struggle, with the effect upon them of the contest and the defeat; for, after all, the unsuccessful will always represent the majority of the citizens, and it is with the large majority that self-government must eventually deal whatever course of action other governments may legitimately determine for themselves.

Source: Addams, Jane. *Newer Ideals of Peace*. New York: The Macmillan Company, 1907. 62.

5. Based on the document, explain *one* point of view of Addams concerning immigrants serving their governments.

_____

_____

Document 6

Source: Library of Congress, Prints & Photographs Division, National Child Labor Committee Collection, [reproduction number, LC-DIG-nclc-04960]

6. Based on the document, explain *one* way the government acted to help immigrant and native born Americans.

_____

_____

Get a guided look at this essay on page 138

Ideas For Civic Literacy Document-Based Essay: African American Rights

For this essay, the *historical circumstances* involved the antebellum period, through the Civil War, and into Reconstruction. The human rights violation of slavery existed for hundreds of years, as we can see in the narrative of Frederick Douglass (Doc 1). The Supreme Court supported the notion that slaves were property in the Dred Scott Case (Doc 2). The issue ultimately boiled over into the Civil War between North and South, where the beginnings of freedom can be seen with the Emancipation Proclamation (Doc 3). When the North (Union) won, slavery ended, and freed blacks gained rights. But did they? After Reconstruction, a period of Home Rule took place where Jim Crow laws were prevalent, as was disenfranchisement (being denied the right to vote).

The second part of the task calls for *efforts (plural) to address the constitutional or civic issue*. For this, the government passed several amendments (Doc 4a, Doc 4b, and Doc 6a). Even earlier, Abraham Lincoln's Emancipation Proclamation (Doc 3) supported the freeing of slaves in the Confederacy. There's much to choose from here!

The third part of the task looks to *evaluate the extent of success of the efforts*. Although there was certainly success because slavery didn't exist anymore and citizenship and suffrage were gained, rights were still denied in the American South during Home Rule. *Plessy* v. *Ferguson* (Doc 5) defended "separate but equal," while literacy tests and grandfather clauses prevailed at the polls (Doc 6b). Thus, there was mixed success.

As for *outside information*, there is much you could include in your essay such as: Abolitionist writings, Slavery Compromises (1820, 1850, 1854), slave rebellions, John Brown's Raid, secession, Reconstruction Act of 1867, Freedmen's Bureau, poll taxes, violence at the polls, sharecropping, and the Election of 1876. You are not limited to these ideas, but they are a few to consider.

Ideas For Civic Literacy Document-Based Essay: Immigrant Rights & Adjustment

For this essay, the *historical circumstances* involve the great waves of immigration in the nineteenth century. As can be seen in (Doc 1), there were thousands of people who could trace their birth to various places around the world. Despite their contribution of labor that helped fuel the Industrial Revolution, immigrants suffered socially, economically, and politically as they adjusted to life in the United States during the Gilded Age and Progressive Era.

The second part of the task calls for *efforts (plural) to address the constitutional or civic issue*. People and the government looked to address immigrant rights in different ways. First, to solve the tenement crisis (Doc 3a), New York City passed legislation to make housing safer (Doc 3b). In addition, settlement houses such as Hull House began to pop up around the country to help immigrants adjust to society (Doc 4). Leaders such as Jane Addams encouraged immigrants to have more of a say in government (Doc 5). However, another way that government addressed immigration was through more nativist policies such as the Chinese Exclusion Act and immigrant quota laws (Doc 2a and 2b).

The third part of the task looks to *discuss the impact of the efforts*. First, making housing safer is certainly a major impact (Doc 3b). In addition, the efforts of Hull House and Mothers' Pensions made it easier for immigrants to adjust to society (Doc 4) (Doc 6). However, one can also see a decrease in rights, as laws were passed by the government to limit immigration (Doc 2a and 2b). Furthermore, there was nativist sentiment in the country as explained by Jane Addams (Doc 5).

As for *outside information*, there is much to include such as: nativism, Gentlemen's Agreement, Quota Acts of the 1920s, Red Scare, and the rise of the KKK. Furthermore, unionization, worker's rights, the Social Gospel, and the immigrant experiences at Ellis Island could help bolster your essay. You are not limited to these ideas, but they are a few to consider.

Concrete Examples of Continuity/Change, Causation, and Comparison

Understanding Turning Points and Related Continuity and Change Over Time

When it comes to important turning points, you could analyze continuity *and* change over time. Here are some examples concerning such ideas.

Declaration of Independence: Life in the colonies CHANGED as there was now independence, but African Americans, American Indians, and women CONTINUED to experience inequality.

Fourteenth Amendment: Although the amendment CHANGED the citizenship status of African Americans, they still CONTINUED to be denied rights during the period of Home Rule.

Fifteenth Amendment: Although African American males had their lives CHANGED because they were granted suffrage, discrimination at the polls CONTINUED in the form of literacy tests, grandfather clauses, and poll taxes. Furthermore, not all women could vote until 1920.

Imperialism: Although the Spanish-American War ushered in a CHANGE in terms of a foreign policy of building a world empire, one might consider it to be a CONTINUATION of domestic manifest destiny in the first half of the nineteenth century.

Counterculture: Although the counterculture of the 1960s brought about CHANGE with protests for Civil Rights and against the Vietnam War, one might consider the movement to be a CONTINUATION of the non-conformity seen with the Beatniks, Lost Generation, or going back much earlier, the transcendentalists.

New Deal: Despite the New Deal being an incredibly large program which CHANGED the way government conducted economic policy, one can see it as a CONTINUATION of the Progressive Era which increased the size of the bureaucracy. In the 1960s, the Great Society saw a CONTINUED increase in government size and spending as well.

Civil Rights: The Civil Rights Era of the 1960s brought much CHANGE after the Civil Rights Act of 1964 and Voting Rights Act of 1965. But, one might see it as a CONTINUATION of the goals of Reconstruction legislation and the actions of early twentieth century leaders such as Booker T. Washington and W.E.B. Du Bois.

Containment: Although George Kennan's containment policy was a foreign policy CHANGE in that the United States looked to stop the spread of communism in Europe and Asia after World War II, it can be considered a CONTINUATION of the slow progression of becoming a world power going back to the Monroe Doctrine, its Corollary, and entrance into the two World Wars.

Democracy: Although the United States CHANGED from being merely colonies when they created their representative democracy after the American Revolution, there was a CONTINUA-

TION of freedom of speech (Zenger Trial), freedom of religion (Rhode Island), and a bicameral legislature (House of Burgesses) experienced during the colonial period.

Feminism: Although the feminist movement of the 1970s brought CHANGE through Betty Friedan's philosophy and Title IX, women CONTINUED to be without an Equal Rights Amendment and historically received unequal wages. Furthermore, one might consider such feminism to be a CONTINUATION of earlier women's rights movements, such as the flapper of the 1920s, suffrage, and even Seneca Falls.

Immigration and Nativism: New immigration (c1890-c1920) brought CHANGE and diversity to the populations of eastern seaboard cities, as large numbers of Eastern Europeans entered the workforce. However, these new immigrants CONTINUED to suffer the effects of nativism just as earlier immigrants had.

Gilded Age: Although acts such as the Sherman Anti-Trust Act and Interstate Commerce Act brought CHANGE, as they sought to decrease the power of the robber barons during the late nineteenth century, business leaders CONTINUED to exploit consumers for their own gain until stronger reforms occurred during the Progressive Era.

Segregation: Although the decision of *Brown* v. *Board of Education* CHANGED the legalities of "separate but equal" in schools, segregation CONTINUED in several forms, and politicians CONTINUED to campaign on pro-segregationist platforms.

Government: Although the Articles of Confederation and the Constitution brought a major CHANGE to what had been life under the British Crown, there was still a CONTINUATION of Enlightenment ideas such as freedom of religion and speech which had long-since been considered by Great Britain.

Great Migration: Although African Americans experienced CHANGE when they moved north for economic growth and to escape Jim Crow hostilities, racism CONTINUED in the North as there was still discrimination and violence.

Religious Tolerance: Although the Puritans in Massachusetts Bay CONTINUED to refrain from tolerance, CHANGE occurred in New England as religious freedom extended to Rhode Island. Furthermore, a similar CHANGE for tolerance occurred in Maryland and Pennsylvania.

John Marshall: Once the weakest of the three branches, John Marshall CHANGED the power and strength of the Supreme Court after the decision of *Marbury* v. *Madison*. However, a CONTINUITY of a lack of judicial might would be experienced when Andrew Jackson refused to enforce the *Worcester* v. *Georgia* decision.

Korea and Vietnam: Although the deployment of troops into Asian wars was a CHANGE in US policy, it can be considered a CONTINUATION of containment policies applied to Europe after World War II.

Rachel Carson: Although Rachel Carson's book can be considered a CHANGE in the modern environmental movement because it led to the banning of certain chemical agents, it can also be seen as a CONTINUATION of an earlier movement for conservation. In addition, her writing can be seen as a CONTINUATION of muckraking seen during the Progressive Era.

Continuity Ideas to Consider

The actions of Joseph McCarthy can be seen as a CONTINUATION of the Red Scare actions of A. Mitchell Palmer.

The Civil Rights Movement for African Americans CONTINUED to affect women and American Indians in the decades which followed.

The protests during the Vietnam War were not unique to that conflict, as they can be considered a CONTINUATION of war discontent going back to the Civil War draft riots, and CONTINUING to isolationist concerns before WWI.

John C. Calhoun's *South Carolina Exposition and Protest*, suggesting the tariff to be legislation that states should consider to be "null and void," was a CONTINUATION of the arguments of Jefferson and Madison in their *Kentucky and Virginia Resolutions* which protested the Alien and Sedition Acts.

The *Korematsu* decision, which led to a limit of civil liberties during World War II, can be seen as a CONTINUATION of earlier increases of executive strength during wartime, such as Lincoln suspending habeas corpus during the Civil War and the passage of the Alien and Sedition Acts during the Quasi War with France.

Events such as the Sand Creek Massacre and Wounded Knee can be seen as a CONTINUATION of Indian Removal, the Trail of Tears, and what Helen Hunt Jackson considered to be *A Century of Dishonor*.

The Progressive Era reforms of a graduated income tax, railroad regulation, direct election of senators, and a secret ballot can be seen as a CONTINUATION of Populist concerns brought about during the 1890s.

The Presidential scandals of Richard Nixon and Bill Clinton can be considered a CONTINUATION of earlier scandals that plagued the Presidencies of Ulysses S. Grant and Warren G. Harding.

Change Ideas to Consider

When the contracts of tobacco-farming indentured servants expired in the seventeenth century, there was a CHANGE in labor, as the presence of African slavery increased on colonial plantations. By the early nineteenth century, there was a CHANGE as well, as cotton became the major cash crop of the South after the invention of the cotton gin.

The Stonewall Riots marked a CHANGE as it led to an increased fight for LGBT rights. Furthermore, the repeal of "don't ask, don't tell" marked a CHANGE in government policy, as all citizens were permitted to openly serve in the military.

The French and Indian War ushered in a new CHANGE in the way the British dealt with the colonies. Taxes, restriction of settlement, and quartering of troops coincided with an end to salutary neglect and a tightening grip over colonial life.

The Warren Court not only established CHANGE regarding civil rights, but it also extended CHANGES regarding the way that accused criminals are handled during the judicial process.

Because the Constitution CHANGED the government's power to oversee a national army, the Whiskey Rebellion was put down…unlike Shays' Rebellion years earlier under the weaker Articles of Confederation.

Causation – Understanding BOTH Long-Term and Short-Term Causes and Effects

The Civil War had *long-term* causes such as slavery, economic and ideological differences, and political discord. Yet, the *short-term* cause of Lincoln's election led to secession. The *short-term* effects of the war included the elimination of slavery and the return of Southern states into the Union. However, there would still be *long-term* uncertainty as to the extent of civil rights for another century. Furthermore, there was an effect known as the New South, as certain cities such as Atlanta experienced greater industrialization.

The *long-term* causes of the Civil Rights Era can be traced back to slavery, the Civil War, and the unfulfilled promises of Reconstruction. In addition, there were earlier leaders such as Booker T. Washington and W.E.B. Du Bois who held different ideas as to how African Americans could gain rights. *Short-term* causes included the Montgomery Bus Boycott and the *I Have a Dream* speech. The *short-term* effects included the Civil Rights Act, Voting Rights Act, and an end to poll taxes. A *long-term effect* was inspiration for other rights movements including LGBT rights, feminism, and the rights of American Indians.

The Progressive Era reforms were caused by *long-term* issues such as exploitation of consumers, a lack of worker rights, and the massive power of robber barons during the Gilded Age. *Short-term* causes included the works of muckrakers such as Upton Sinclair and Ida Tarbell. The *short-term* effects were legislation such as the Pure Food and Drug Act, 16th and 17th Amendments, and the Clayton Anti-Trust Act. *Long-term effects* included an increase in size of the government's bureaucracy which would continue into the New Deal Era, and President Johnson's Great Society.

The *short-term* causes of the American Revolution included the post-French and Indian War tax acts and continued denial of representation. However, *long-term* causes show that there was an evolution of the cutting of ties, as colonists set up their own political, economic, and social structures long before shots were fired at Lexington and Concord. The *short-term* effects of winning the war included a weak Articles of Confederation, and then a stronger Constitution. The *long-term* effects included the creation of political parties, each with a different idea as to how the new government should operate.

The *short-term* cause for Indian Removal was the desire for the United States to expand onto land previously held by American Indians. There were also *long-term* causes such as cultural differences and violent clashes which went back hundreds of years. The *short-term* effect of the Indian Removal Act was US acquisition of land and eventually, the Trail of Tears. *Long-term* effects included the continued break up of tribal landholdings with the

Dawes Act, and denial of citizenship for all American Indians until the twentieth century.

Compare and Contrast: Understanding *BOTH* Similarities and Differences

Comparing Time Periods: Immigration from c1840-1860 was generally from Western Europe while immigration c1890-1920 was mostly from Southern and Eastern Europe. They were *similar* in that both groups tended to immigrate to urban areas where jobs were more available. In addition, both suffered the effects of nativism. However, they were *different* because the first wave tended to be more skilled, smaller in size, and likely to be more Americanized. In addition, the newer immigrants would eventually become subject to quotas, as a time of open immigration ended.

Comparing Time Periods: The Reconstruction Era was *similar* to the Civil Rights Era in that both time periods looked to expand rights to minorities. In addition, both time periods were met with fierce resistance from those looking to deny upward social mobility. However, the movements were *different* in that the Reconstruction Era was predominantly concerned with African Americans, while the later Civil Rights Movement led to rights for both women and minorities. Furthermore, the Civil Rights Era would have greater success, as Reconstruction legislation was undermined by Jim Crow laws and voting obstacles enforced later during Home Rule.

Comparing Time Periods: Women reformers during both the antebellum period and Progressive Era were *similar* in that both wanted expansion into the political sphere. For example, the antebellum women looked to become engaged in temperance and the abolitionist crusade. The Progressive Era women hoped to gain suffrage, achieve prohibition, and bring about an end to child labor. However, both eras were *different* in that the Progressive Era women were more likely to be working in factories alongside men, and specifically saw much opportunity during World War I. Furthermore, Progressive Era women such as Jane Addams had opportunities helping out immigrants in settlement houses.

Comparing Rights in Time of War: Both the Patriot Act after 9/11, and Executive Order 9066 during World War II were *similar* in that they expanded the power of the government to limit civil liberties in a time of war. Both had the intention of keeping Americans safe. However, they were *different* in that the Patriot Act looked to give more power to the government to investigate suspected terrorists, while the Executive Order was more extreme, detaining a large population of Japanese Americans on the west coast.

Comparing Early European Settlement: Both the Spanish and English were *similar* in that they were involved in the mercantilist system in the early years of colonization. They looked to extract raw materials and sell finished goods to benefit the Mother Country. However, they were *different*, as while the Spanish were more concerned with extracting gold and enforcing the *encomienda* labor system, the English turned to indentured servants and later slaves to work tobacco fields on the east coast. In addition, whereas the Spanish intermarried with American Indians to create a Mestizo culture, the English in New England tended to settle into families of European descent.

Comparing Presidents: Andrew Jackson and Thomas Jefferson were **_similar_** in that both supported the interests of the common man, as Jefferson hoped to limit the powers of the wealthy elite, and Jackson vetoed the recharter of the Bank of the US. However they were also **_different_** with regard to trade, as Jefferson hurt merchants with the Embargo Act, while Jackson looked to protect domestic businesses by enforcing controversial tariffs in the early 1830s.

Comparing Types of Government: The Articles of Confederation and Constitution were **_similar_** in that they provided for a way for laws to be passed, an amendment process, and conducted foreign diplomacy. However, they were very **_different_**, as the Constitution provided for a more efficient taxation system, a President, a bicameral legislature, and an easier process to pass laws and amendments.

100 "Old Style" Questions ...
These are NOT Regents style, but people tell us they help ... so here!

1. Thomas Paine's *Common Sense*
   A) condoned revolutions in France after the rise of the Jacobins
   B) said that a small island should not control a large continent thousands of miles away
   C) believed that citizens of the colonies had certain unalienable rights that could not be denied
   D) agreed that a monarchy could survive, but only if consent of the governed was reflected

2. The British enacted the Stamp Act in 1765 which
   A) was an internal tax on tea
   B) extended Parliamentary rule over the lands west of the Appalachian Mountains
   C) made it mandatory for soldiers to reside in private homes
   D) taxed legal and other paper documents

3. Which of the following was true of the Northwest Ordinance of 1787?
   A) the land was received in the Louisiana Purchase
   B) slavery was banned in new western states
   C) it was overridden by the Webster-Ashburton Treaty
   D) It led directly to the annexation of Texas

4. All are true of the Constitution's Great Compromise EXCEPT:
   A) It created a bicameral legislature
   B) The compromise is still in effect today
   C) It gave equal representation to states within the House of Representatives
   D) New Jersey's plan, part of the compromise, provided for equal representation

5. Which legislative idea of the seventeenth century became a model for the current United States Congress?
   A) House of Burgesses
   B) Mayflower Compact
   C) New England Town Meetings
   D) House of Commons

6. The purpose of the Bill of Rights was to
   A) appease the Federalists who refused to ratify the Constitution
   B) emphasize the importance of protecting individual rights in the Constitution
   C) guarantee the right to vote to all citizens
   D) increase the power of the Executive Branch

7. The *Kentucky and Virginia Resolutions* can be compared to what other writing of the mid-nineteenth century?
   A) *South Carolina Exposition and Protest*
   B) Jackson's Bank Veto
   C) *The Federalist*
   D) *The Liberator*

8. Which of the following called for America to be economically self-sufficient in the first half of the nineteenth century?
   A) James Monroe's Doctrine
   B) Henry Clay's American System
   C) Andrew Jackson's Spoils System
   D) Abraham Lincoln's House Divided speech

9. What action of Andrew Jackson led to a split in political parties in 1832?
   A) Force Bill
   B) Indian Removal Act
   C) Veto of the Bank of the United States
   D) Signing of the Tariff of 1832

10. The Seneca Falls Convention of 1848
   A) was the first ever formal gathering held for abolition
   B) led to a Women's Declaration of Sentiments
   C) brought Unitarians and Mennonites together for religious compromise
   D) promoted the thoughts of Charles Grandison Finney

11. The Second Great Awakening directly influenced the
   A) utopian community at Brook Farm
   B) Equal Rights Amendment
   C) Lowell Factory system
   D) settlement house movement

12. States legislating for education and driving laws is an example of
   A) checks and balances
   B) separation of powers
   C) federalism
   D) judicial review

13. The Wilmot Proviso of 1846 called for
   A) Washington, DC to end the practice of trading slaves
   B) an end to the expansion of slavery into certain territories
   C) nullification of the Tariff of Abominations
   D) annexation of Texas as a slave state

14. The Compromise of 1850 provided for
   A) popular sovereignty in Kansas, but not Nebraska
   B) Missouri to enter the Union as a slave state
   C) an outlaw of all slavery north of the 36° 30' line
   D) a strict fugitive slave act

15. John Brown and Nat Turner were similar in that both
   A) supported states' rights
   B) led unsuccessful slave rebellions
   C) protested against the Tariff of Abominations
   D) ran as a third party candidate in a Presidential Election

Use the map below to answer questions 16 and 17.

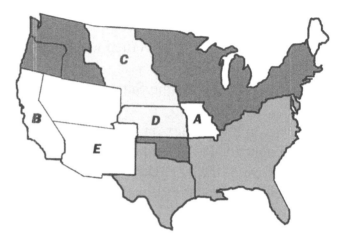

16. Space "A" became a slave state after the
   A) Missouri Compromise
   B) Kansas-Nebraska Act
   C) Compromise of 1850
   D) Dred Scott Decision

17. Popular Sovereignty led to the Lecompton Constitution in
   A) A
   B) B
   C) C
   D) D
   E) E

18. All of the following regarding slaves in the Civil War were true EXCEPT:

A) Many were confiscated as contraband by the Union Army

B) African American regiments were formed in the North

C) Slaves who were freed in the border states after the Emancipation Proclamation flocked to the Union army

D) Many slaves remained loyal to their masters in the South and helped with the Confederate war-effort

19. How did Presidential Reconstruction differ from Radical Reconstruction?

A) Presidents Lincoln and Johnson wanted to treat the South as conquered territory

B) Radical Republicans supported a 10% oath

C) Both the Presidents and Radical Republicans wanted to be lenient to the South

D) Radical Republicans supported military rule to enforce legislation

20. After the end of Reconstruction in 1877, Southerners did everything below EXCEPT:

A) Instituted the Mississippi Plan to intimidate black voters

B) Promoted the use of literacy tests

C) Supported Jim Crow legislation

D) Did not obey the Thirteenth Amendment

21. *"In bestowing charity, the main consideration should be to help those who will help themselves; to provide part of the means by which those who desire to improve may do so; to give those who desire to use the aids by which they may rise; to assist, but rarely or never to do all."*

Which robber-baron was most associated with this quote?

A) Andrew Carnegie

B) John D. Rockefeller

C) Cornelius Vanderbilt

D) Jay Gould

22. Which of the following is an example of using implied powers, or loose interpretation of the Constitution?

A) Congress declared war on Spain in 1898

B) The Senate did not ratify the Treaty of Versailles

C) The Presidential Election of 1824 was decided by the House of Representatives

D) Thomas Jefferson purchased Louisiana with a treaty

23. Most immigrants in the Second (New) Wave of immigration of the late nineteenth century-early twentieth century moved to

A) cities in the North

B) farms

C) rural areas west of the Mississippi

D) Canada

24. *"Silver, which has been accepted as coin since the dawn of history has been demonetized to add to the purchasing power of gold by decreasing the value of all forms of property as well as human labor, and the supply of currency is purposely abridged to fatten usurers, bankrupt enterprise and enslave industries."*

The above was discussed as part of

A) *The Jungle*
B) The Omaha Platform
C) The Hepburn Act
D) The Sherman Anti-Trust Act

25. How did Theodore Roosevelt's handling of the Anthracite Coal Strike of 1902 compare to Grover Cleveland's actions during the Pullman Strike of 1894?

A) Both used force to break up the strike
B) Cleveland sided with the employees
C) Both Presidents sided with the employers
D) Whereas Cleveland broke up the strike, Roosevelt sided with the workers

26. All of the following were aims of the Progressive Era of the early twentieth century EXCEPT:

A) Cleaning up the abuses of the Gilded Age
B) Bringing more government to the people
C) Narrowing the gap between the rich and poor
D) Eliminating the closed-shop

27. The New South refers to

A) the end to segregation after 1954
B) a repeal of the literacy test
C) an increase in Jim Crow laws
D) creation of industry after Reconstruction

28. The goal of the Open Door Policy was to

A) allow all immigrants to enter the United States, regardless of their country of origin
B) trade with Britain before World War II, despite the desire for neutrality
C) protect United States trade in China
D) prevent railroads from securing a monopoly

29. The Gentlemen's Agreement of 1907 limited immigration from

A) China
B) Japan
C) Poland
D) Russia

30. During the New Deal, the Supreme Court

A) approved of economic, but not the political issues of Franklin Roosevelt
B) declared several key acts unconstitutional
C) supported Congress and the President in all forms of legislation
D) declared Social Security unconstitutional

31. During both World War I and World War II, American women

A) fought overseas
B) became isolated in their homes
C) entered factories to fill jobs left vacant by men fighting abroad
D) demanded equal pay for equal work in the private sector

32. American foreign policy in the second half of the twentieth century can best be described as

A) imperialism in the Caribbean
B) containment in Europe and Asia
C) noninvolvement
D) Dollar Diplomacy in China

33. The actions of the House Un-American Activities Committee and Senator Joseph McCarthy were similar in that both

A) advocated for a policy of détente

B) believed in absolute freedom of speech

C) condoned the deployment of nuclear weapons

D) believed potential communist government officials should be targeted

34. Which of the following books would be an example of nonconformity in the Beat Generation?

A) Jack Kerouac - *On the Road*

B) Rachel Carson - *Silent Spring*

C) Jacob Riis - *How the Other Half Lives*

D) Ralph Nader - *Unsafe at Any Speed*

35. President Eisenhower's Administration created the

A) Marshall Plan

B) plan for interstate highways

C) Mars rover

D) Peace Corps

36. The escalation of the war in Vietnam was a result of the

A) firing of General MacArthur

B) Gulf of Tonkin Resolution

C) Nixon Doctrine

D) Eisenhower Doctrine

37. Richard Nixon's policy of Vietnamization called for

A) a gradual reduction of the reliance on US ground troops in Vietnam

B) an end to the policy of using napalm in the war

C) a surrendering of forces after the Tet Offensive

D) expansion of the draft

38. George Wallace was best known for his ideas of

A) taking a more open approach about limiting nuclear weapons with the Soviet Union

B) reintroducing segregationist ideas to the South

C) ending the War in Vietnam

D) increasing educational opportunities for minority students

39. Which of the following best describes the actions of Rosa Parks, SNCC and CORE?

A) Calling for reparations for all citizens who were the children of former slaves

B) Disobeying unjust laws of segregation

C) Protesting the *Brown* v. *Board of Education* decision

D) Promoting de facto, or voluntary, segregation of the races

40. The Presidency of Jimmy Carter of the late 1970s involved all of the following EXCEPT:

A) High prices on oil

B) Conflict in the Middle East

C) Stagflation

D) Vietnam War protests

41. Modern-Day environmentalism was influenced by which author?
    A) Jacob Riis
    B) Rachel Carson
    C) Betty Friedan
    D) Jack Kerouac

42. The decisions of the Warren Court such as *Miranda* v. *Arizona* and *Mapp* v. *Ohio* were best known for
    A) expanding rights of the accused
    B) limiting free speech
    C) segregating the South
    D) eliminating the powers of corporate trusts

43. The demonstrations and massacre at Kent State University were related to
    A) segregation
    B) the broadening of civil rights
    C) labor protests for greater union rights and collective bargaining
    D) discontent with the Vietnam War

44. Richard Nixon's Administration saw all of the following occur EXCEPT:
    A) The end to the Vietnam War
    B) His impeachment
    C) SALT Treaty
    D) A visit to China

45. Which of the following pushed for the creation of the Equal Rights Amendment?
    A) Phyllis Schlafly
    B) Betty Friedan
    C) Elizabeth Cady Stanton
    D) Susan B. Anthony

46. Woodrow Wilson's Fourteen Points aimed to
    A) lower tariffs
    B) allow consumers the right to fair prices
    C) bring peace to the world after World War I
    D) contain communism

47. Which of the following is paired with the proper writing?
    A) Phyllis Schlafly -*The Feminine Mystique*
    B) Rachel Carson - *On The Road*
    C) Jacob Riis - *The Jungle*
    D) William Lloyd Garrison - *The Liberator*

48. Where would the influence of the Zenger trial decision be seen in the Bill of Rights?
    A) The First Amendment which protects freedom of the press
    B) The Fourth Amendment that protects against unreasonable searches and seizures
    C) The Tenth Amendment which addresses division of powers
    D) The Eighth Amendment that protects against cruel and unusual punishment

49. Why did the English monarchy establish a rule of salutary neglect in the American colonies?
    A) Agricultural dominance in the South meant an abandonment of mercantilist policies
    B) The Great Awakening caused the king to intervene on behalf of the Church
    C) Britain was economically satisfied, so they looked the other way on certain social and political affairs
    D) The House of Burgesses was permitted to operate so long as a bicameral legislature was present

50. All of the following were results of the French and Indian War EXCEPT:

A) The removal of the Spanish from North America

B) The end of France as a major power in the 13 colonies

C) The emergence of George Washington as a recognizable name in the colonies

D) The need for Britain to raise money to support its army

51. John Marshall's major Supreme Court decisions generally

A) favored states' rights

B) supported Presidential power

C) expanded the power of the federal government

D) limited free speech and taxation rights

52. Henry David Thoreau and Ralph Waldo Emerson were most associated with

A) higher tariffs to protect American jobs

B) a reliance on nature and peace

C) a state of perfection which would lead to a millennium

D) a "city upon a hill"

53. All of the following were associated with abolitionism EXCEPT:

A) William Lloyd Garrison

B) Frederick Douglass

C) Harriet Beecher Stowe

D) Stephen Douglas

54. The Haymarket Affair and Taft-Hartley Act were similar in that both

A) led to increases in nativism

B) limited the power of labor unions

C) favored poor laborers

D) illustrated the need for suffrage reform

55. In the Freeport Doctrine, Stephen Douglas affirmed his belief that

A) Blacks should not own property

B) Slavery should not expand to newly formed states in the west

C) All territories gained in the Mexican War should be closed to slavery

D) Popular sovereignty should be favored over the Dred Scott decision

56. The spark that led to the secession of the Southern states was the

A) Compromise of 1850

B) Dred Scott decision

C) Harper's Ferry slave rebellion

D) Election of Abraham Lincoln

57. Which of the following acts that provided for popular sovereignty was passed in the antebellum period?

A) Missouri Compromise

B) Kansas Nebraska Act

C) Ostend Manifesto

D) Fugitive Slave Act

58. All of the following were examples of nativism EXCEPT:

A) Red Scare

B) Emergency Quota Act

C) Sacco-Vanzetti Case

D) Roosevelt Corollary

59. The Supreme Court decision of *Engel* v. *Vitale* dealt with the public school issue of

A) freedom of speech

B) search and seizure

C) prayer

D) dress code

60. *Plessy* v. *Ferguson* affirmed which of the following?

A) Separate but equal was constitutional
B) The Civil Rights Act of 1866 was unconstitutional
C) Jim Crow laws were unconstitutional
D) Schools in Kansas could be segregated with the consent of the people

61. Booker T. Washington's Atlanta Compromise called for

A) an immediate end to Jim Crow
B) anti-lynching legislation
C) a hope for gradual freedom and equality
D) the integration of schools

62. All of the following are paired with the proper author EXCEPT:

A) Rachel Carson - *Silent Spring*
B) Harriet Beecher Stowe - *Uncle Tom's Cabin*
C) Frederick Jackson Turner - *Common Sense*
D) William Lloyd Garrison - *The Liberator*

63. All of the following were leaders of slave rebellions EXCEPT:

A) Denmark Vesey
B) John Brown
C) Nat Turner
D) Frederick Douglass

64. Folk singers of the late 1960s such as Phil Ochs and Tom Paxton mostly disagreed with which of the following actions of President Johnson?

A) Medicare
B) The Great Society
C) Escalation of the war in Vietnam
D) Gun Control Act

65. The majority of workers in the Lowell Factory System in 1835 were

A) married men
B) Russian immigrants
C) young women
D) Chinese immigrants

66. All of the following were parts of the Omaha Platform of 1892 EXCEPT:

A) Free and unlimited coinage of silver at a rate of 16:1 with gold
B) Direct election of United States Senators
C) A graduated income tax
D) The raising of tariffs to support big business

67. Legislation regarding immigration in the 1920s looked to

A) increase the number of immigrants to fill unskilled jobs
B) end immigration from all countries in Western Europe
C) increase the amount of immigration coming from Asia
D) limit immigration from Southern and Eastern Europe

68. Which event led to the resignation of Richard Nixon?

A) The tax-evasion scandal of his Vice President
B) Failure to end the War in Vietnam
C) Accusations of obstruction of justice
D) Illegally taking money out of a campaign fund

69. In the early nineteenth century, the American Colonization Society looked to

A) provide "40 acres and a mule" to all newly freed slaves

B) send freed slaves to Liberia in Africa

C) establish a policy of sharecropping

D) support the settlement of western lands by African Americans

70. Andrew Jackson did not admit Texas into the Union because

A) Texas would disrupt the balance of free and slave states

B) any admission of Texas would incite Spain into fighting a war

C) Santa Anna had reclaimed Texas as part of Mexico

D) parts of Texas north of the Rio Grande were still under dispute

71. The reaction of the US Government after the Soviet launch of Sputnik in 1957 was

A) the sending of aid to West Berlin

B) an increase in spending on American education and technology

C) a moon launch later that same year

D) the execution of Americans who gave the Soviets information on rockets

72. *"There would be meat stored in great piles in rooms; and the water from leaky roofs would drip over it, and thousands of rats would race about on it. It was too dark in these storage places to see well, but a man could run his hand over these piles of meat and sweep off handfuls of the dried dung of rats."*

The above quote could be found in

A) *The Impending Crisis of the South* by Hinton Rowan Helper

B) *How the Other Half Lives* by Jacob Riis

C) *The Jungle* by Upton Sinclair

D) *On the Road* by Jack Kerouac

73. George Washington set a precedent on foreign policy by advocating

A) imperialistic opportunities in the Western Hemisphere

B) annexation of land in the Pacific northwest

C) neutrality in terms of alliances with foreign nations

D) protecting American naval rights in the Mediterranean

74. The Great Compromise dealt with what issue during the Constitutional Convention?

A) Representation of the states

B) Taxes for owning slaves

C) Import and export tariffs

D) The impeachment process

75. All of the following are a part of the process to become President EXCEPT:

A) Electoral College

B) Primary

C) Referendum

D) Nominating Convention

76. Which event was partially responsible for the United States declaring war on Spain in 1898?

A) Interception of the Zimmermann Telegram

B) Unrestricted submarine warfare in the Atlantic

C) Platt Amendment

D) Sinking of the USS *Maine*

77. As a Presidential candidate, Abraham Lincoln believed that slavery

A) should be abolished in the border states

B) could be abolished in states added after 1800

C) could stay where it was, but not expand to new states in the west

D) should be abolished everywhere in America

78. After John Marshall's decision in *Worcester* v. *Georgia*, President Andrew Jackson

A) stopped the removal of all Native Americans

B) ignored Marshall's recommendations

C) reworded the Indian Removal Act for Congressional approval

D) allowed Cherokees to return to their land

79. Alexander Hamilton's national bank was passed

A) with the help of the Elastic Clause

B) after a joint session of Congress and the Supreme Court

C) as a compromise which moved the nation's capital to New York

D) as part of the Treaty of Paris

80. The Pendleton Act of 1883 was successful in ending

A) unrestricted submarine warfare

B) the patronage system of appointing supporters to office

C) unionization of workers after the Haymarket Affair

D) the gold standard as a means of backing the US currency

81. After the President appoints a member to the cabinet, that appointee must be approved by the

A) Supreme Court

B) Senate

C) State legislatures

D) House of Representatives

82. In the first few decades of the seventeenth century, the Chesapeake Bay area was an agricultural center where

A) slaves harvested cotton

B) Native Americans planted rice

C) indentured servants farmed tobacco

D) free blacks planted sugar

83. Which of the following was true of women with regard to the right to vote before 1920?

A) They could not vote

B) Some states allowed them to vote in different types of elections

C) All women could vote in Presidential elections

D) Southern states allowed women to vote in all elections

84. After the Boston Tea Party of 1773, Britain implemented the
   A) Sugar Act
   B) Tea Act
   C) Declaratory Act
   D) Intolerable Acts

85. The American Federation of Labor was known to support which of the following?
   A) High tariffs
   B) Tax breaks for the wealthy
   C) Collective Bargaining
   D) Passage of the Fourteenth Amendment

86. Which of the following best defends the idea of Social Darwinism in the late nineteenth century?
   A) The decision of the Scopes Trial
   B) Existence of monopolies
   C) Use of the spoils system
   D) Completion of the Transcontinental Railroad

87. The Stonewall Riots were influential in
   A) repealing the Defense of Marriage Act
   B) bringing attention to the gay rights movement
   C) gaining support for the Equal Rights Amendment
   D) ending US involvement in Vietnam

88. In its decision of *Korematsu* v. *United States*, the Supreme Court
   A) limited civilian Constitutional rights in a time of war
   B) extended the belief that the protections of the Fourteenth Amendment were absolute
   C) stated that free speech was not absolute
   D) declared that persons naturalized in America were citizens

89. The Dawes Severalty Act of 1887
   A) was passed to give reparations after the Wounded Knee massacre
   B) offered citizenship and land in exchange for abandoning aspects of tribal culture
   C) promised free land to African Americans in accordance with the Homestead Act
   D) was declared unconstitutional by the Supreme Court

90. The United States did not join the League of Nations or ratify the Treaty of Versailles because
   A) they refused to keep Germany divided after World War I
   B) there were reservations to the idea of making firm alliances with foreign nations
   C) the United States did not want to donate troops to the League of Nations army
   D) France and Germany had not signed the treaty

91. Traditionally before World War I, the Republican Party attracted all of the following voters EXCEPT:
   A) Northern industrialists
   B) Southern African Americans
   C) Wall Street executives
   D) Immigrants in urban areas

92. In *Marbury* v. *Madison*, Chief Justice John Marshall
   A) used the principle of judicial review
   B) upheld the constitutionality of the Judiciary Act of 1789
   C) voiced strong misgivings to the creation of a national bank
   D) denied the states the right to make contracts

93. Unlike Thomas Jefferson, Alexander Hamilton believed

A) in a loose interpretation of the Constitution, and use of the Elastic Clause
B) that a strong army would deprive citizens of their rights
C) the educated commoner should rule
D) the US should support France in accordance with the alliance of 1778

94. Discontent over the gap between the rich and the poor could be seen in which colonial event?

A) Bacon's Rebellion
B) Salem Witch Trials
C) King Philip's War
D) Pequot War

95. In *Federalist #10*, James Madison argued that

A) a large republic could never successfully exist
B) the Electoral College would protect the voting rights of all
C) tyranny of factions could be controlled in a large republic
D) the Articles of Confederation could succeed if there was a stronger army

96. Which of the following was a result of the eighteenth century Great Awakening?

A) Increase in the number of Quakers in Rhode Island
B) Creation of the Half-Way Covenant
C) Increase in religious practice
D) Creation of the colony of Rhode Island

97. The Patriot Act and Department of Homeland Security were created

A) during the Red Scare before 1920
B) after terrorist attacks on the United States in 2001
C) before American involvement in World War II
D) during the Cold War

98. All of the following women were associated with the suffrage movement EXCEPT:

A) Susan B. Anthony
B) Mary Chapman Catt
C) Jane Addams
D) Lucy Stone

99. Social society during the Presidency of Dwight Eisenhower was best characterized as a time period where

A) women questioned traditional morals
B) there was a decrease in marriage
C) public education was reserved for the rich
D) conformity and moves to suburbia were quite common

100. The "graying" of America has led to problems with the

A) Federal Deposit Insurance Corporation
B) Social Security fund
C) Reconstruction Finance Corporation
D) National Defense fund

Answers and Explanations

1. **B**. Thomas Paine believed that it was "common sense" for America to be independent from Britain, as it was miles away and larger.

2. **D**. The Stamp Act was a direct tax on all paper materials and legal documents.

3. **B**. The Northwest Ordinance provided for the admission of new states, which would be free of slavery.

4. **C**. The House of Representatives is based on population. The states with a greater population have more representatives. The Senate has equal representation.

5. **A**. The House of Burgesses was a representative assembly in Virginia. The House of Representatives created by the Constitution provides for a similar representative government.

6. **B**. The Bill of Rights, added in 1791, was an appeal to Anti-Federalists who believed the Constitution would infringe upon individual rights. The Bill of Rights came after the Constitution was ratified.

7. **A**. John C. Calhoun's *South Carolina Exposition and Protest* said that states should be able to declare acts of Congress "null and void." This was similar to what Thomas Jefferson and James Madison wrote in 1798-99 in their *Kentucky and Virginia Resolutions*.

8. **B**. Henry Clay believed the United States could be economically self-sufficient. He supported higher tariffs, a bank, and internal improvements with infrastructure projects like bridges and roads.

9. **C**. Issues with the national bank caused the first two major splits in American History. The split in the 1830s led to the formation of the Whig Party.

10. **B**. Women drafted a Declaration of Sentiments at the convention, and stated that men and women were created equal.

11. **A**. The Second Great Awakening led to education reform, temperance, abolition, and utopian communities. The utopian community at Brook Farm was one. You might also see the name Robert Owen for New Harmony, Indiana. Both looked to create a perfect society based on communal work.

12. **C**. Don't get these confused. Federalism is the division of power between the states and the federal government. Checks and balances and separation of powers are for controlling tyranny within the federal government. Judicial review gives the Supreme Court the power to declare acts of the Legislative or Executive Branches unconstitutional.

13. **B**. David Wilmot's Proviso (stipulation) said that no slavery should spread to lands that might be acquired in the War with Mexico. The Proviso never became law, but it put the slave issue on the table. Soon after, a Northern Free-Soil Party would emerge.

14. **D**. The Fugitive Slave Act in the Compromise of 1850 provided for the capture and return of runaway slaves.

15. **B**. John Brown (1859) and Nat Turner (1831) led failed slave rebellions.

16. **A**. Space A is showing the state of Missouri, which became a slave state in 1820.

17. **D**. The Lecompton Constitution approved slavery for the state of Kansas. "Bleeding Kansas" was a violent series of events that occurred during the process of popular sovereignty stemming from the Kansas-Nebraska Act.

18. **C**. The Emancipation Proclamation did not free any slaves in the northern or border states that were loyal to the Union. It only "freed" slaves in the rebelling states who did not listen to federal law.

19. **D**. Highlighted by the Reconstruction Act of 1867, Radical Republicans favored military rule to enforce legislation.

20. **D**. The Thirteenth Amendment abolished slavery. This was never in question after Reconstruction.

21. **A**. Andrew Carnegie is explaining the "Gospel of Wealth," or the idea that robber barons like himself should be charitable with their fortune and help those who wish to rise to prominence.

22. **D**. Thomas Jefferson, though not a Federalist, acted like one when he purchased Louisiana from Napoleon. There's nothing in the Constitution regarding such a purchase. Therefore, he used implied powers by making a treaty to secure the land.

23. **A**. Immigrants moved to cities because that's where the jobs were.

24. **B**. Anything you see regarding silver, or a 16:1 ratio of silver to gold, has to do with the Populists' Omaha Platform of 1892.

25. **D**. Theodore Roosevelt said he gave those coal miners a "square deal" by making employers accept arbitration. Cleveland broke up the Pullman Strike in 1894.

26. **D**. Closed shops were not eliminated until the 1947 Taft-Hartley Act. A closed shop meant that one could not work a job unless they were in a specific union.

27. **D**. The New South has nothing to do with race or Jim Crow. It meant an increase in industry for the late nineteenth century agrarian South. Cheap land and resources made industry an appealing alternative there.

28. **C**. Because John Hay wanted to protect American interests in China, he declared it open to all foreign trade. European nations had carved China into spheres of influence, or areas of imperialistic control.

29. **B**. The Gentlemen's Agreement was between the US and Japan. It restricted emigration from Japan to the United States.

30. **B**. Congress and the President were on the same page, but not the Supreme Court. *Schechter Poultry Corporation* v. *US* led to the end of the National Industrial Recovery Act. *US* v. *Butler* struck down the Agricultural Adjustment Act.

31. **C**. Women helped out first during World War I. They received the right to vote at the end of the war. Rosie the Riveter was the name for women who worked in the factories during World War II.

32. **B**. From 1945-1991, America's foreign policy was to stop the spread of communism. This was known as containment.

33. **D**. Both HUAC and McCarthy looked to remove suspected communists. This turned into a witch-hunt, oftentimes with faulty evidence leading to convictions.

34. **A**. Jack Kerouac's *On The Road* is typically the book to know on the Beatniks. Beat Generation members were non-conformists who renounced materialism and modern society in the 1950s.

35. **B**. After World War II, there was a great move to the suburbs. The Federal-Aid Highway Act of 1956 created the modern-day interstate highway system.

36. **B**. The Gulf of Tonkin Resolution gave President Johnson a "blank check" as Commander-in-chief of the Vietnam conflict. This meant an escalation of the use of ground troops.

37. **A**. Nixon's policy aimed to give control of the war to Vietnamese soldiers in South Vietnam.

38. **B**. Governor Wallace of Alabama ran for President several times as a segregationist candidate from the South.

39. **B**. Rosa Parks refused to give up her bus seat for a white. SNCC (Student Nonviolent Coordinating Committee), and CORE (Congress of Racial Equality) were two civil rights organizations involved in many activities including the freedom rides and sit-ins.

40. **D**. The Vietnam War ended years earlier under President Nixon.

41. **B**. Rachel Carson's 1962 book *Silent Spring*, which is about environmentalism, led to the banning of certain pesticides.

42. **A**. Earl Warren expanded the rights of the accused in court decisions such as *Miranda* v. *Arizona*, *Gideon* v. *Wainwright*, and *Mapp* v. *Ohio*.

43. **D**. In 1970, four students were shot and killed while they were protesting the Vietnam War at Kent State University in Ohio.

44. **B**. Nixon was never impeached. He resigned before he could be impeached for obstruction of justice associated with the Watergate Scandal.

45. **B**. Betty Friedan was a feminist leader who supported the Equal Rights Amendment. She wanted women to be "Frieee dan." Choice A, Phyllis Schlafly, favored the opposite. She wanted women to be in a traditional role.

46. **C**. Wilson's Fourteen Points looked to bring peace to war-torn Europe. His fourteenth point was to create a League of Nations. Because of this idea, the Senate ultimately never ratified the Treaty of Versailles.

47. **D**. Abolitionist William Lloyd Garrison wrote *The Liberator*.

48. **A**. The Zenger decision said that if something is true, then it can't be libel (crime for printing false claims). Zenger was a journalist, and the decision helped establish freedom of the press.

49. **C**. Salutary neglect took place at a time when the profiting British Government did not enforce trade laws extensively. They also let their guard down on social and political movements in the colonies. Salutary neglect ended after the French and Indian War.

50. **A**. Spain remained in places like Mexico. This included parts of the modern-day west coast of the United States.

51. **C**. John Marshall's decisions generally increased the power of the federal government. For example, in *McCulloch* v. *Maryland*, he said that Maryland could not tax the Bank of the United States. In *Gibbons* v. *Ogden*, he declared that the federal government regulated commerce between the states.

52. **B**. Transcendentalist philosophy meant embracing nature, renouncing materialism, and finding inner peace.

53. **D**. Don't get your Douglases confused. Frederick Douglass (2 S's, African American) was for abolition. Stephen Douglas (1 S, white) championed popular sovereignty, or the right for territories to choose to have slavery or not.

54. **B**. In 1886, a bomb went off in Haymarket Square in Chicago. Unions were blamed and labeled as anarchists. Union membership declined. The Taft-Hartley Act took away some union rights in 1947. Notably, closed shops were outlawed. A closed shop meant that one had to be in a union to work a certain job.

55. **D**. Douglas defended popular sovereignty, or the right of people in a territory to choose if they would have slavery or not. He believed it to be more binding to the states than Roger Taney's decision in the *Dred Scott* case that said slave ownership could not be denied. The Freeport Doctrine was explained in a speech during the 1858 Lincoln-Douglas debates.

56. **D**. Lincoln was a Republican. The Republican Party was viewed by the South as a threat towards the institution of slavery. South Carolina seceded from the Union in 1860, followed by the rest of the Confederacy.

57. **B**. Though the concept of popular sovereignty existed before 1854, the Kansas Nebraska Act would be its most famous application. The event would lead to Bleeding Kansas.

58. **D**. Nativism involved anti-immigrant sentiment. The Roosevelt Corollary was a foreign policy statement, not related to nativism.

59. **C**. *Engel* v. *Vitale* dealt with school prayer. The court found that prayer in public schools was unconstitutional.

60. **A**. *Plessy* v. *Ferguson* is the opposite of Brown v. Board of Education. In Plessy, "separate but equal" was seen as constitutional. This meant that as long as blacks and whites had the same type of facilities, they could be separate. Brown reversed that in 1954.

61. **C**. Washington's speech was criticized by civil rights leaders like W.E.B. Du Bois. Du Bois, and his Niagara Movement, believed African Americans should receive immediate rights of equality. Washington wanted to gradually gain freedoms, while being subservient to whites in political affairs.

62. **C**. Frederick Jackson Turner wrote a thesis about the frontier. *Common Sense* was written by Thomas Paine during the American Revolution.

63. **D**. Frederick Douglass was an abolitionist who looked to end slavery by conventional means, not violence. His slave narrative was widely read in the North.

64. **C**. The Gulf of Tonkin Resolution escalated the War in Vietnam, and led to deployment of more troops. This upset many of the folk singers and the young generation of draftees who listened to them.

65. **C**. Young women, or mill girls, worked in Lowell, Massachusetts. After the first Great Wave of Immigration of the 1840s, many Irish immigrants took over.

66. **D**. The Populists were similar to Democrats in that they did not want to raise tariffs.

67. **D**. In the 1920s, it was believed that immigrants from Southern and Eastern Europe were inferior to those from Western Europe. A pseudoscience called eugenics fueled these beliefs. Quotas were created to limit immigrants seen as "undesirable."

68. **C**. Nixon lied about what he knew concerning the Watergate Scandal. He was targeted for obstruction of justice, but resigned before he could be impeached.

69. **B**. Many believed that African Americans should be sent back to their continent of ancestry. The American Colonization Society was a mix of abolitionists, politicians, and slave owners who didn't want impoverished freed slaves nearby.

70. **A.** Jackson did not want to annex Texas because it would have opened up a can of worms concerning the slave state vs. free state imbalance. Texas would be annexed as a slave state in 1845 by President Tyler.

71. **B.** After being embarrassed by the superior technology of the Soviets, the US stepped up funding for education and scientific research. In 1969, the US won the race to the moon.

72. **C.** Rats, dangerous working conditions, or something disgusting means the passage is from *The Jungle*. The book led to the Meat Inspection Act and the Pure Food and Drug Act (which created the Food and Drug Administration).

73. **C.** Washington wanted to avoid foreign alliances. The belief was that the United States was too fragile a nation to meddle greatly in foreign affairs.

74. **A.** The Great Compromise created a bicameral (two house) legislature. Today, the House of Representatives is based on population (similar to the Virginia Plan). The Senate is based on equality (similar to the New Jersey Plan).

75. **C.** A referendum is held in certain states whereby the citizens vote for a law. The President is not directly elected by the people. In the Presidential Election, citizens vote for electors of the Electoral College, who choose the President.

76. **D.** We now know that the *Maine* sank on its own. In 1898, the event was blamed on the detonation of a Spanish mine.

77. **C.** You need to know that Lincoln was against the spread of slavery, but was not an abolitionist in 1860.

78. **B.** Jackson did not listen to Marshall when he said that Georgia could not pass laws regarding Cherokee lands. Jackson said, "John Marshall has made his decision, now let him enforce it."

79. **A.** The Elastic Clause allows Congress – and only Congress – to do anything "necessary and proper."

80. **B.** The patronage system was synonymous with the spoils system where elected officials appointed their supporters and friends to government jobs. This ended in 1883 when the Pendleton Act was passed. The act was created after an angry office seeker assassinated President James Garfield in 1881.

81. **B.** The Senate approves appointments. They can also ratify treaties.

82. **C.** The Chesapeake Bay area of Maryland and Virginia was populated by indentured servants who harvested tobacco for the Virginia Company.

83. **B.** A common misconception is that women could not vote before the Nineteenth Amendment was ratified in 1920. Women could vote in certain states, including Wyoming which was the first. Typically, it was the lower populated western states that allowed women to vote. Some states only allowed them to vote in Presidential elections.

84. **D**. The Intolerable, or Coercive, Acts of 1774 punished the colonies by closing down Boston Harbor and making them pay for the destroyed tea. In addition, a new quartering act was put in place that allowed troops to stay in the homes of citizens. The Quebec Act was also passed which expanded the Roman Catholic region of Quebec, which the predominantly Protestant colonists were against.

85. **C**. Collective bargaining meant that employees and employers could communicate their differences. This would hopefully prevent a strike, or work stoppage. Samuel Gompers of the AFL believed in arguing for "bread and butter" issues, such as an 8-hour day.

86. **B**. Social Darwinism was used to defend the existence of monopolies. The belief was that "survival of the fittest" would exist in business, similar to what would happen in nature according to Charles Darwin.

87. **B**. The Stonewall Riots led to the creation of gay rights activist organizations, and rallied the LGBT community.

88. **A**. Executive Order 9066 gave the government the power to round up Japanese Americans on the west coast, and relocate them to internment camps during World War II. The Supreme Court agreed that these actions were justified in a time of war. The decision showed the limits of the Fourteenth Amendment, as Japanese Americans were not given the same rights as other ethnic groups.

89. **B**. The goal of this act was to assimilate Native Americans and break up reservation tribal lands in favor of individual ownership. Land and citizenship were offered in return.

90. **B**. Senator Henry Cabot Lodge had "reservations" about joining the League, because it would violate neutrality rights of America. If you said choice C, sorry...the League had no army. The United Nations would organize peacekeeping troops after WW II.

91. **D**. Immigrants in urban areas typically voted Democratic. This was especially true in New York City where the Tammany Hall political machine flourished.

92. **A**. Judicial review gives the Supreme Court the power to declare an act of the Legislative or Executive Branch unconstitutional. Marshall used it for the first time in this 1803 case.

93. **A**. Hamilton wanted a strong government which would have flexibility in creating laws to meet the needs of the people.

94. **A**. Bacon's Rebellion saw Nathaniel Bacon leading discontented farmers against the wealthy planter class and the governor. King Philip (Metacom), and the Pequot War were conflicts between colonists and Native Americans. The other choices involved religion.

95. **C**. Madison contended that factions, or groups of individuals with special interests, would be kept in check.

96. **C**. The Great Awakening was a religious revival that spread throughout the northern colonies. It was the first true mass-movement in colonial history. The American Revolution would spread to all of the colonies a few decades later.

97. **B**. Both were created for protecting the safety of Americans after the terrorist attacks of September 11, 2001.

98. **C**. Jane Addams was known for her work at Hull House in Chicago, a settlement house which aided poor immigrants in the late nineteenth century.

99. **D**. The Baby Boom began after World War II. Generally, women returned to the home to raise children. There was an exodus from the cities into the suburbs. In addition, many moved to the "Sun Belt" to live in the American South and Southwest.

100. **B**. "Graying" means getting older. As people live longer and healthier lives, there will be problems paying out Social Security. Social Security was founded in 1935 as a pension fund to help the elderly. As life expectancy has increased since the 1930s, these payments have become increasingly harder to make.

Now we're ready to begin!

NO BULL
~~NOBLE~~ REVIEW
SHEET

Here are my Review Sheets. Use them often to help you study.

You will notice numbers in brackets after a word or paragraph. These are the pages where you can find more detailed information.

Good luck!

Your friend,
Nobley

Most Important Terms of the Course

1. Columbian Exchange [5]
2. Indentured Servant [5]
3. Bacon's Rebellion [6]
4. House of Burgesses, Mayflower Compact [6]
5. Separatists [6]
6. City Upon a Hill [6]
7. Anne Hutchinson [6]
8. Fundamental Orders of Connecticut [6]
9. Metacom (King Philip) [7]
10. Great Awakening [7]
11. Middle Passage [7]
12. Stono Rebellion [8]
13. Zenger Trial [7]
14. Mercantilism [8]
15. Albany Plan of Union [9]
16. Salutary Neglect [8]
17. Navigation Acts [8]
18. French and Indian War [9]
19. Proclamation of 1763 [12]
20. Stamp Act [12]
21. Townshend Acts [12]
22. Boston Massacre [12-13]
23. Committees of Correspondence [13]
24. Boston Tea Party [13]
25. Intolerable Acts [13]
26. *Common Sense* [14]
27. Continental Congress [14]
28. Olive Branch Petition [14]
29. Declaration of Independence [14]
30. Battle of Saratoga [14-15]
31. Republican Motherhood [15]
32. Articles of Confederation [15]
33. Land Ordinances [16]
34. Shays' Rebellion [15-16]
35. Philadelphia Convention [16]
36. Federalists & Anti-Federalists [16-17]
37. Federalist Papers [17]
38. Federalist #10 [17]
39. Great Compromise [16]
40. 3/5 Compromise [16]
41. Commercial Compromise [16]
42. Elastic Clause [22]
43. Bill of Rights [17]
44. Whiskey Rebellion [27-28]
45. Jay Treaty [28]
46. Pinckney Treaty [28]
47. Proclamation of Neutrality [28]
48. XYZ Affair [28]
49. Alien and Sedition Acts [28]
50. Kentucky and Virginia Resolutions [29]
51. Louisiana Purchase [29]
52. Judicial Review [30]
53. Embargo Act [30]
54. The *Chesapeake* [30]
55. Hartford Convention [31]
56. American System [32]
57. Monroe Doctrine [32]
58. Corrupt Bargain [35-36]
59. Sectionalism [35]
60. Spoils System [36]
61. Caucus & Nominating Conventions [36]
62. Jacksonian Democracy [36]
63. Alexis deTocqueville [36]
64. Tariff of Abominations [38]
65. *South Carolina Expostion & Protest* [38]
66. Ordinance of Nullification [38]
67. Indian Removal Act [39]
68. Trail of Tears [39]
69. Second Great Awakening [40]
70. Transcendentalism [40]
71. Hudson River School [41]
72. Seneca Falls Convention [40]
73. Temperance [40]
74. Mormons [41]
75. Brook Farm [41]
76. Abolitionism [48]
77. Missouri Compromise [44]
78. Manifest Destiny [45]
79. Wilmot Proviso [46]
80. Compromise of 1850 [46]
81. Kansas-Nebraska Act [47]
82. Bleeding Kansas [47-48]
83. Lecompton Constitution [48]
84. Republican Party [48]
85. *Dred Scott* Case [48-49]
86. Lincoln-Douglas Debates [49]
87. John Brown [49]
88. Election of 1860 [49-50]
89. Secession [50]
90. Anaconda Plan [53]
91. Emancipation Proclamation [54]
92. Civil War Draft [54-55]
93. Homestead Act [68]
94. Black Codes [57]
95. Freedmen's Bureau [57]
96. Impeachment of Andrew Johnson [58]

97. Reconstruction Act of 1867 [58]
98. Carpetbaggers and Scalawags [58]
99. Literacy Tests [59]
100. Ku Klux Klan [58, 88]
101. Jim Crow Laws [59]
102. Sharecropping [59]
103. Home Rule [59]
104. New South [60]
105. Nativism [67]
106. Robber Barons [63]
107. Social Darwinism and Edward Bellamy [63]
108. *The Gospel of Wealth* [63]
109. Transcontinental Railroad [66, 68]
110. Knights of Labor [64]
111. AFL [64]
112. IWW [65]
113. Pendleton Act [64]
114. Railroad Strike of 1877, Pullman Strike [65]
115. Haymarket Affair [65]
116. Interstate Commerce Act [66]
117. Sherman Anti-Trust Act [66]
118. Granger Movement [72]
119. Dawes Severalty Act [68-69]
120. Wounded Knee [69]
121. Roosevelt Corollary [82-83]
122. Big Stick Diplomacy [82]
123. Panama Canal [82]
124. Teller and Platt Amendments [82]
125. Open Door Policy [82]
126. Conservation [75]
127. Triangle Shirtwaist Fire [76]
128. Election of 1912 [76]
129. Underwood Tariff [76]
130. FDA, FTC, Federal Reserve [75-77]
131. Red Scare [84]
132. Lost Generation [87]
133. Flapper [87]
134. Sacco-Vanzetti [88]
135. Great Migration [87-88]
136. Harlem Renaissance [88]
137. Teapot Dome Scandal [89]
138. Scopes Trial [88]
139. Dust Bowl [90]
140. Bonus Army [90]
141. Reconstruction Finance Corporation [89]
142. Smoot-Hawley Tariff [89-90]
143. Fireside Chats [93]
144. AAA [94]
145. NIRA [95]
146. SEC [94]

These terms are important to know!

147. Court Packing [95]
148. Wagner Act [95]
149. Good Neighbor Policy [99]
150. Lend Lease Act [99]
151. Zoot Suit Riots/Braceros [102]
152. Yalta Conference [100]
153. Atomic bomb [100]
154. GI Bill [102]
155. Taft-Hartley Act [103]
156. United Nations [103]
157. Containment [106]
158. Truman Doctrine [107]
159. Marshall Plan [107]
160. Berlin Airlift [107]
161. NATO [107]
162. Sputnik [107]
163. McCarthyism [107]
164. Domino Theory [110-111]
165. The Rosenbergs [107]
166. U-2 [107-108]
167. Election of 1960 [119]
168. Bay of Pigs Invasion [109]
169. Cuban Missile Crisis [109]
170. Gulf of Tonkin Resolution [111]
171. Tet Offensive [111-112]
172. Beatniks and Hippies [102, 112]
173. Détente [109]
174. Kent State [112]
175. Little Rock Nine [117]
176. Civil Rights Act and Voting Rights Act [117-118]
177. Stonewall Riots [118]
178. War Powers Act [120]
179. Watergate [120]
180. Oil Embargo [122]
181. Camp David Accords [122]
182. Equal Rights Amendment [120]
183. *Silent Spring* [121]
184. César Chávez [121]
185. Iran Hostage Crisis [122]
186. Reaganomics [122]
187. Christian Right [122]
188. Operation Desert Storm [123]
189. North American Free Trade Agreement [123]
190. War on Terror [124]

Key Questions

1. What were the causes of the American Revolution? [13]

2. What were the weaknesses of the Articles of Confederation? [15-16]

3. What were the precedents and foreign policy of George Washington? [26, 28]

4. Describe the aspects of Hamilton's financial plan. [26-27]

5. What were the major causes and results of the War of 1812? [30-31]

6. Why did Andrew Jackson veto the Bank of the US? What happened to the economy after the veto? [37]

7. What economic changes occurred during the market revolution c1830? [36-37]

8. What were some of the effects of the Second Great Awakening on Reform Movements? [40-41]

9. What should I know about slave life? [44]

10. What were the causes of the Civil War? [49-50]

11. What was Lincoln fighting for at the beginning of the Civil War? [53]

12. How did African American troops make an impact in the Civil War? [54]

13. How did Presidential Reconstruction differ from Radical Reconstruction? [57]

14. How did Reconstruction end? [58-59]

15. What were the two Great Waves of immigration? What immigration laws should I know? [66-67]

16. What were the causes and results of the Spanish-American War? [81-82]

17. What did the Populists want? [72]

18. How did Populist ideas become Progressive Era reforms? [73]

19. What were some important reforms of the Progressive Era? [77]

20. What muckrakers do I need to know about? [75]

21. What famous women reformers of the Progressive Era should I know about? [77-78]

22. What was Theodore Roosevelt's stance on both trusts and labor? [74-75]

23. Why did the US maintain a foreign policy of imperialism in the late nineteenth century? [81]

24. Why didn't the US ratify the Treaty of Versailles? [84]

25. What were the causes of the Great Depression? [89]

26. What programs did FDR create to help the unemployed? [94-95]

27. How did the Supreme Court respond to the New Deal? [95]

28. Why did Truman order the dropping of the atomic bomb? [100-101]

29. Who were some of the most important civil rights leaders? [115-116]

30. What were major examples of containment during the Cold War? [108]

31. What's important to know about the global economy? [123-124]

Government...what you need to know

1. What are the three branches of government? [20]

2. What are the powers of each branch? [20]

3. How does a bill become a law? [21]

4. What is Federalism? [21-22]

5. What is the elastic clause? [22]

6. How does the President get elected? [23]

7. What is impeachment? [23]

8. How can the Constitution be changed? [23]

9. What are the powers of the Supreme Court? [23-24]

How do Checks and Balances Work?

	LEGISLATIVE	EXECUTIVE	JUDICIAL
LEGISLATIVE CHECKS		1. Can override vetoes by 2/3 vote 2. Senate can refuse to confirm a Presidential appointment	1. Can change the size of the Supreme Court 2. Can impeach and convict justices (as well as the President)
EXECUTIVE CHECKS	1. Can veto bills 2. Can call Congress into special session		1. Appoints Supreme Court justices 2. Grants pardons and reprieves
JUDICIAL CHECKS	1. Can declare an act of Congress to be unconstitutional (judicial review)	1. Can declare an act of the President to be unconstitutional	

Constitutional Compromises

The Great Compromise

Virginia Plan (bicameral based on population) vs. New Jersey Plan (equal representation). The Compromise provided for a two-house (bicameral) legislature where the House of Representatives is based on population, and the Senate has equal representation (2 Senators per state).

3/5 Compromise

Slaves counted as 3/5th of a person for both taxation and representation.

Commercial Compromise

The federal government will regulate interstate commerce, and tax imports, not exports.

Amendments to Know

Including the Bill of Rights, you need to know the following Amendments. Remember: The Bill of Rights was ratified in 1791, two years after the Constitution went into effect. Of the ten, these tend to be the most important:

Bill of Rights Amendments (1791)

1st – Freedoms of speech, press, religion, assembly, and right to petition the government.
2nd – Right to bear arms.
4th – Freedom from unreasonable searches and seizures.
5th – Due process rights (right to fair justice, and freedoms from self-incrimination). Also, one cannot be tried twice for the same crime. This is a freedom from "double-jeopardy."
6th – Right to a fair trial and attorney.
10th – Division of power between the states and federal government (called federalism).

Civil War Amendments

13th Amendment (1865) – Abolition of Slavery [57]
14th Amendment (1868) – Equality [57]
15th Amendment (1870) – Universal Male Suffrage [57]

Progressive Era Amendments

16th Amendment (1913) – Income Tax [73-74]
17th Amendment (1913) – Direct Election of Senators [74]
18th Amendment (1919) – Prohibition…Was it successful? [77, 88]
19th Amendment (1920) – Women's Suffrage [78]

Other Important Amendments

22nd Amendment (1951) – Two Term Limit for Presidents [102]
24th Amendment (1964) – Ended the poll tax [59]
26th Amendment (1971) – Lowered the voting age to 18 [112]

Supreme Court Cases — A Short Synopsis

Marbury v. *Madison* (1803) - First use of judicial review. [30]

McCulloch v. *Maryland* (1819) - Maryland could not tax the Bank of the United States because of federal supremacy, and the right of the national government to charter a bank. [This, and other Marshall Court decisions are found on pg. 32.]

Worcester v. *Georgia* (1832) - The Supreme Court ruled that Georgia could not pass legislation regarding Cherokee land. [39]

Dred Scott v. *Sandford* (1857) - Chief Justice Roger B. Taney said that slaves were property, and owners could not be deprived of them. [48-49]

Slaughterhouse Cases (1873) - The Fourteenth Amendment did not protect slaughterhouse workers attempting to conduct a business. [60]

Plessy v. *Ferguson* (1896) - Justified Jim Crow laws. "Separate but equal" was fine. [116]

Insular Cases (early 1900s) - Stated that Constitutional rights did not necessarily extend to US territories acquired during the Age of Imperialism. [82]

Muller v. *Oregon* (1908) - The Court ruled that women were not permitted to work such long hours because they might damage their bodies for maternity. [78]

Schenck v. *US* (1919) - Said that free speech was not absolute. One can't utter something that creates a "clear and present danger," as someone can't shout "FIRE!" in a crowded theater. [83]

Schechter Poultry Corp. v. *US* (1935) - Declared the New Deal's NIRA unconstitutional. [95]

Korematsu v. *US* (1944) - Japanese internment was constitutional, as in times of war, rights can be limited. [101-102]

Dennis v. *US* (1951) - Upheld the Smith Act during the Cold War which made it illegal to speak about overthrowing the government. Due process was limited because of a fear of communism. This was similar to the "clear and present danger" decision of the *Schenck* case. [107]

Brown v. *Board of Education of Topeka, Kansas* (1954) - Ended segregation in schools. "Separate but equal" is inherently unequal. [116]

Miranda* v. *Arizona (1966), ***Gideon* v. *Wainwright*** (1963), ***Mapp* v. *Ohio*** (1961) – All of these decisions of the Warren Court protected rights of the accused. [116-117]

Heart of Atlanta Motel* v. *US (1964) - Public accommodations, such as hotels, can't reject customers based on race. The Civil Rights Act of 1964 does not violate the commerce clause.

NY Times* v. *US (1971) - Publication of the Pentagon Papers was protected by freedom of the press. [119]

Roe* v. *Wade (1973) - Legalized abortion in 1973, but not in all cases. Most important to know is that a woman's right to privacy is protected by the Constitution. Note: Though *Planned Parenthood* v. *Casey* (1992) affirmed the major points of the *Roe* decision, the Supreme Court ruled that states could also regulate abortions with requirements such as parental consent. [120]

United States* v. *Nixon (1974) - President Richard Nixon was not protected by executive privilege, and had to hand over tape-recordings. Nixon remains the only President to resign the office. [120]

Regents of the University of California* v. *Bakke (1978) - Race can be considered in the university admissions process, but distinct racial quotas are illegal. [121]

Texas* v. *Johnson (1989) - Burning of the American flag was protected by the First Amendment.

Cases Involving a School

Engel* v. *Vitale (1962) - The Supreme Court ruled that official school-sponsored prayer is a violation of the free exercise clause of the First Amendment. Even if the prayer was non-denominational and optional, it was still unconstitutional.

Tinker* v. *Des Moines (1969) - Students wanting to protest the Vietnam War wore a black armband to school. They were suspended for making such a political statement. The Supreme Court ruled that clothing is an extension of free speech (First Amendment), and the students did not lose that right when entering the school.

New Jersey* v. *T.L.O. (1985) - T.L.O. was a girl smoking in the bathroom. The principal came in and confiscated her pocketbook, which had rolling-papers for drugs and a list of contacts to sell them to. She was suspended. T.L.O. believed her rights were violated, and the search was illegal. However, the Supreme Court ruled that freedom against searches and seizures in schools may be limited to protect the student body. Thus, this decision curtails the Fourth Amendment rights of students.

Hazelwood v. *Kuhlmeier* (1988) - This was another freedom of speech case. The school newspaper was printing material about the private lives of teenagers. Such information reported on was teen-pregnancy and parental divorce. The principal deleted the controversial articles from the paper. Students felt their rights were violated and the case went as far as the Supreme Court. The court ruled that the principal was allowed to censor said materials because of "legitimate pedagogical concerns" in school procedure.

Differences Between Thomas Jefferson and Alexander Hamilton

Issue	Thomas Jefferson	Alexander Hamilton
Who should have power in government?	The educated/ commoners	The propertied aristocracy
Give most power to the:	States	Federal or Central Gov't. (Strong Federal Gov't.)
Constitutional Interpretation	Strict — Don't give the Federal Government too much power to legislate	Loose — Allow the Federal Government to do whatever is "necessary and proper"
Stance on Army	Against! Gives government too much power	For! Will make the government powerful
National Bank	Con: Favors the rich	Pro: Stabilizes the economy
Favored foreign nation	France — They supported our revolution	England — the strongest nation; similar heritage
Preferred Economy	Agriculture	Industry and Commerce

How Did Our Two-Party System Develop?

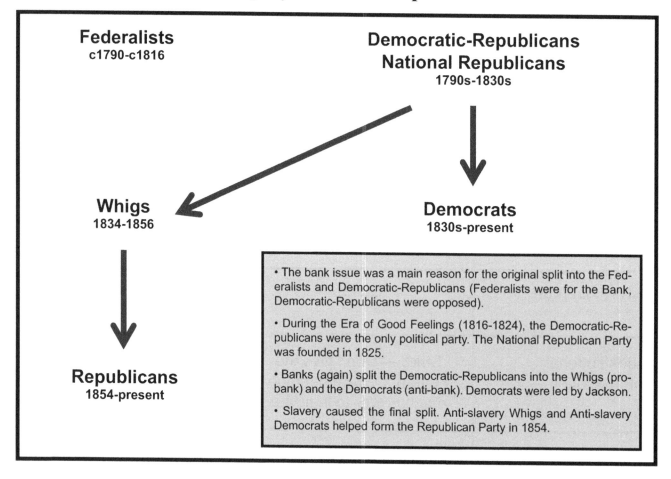

Federalists
c1790-c1816

Democratic-Republicans
National Republicans
1790s-1830s

Whigs
1834-1856

Democrats
1830s-present

Republicans
1854-present

• The bank issue was a main reason for the original split into the Federalists and Democratic-Republicans (Federalists were for the Bank, Democratic-Republicans were opposed).

• During the Era of Good Feelings (1816-1824), the Democratic-Republicans were the only political party. The National Republican Party was founded in 1825.

• Banks (again) split the Democratic-Republicans into the Whigs (pro-bank) and the Democrats (anti-bank). Democrats were led by Jackson.

• Slavery caused the final split. Anti-slavery Whigs and Anti-slavery Democrats helped form the Republican Party in 1854.

Look What the Jay Treaty with Britain Caused!

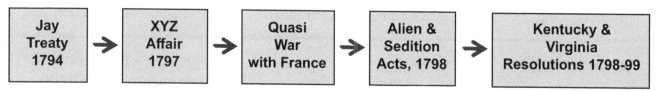

| Jay Treaty 1794 | → | XYZ Affair 1797 | → | Quasi War with France | → | Alien & Sedition Acts, 1798 | → | Kentucky & Virginia Resolutions 1798-99 |

A Quick Review of Tariffs, Early 1800s-World War II

1. 1828 Tariff of Abominations raised rates, and nearly caused South Carolina to secede.

2. The Underwood Tariff of 1913 decreased rates after the Democrats took office.

3. The Smoot-Hawley Tariff of 1930 raised tariffs to the highest point since the Tariff of Abominations. This was done originally to protect the agriculture industry.

D ... **D**emocrats, Tariffs go **D**own, Help **D**ee poor, **D**eep or Solid South.

R ... **R**epublicans, **R**aise Tariffs, Less Taxes for the **R**ich, Favor **R**ailroads and **R**obber Barons.

Remember: When Democrats were in office, tariffs typically went down. When Republicans were in office, tariffs typically went up. Tariffs eased after World War II.

The Tariff of Abominations Led to...

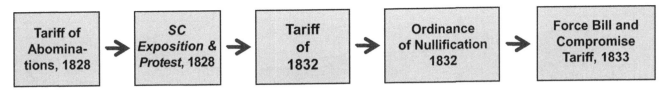

Tariff of Abominations, 1828 → SC Exposition & Protest, 1828 → Tariff of 1832 → Ordinance of Nullification 1832 → Force Bill and Compromise Tariff, 1833

Manifest Destiny

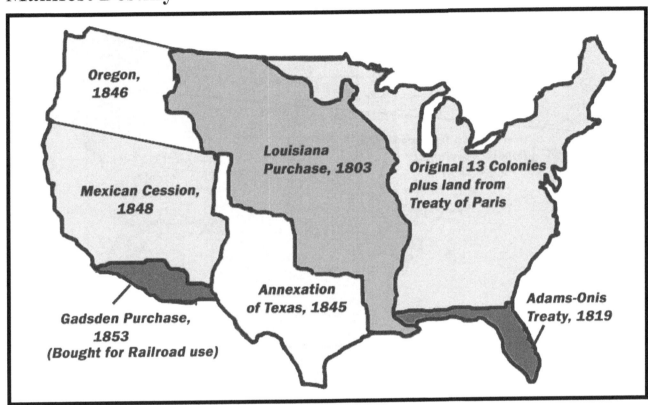

Oregon, 1846

Louisiana Purchase, 1803

Original 13 Colonies plus land from Treaty of Paris

Mexican Cession, 1848

Annexation of Texas, 1845

Adams-Onis Treaty, 1819

Gadsden Purchase, 1853 (Bought for Railroad use)

Slavery Compromises Prior to the Civil War *(Know these well!)*

Missouri Compromise of 1820 - Missouri was a slave state, no slavery north of the 36° 30' latitude line, Maine was a free state. It was brokered by Henry Clay.

Compromise of 1850 - Provided for: A Fugitive Slave Act, no slave trade in DC, the former Mexican Territory of Utah and New Mexico to have popular sovereignty, California to become a free state, Texas to give up western land and receive $10 million to pay off its debt. Authored by Henry Clay.

Kansas-Nebraska Act of 1854 - Provided for popular sovereignty, or the right to choose if a state would have slavery or not. This led to *Bleeding Kansas*, and the *Lecompton Constitution* which approved slavery in Kansas. The compromise was authored by Stephen Douglas.

Slavery Legislation and Compromises, 1820-1854

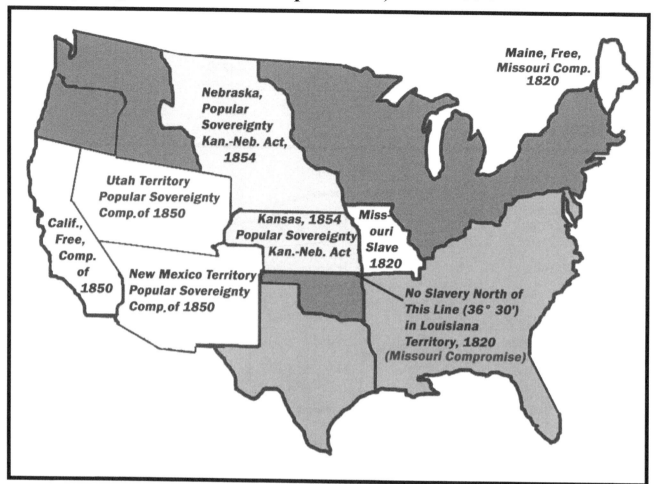

In the map:

- **Maine, Free, Missouri Comp. 1820**
- **Nebraska, Popular Sovereignty Kan.-Neb. Act, 1854**
- **Utah Territory Popular Sovereignty Comp. of 1850**
- **Calif., Free, Comp. of 1850**
- **Kansas, 1854 Popular Sovereignty Kan.-Neb. Act**
- **Missouri Slave 1820**
- **New Mexico Territory Popular Sovereignty Comp. of 1850**
- **No Slavery North of This Line (36° 30') in Louisiana Territory, 1820 (Missouri Compromise)**

Differences Between the American Federation of Labor and the Knights of Labor

American Federal of Labor:
BAGS = **B**read Butter Issues / **A**FL / **G**ompers / **S**trike less with collective bargaining

Knights of Labor:
KUPS = **K**nights / **U**nskilled / **P**owderly / **S**trike more (Unskilled spellers can't spell cups)

Republican Policies, 1865-c1932

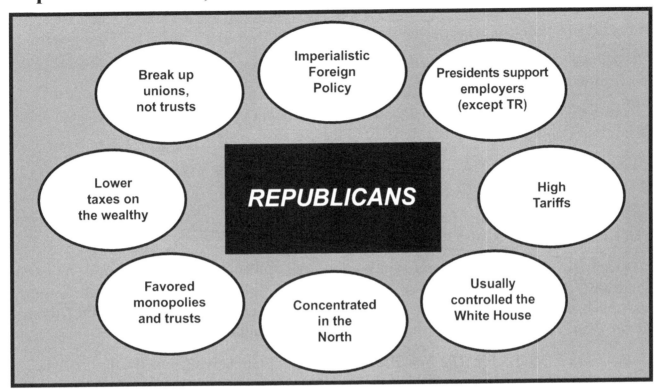

Democratic Policies, 1865-c1932

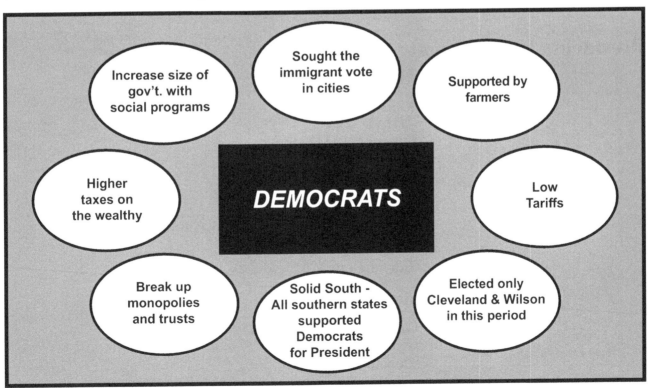

20th Century Presidential Programs and Slogans

Theodore Roosevelt (Rep): A **Square Deal** for Americans. He supported consumers over trusts. [75]

Woodrow Wilson (Dem); His **New Freedom** (defeated TR's **New Nationalism**) promised even more trustbusting. [76]

Warren G. Harding (Rep); Looked to **Return to Normalcy** after World War I. He died in office, and Calvin Coolidge was in office for most of the 20s.

Franklin D. Roosevelt (Dem); **The New Deal** looked for public works, and hands-on government economic change. [93]

Harry S Truman (Dem); **A Fair Deal** for social improvement, civil rights, and expanding education and healthcare. Remember, "Tru" was "Fair." [110]

Dwight Eisenhower (Rep); **Dynamic Conservatism**. The 1950s was a conservative time economically (government supported business), politically (McCarthyism), and socially (women were back at home). You should also know that Eisenhower signed the **Federal-Aid Highway Act in 1956**. This provided for the modern-day **interstate highway system**.

John F. Kennedy (Dem); **The New Frontier** was a hope for solving poverty, racial prejudice, and providing international aid. [108]

Lyndon Johnson (Dem); **The Great Society** offered solutions for poverty, education, and discrimination. [119]

Presidents 1965-Present

Lyndon Johnson [119]

Richard Nixon [120]

Gerald Ford [121]

Jimmy Carter [122]

Ronald Reagan [122-123]

George H. W. Bush [123]

Bill Clinton [123]

George W. Bush [124]

Barack Obama [124-125]

Donald Trump [125]

Foreign Policy: Here's a Handy Timeline

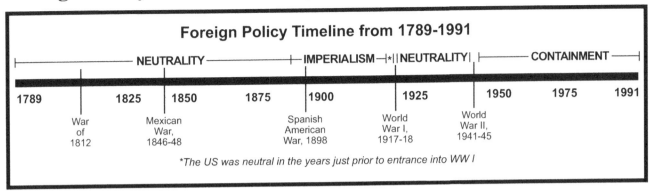

Here are some people you may not know...

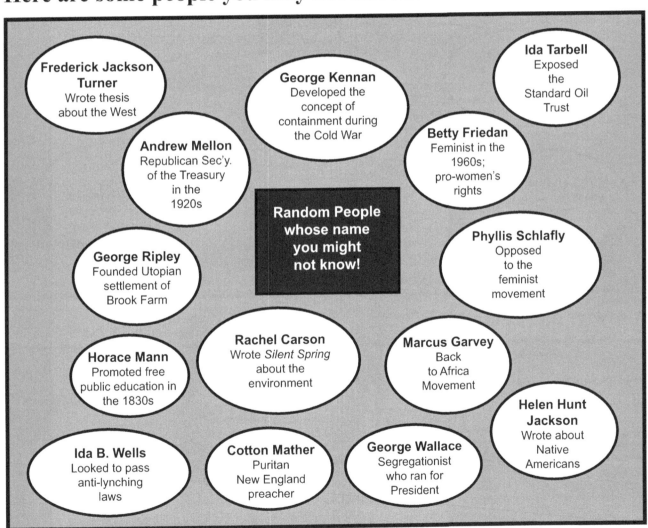

...And here are some more!

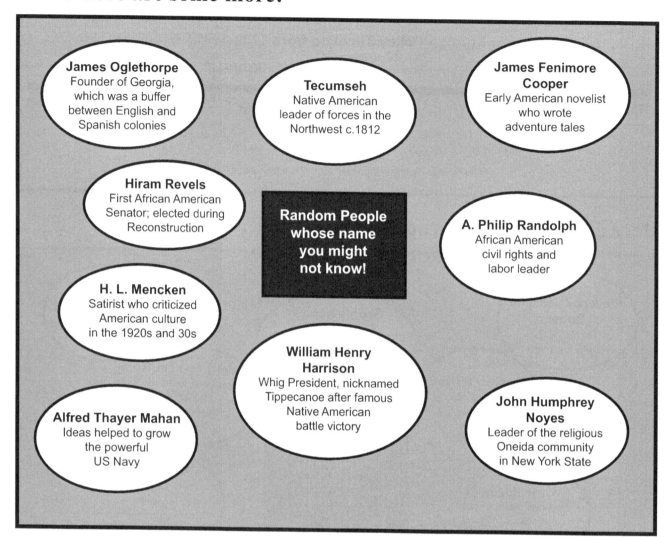

James Oglethorpe
Founder of Georgia, which was a buffer between English and Spanish colonies

Tecumseh
Native American leader of forces in the Northwest c.1812

James Fenimore Cooper
Early American novelist who wrote adventure tales

Hiram Revels
First African American Senator; elected during Reconstruction

Random People whose name you might not know!

A. Philip Randolph
African American civil rights and labor leader

H. L. Mencken
Satirist who criticized American culture in the 1920s and 30s

William Henry Harrison
Whig President, nicknamed Tippecanoe after famous Native American battle victory

John Humphrey Noyes
Leader of the religious Oneida community in New York State

Alfred Thayer Mahan
Ideas helped to grow the powerful US Navy

A few random facts

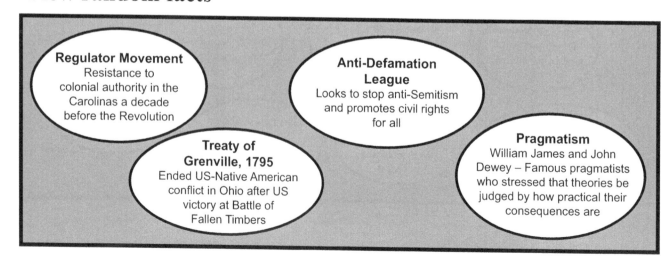

Regulator Movement
Resistance to colonial authority in the Carolinas a decade before the Revolution

Anti-Defamation League
Looks to stop anti-Semitism and promotes civil rights for all

Treaty of Grenville, 1795
Ended US-Native American conflict in Ohio after US victory at Battle of Fallen Timbers

Pragmatism
William James and John Dewey – Famous pragmatists who stressed that theories be judged by how practical their consequences are

13 Colonies Geography c1740

NORTH: Massachusetts, N. Hampshire, Connecticut, & Rhode Island
- Shipbuilding, Agriculture, Trade

MIDDLE: New York, Delaware, New Jersey, Pennsylvania
- Trade, Shipbuilding, Foodstuffs

SOUTH: Virginia and Maryland = Tobacco
North Carolina = Tobacco and Fur
South Carolina = Rice
Georgia = Rice and Indigo

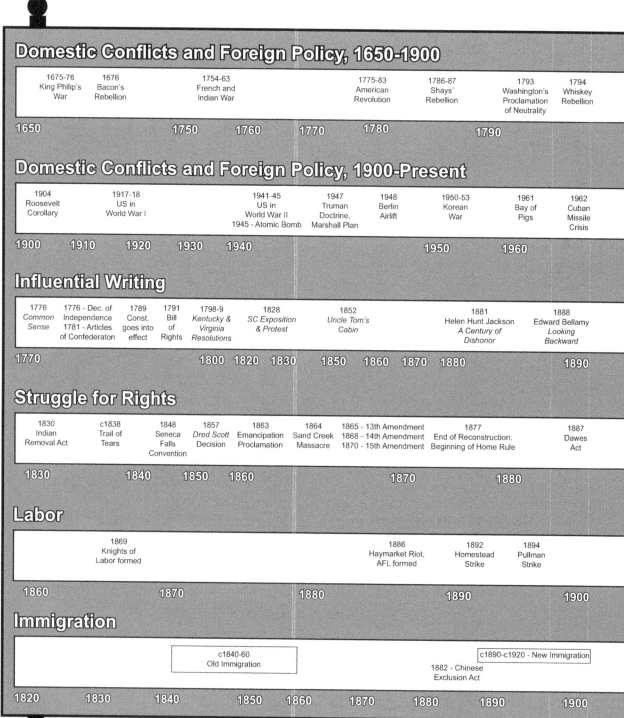

Domestic Conflicts and Foreign Policy, 1650-1900

| 1675-76 King Philip's War | 1676 Bacon's Rebellion | 1754-63 French and Indian War | 1775-83 American Revolution | 1786-87 Shays' Rebellion | 1793 Washington's Proclamation of Neutrality | 1794 Whiskey Rebellion |

1650   1750   1760   1770   1780   1790

Domestic Conflicts and Foreign Policy, 1900-Present

| 1904 Roosevelt Corollary | 1917-18 US in World War I | 1941-45 US in World War II 1945 - Atomic Bomb | 1947 Truman Doctrine, Marshall Plan | 1948 Berlin Airlift | 1950-53 Korean War | 1961 Bay of Pigs | 1962 Cuban Missile Crisis |

1900   1910   1920   1930   1940   1950   1960

Influential Writing

| 1776 *Common Sense* | 1776 - Dec. of Independence 1781 - Articles of Confederaton | 1789 Const. goes into effect | 1791 Bill of Rights | 1798-9 *Kentucky & Virginia Resolutions* | 1828 *SC Exposition & Protest* | 1852 *Uncle Tom's Cabin* | 1881 Helen Hunt Jackson *A Century of Dishonor* | 1888 Edward Bellamy *Looking Backward* |

1770   1800   1820   1830   1850   1860   1870   1880   1890

Struggle for Rights

| 1830 Indian Removal Act | c1838 Trail of Tears | 1848 Seneca Falls Convention | 1857 *Dred Scott* Decision | 1863 Emancipation Proclamation | 1864 Sand Creek Massacre | 1865 - 13th Amendment 1868 - 14th Amendment 1870 - 15th Amendment | 1877 End of Reconstruction. Beginning of Home Rule | 1887 Dawes Act |

1830   1840   1850   1860   1870   1880

Labor

| 1869 Knights of Labor formed | 1886 Haymarket Riot, AFL formed | 1892 Homestead Strike | 1894 Pullman Strike |

1860   1870   1880   1890   1900

Immigration

| c1840-60 Old Immigration | c1890-c1920 - New Immigration 1882 - Chinese Exclusion Act |

1820   1830   1840   1850   1860   1870   1880   1890   1900

More Timelines

1797 XYZ Affair	1812-15 War of 1812	1823 Monroe Doctrine		1846-48 Mexican War		1861-65 Civil War			1898 Spanish- American War
1800	**1810**	**1820**	**1830**	**1840**	**1850**	**1860**	**1870**	**1880**	**1890**

1964 Gulf of Tonkin	1968 Tet Offensive	1970 Kent State	1973-74 Oil Embargo	1978 Camp David Accords	1979-81 Iran Hostage Crisis		1991 Operation Desert Storm	1995 NATO troops to Bosnia	2001 9/11 Attacks
	1970				**1980**		**1990**		**2000**

c1890-c1900 Muckrakers - Tarbell, Sinclair, Wells, Riis, and others			1939 John Steinbeck *The Grapes of Wrath*		1957 Jack Kerouac *On the Road*	1962 Rachel Carson *Silent Spring*	1963 Betty Friedan *The Feminine Mystique*
1900	**1910**	**1920**	**1930**	**1940**	**1950**	**1960**	

1890 Wounded Knee	1896 *Plessy* v. *Ferguson*	1920 Nineteenth Amendment	1954 *Brown* v. *Board of Education*	1963 Martin L. King, Jr. "I Have a Dream" Speech	1964 - Civil Rights Act 1965 - Voting Rights Act	1968 American Indian Movement founded	1969 Stonewall Riots
1890	**1900** **1910** **1920** **1930** **1940** **1950**			**1960**			**1970**

1902 T. Roosevelt supports workers			1933 NIRA	1935 Wagner Act	1938 Fair Labor Standards Act	1947 Taft-Hartley Act
1910	**1920**	**1930**			**1940**	

c1890-c1920 - New Immigration	1921 - Emergency Quota Act				Immigration Act of 1965		1986 Immigration Reform and Control Act
1907 - Gentlemen's Agreement with Japan	1917 Literacy Tests	1924 - National Origins Act					
1910	**1920**	**1930**	**1940**	**1950**	**1960**	**1970**	**1980**

You Should Know

American Indian (Native American) Cultures Before Conquest That You Need to Know

Kwakiutl

Chinook

Tribes in Great Basin and Great Plains were more nomadic as they searched for food sources

Eastern Woodland Tribes (Iroquois)

Navajo

Pueblo

Eastern Woodland (including Iroquois)
   • Crafted items from the trees around them, hunted and gathered in the woods, fished in lakes.

Pueblos and their Anasazi Ancestors
   • Irrigated off the Rio Grande, planted maize (corn) for stable food source. Lived in adobe structures.

Northwest Tribes (Kwakiutl, Chinook)
   • Relied on salmon and whaling near the Pacific Ocean.

Mesoamerican Mayan and Aztec Empires experienced advanced civilizations in modern-day Mexico.

NOTE: Tribes within regions would connect through trade. Native American populations were abruptly diminished after conquest. The tribes were susceptible to European diseases such as smallpox.

Made in United States
North Haven, CT
23 May 2022

19439610R00102